Literature and Degree
in Renaissance England

Literature and Degree in Renaissance England

Nashe, Bourgeois Tragedy, Shakespeare

Peter Holbrook

DELAWARE

Newark: University of Delaware Press
London and Toronto: Associated University Presses

Associated University Presses
440 Forsgate Drive
Cranbury, N.J. 08512

Associated University Presses
25 Sicilian Avenue
London WC1A 2QH, England

Associated University Presses
P.O. Box 338, Port Credit
Mississauga, Ontario
Canada L5G 4L8

1000 627753

The paper used in this publication meets the requirements of the American National Standard for Permanence of Paper for Printed Library Materials Z39.48-1984

Library of Congress Cataloging-in-Publication Data

Holbrook, Peter, 1959–
        Literature and degree in Renaissance England : Nashe, bourgeois tragedy, Shakespeare / Peter Holbrook.
            p. cm.
        Includes bibliographical references and index.
        ISBN 0-87413-474-9
        1. English literature—Early modern, 1500–1700—History and criticism. 2. Social classes in literature. 3. Shakespeare, William, 1564–1616—Political and social views. 4. Literature and society—England—History—16th century. 5. Nashe, Thomas, 1567–1601—Political and social views. 6. English drama (Tragedy)--History and criticism. 7. Domestic drama, English—History and criticism. 8. Renaissance—England. I. Title.
PR428.S65H65   1994
820.9'355—dc20   92–50883
                                                                              CIP

Contents

Preface

This book studies the place of literature in the society of late sixteenth- and early seventeenth-century England: in particular, the relations between literary works and degree, or social stratification. Literary works, I propose, variously symbolize stratification. In the chapter on Nashe I consider how the social situation of a late sixteenth-century humanist shaped his writing, and in chapters on bourgeois tragedy and Shakespeare I deal with the attitudes of particular plays to hierarchy and to modes of discourse identifiable with the idea of hierarchy. Throughout, I am concerned with how some English Renaissance literary works fit into a system of status differences.

The book is substantially the dissertation submitted in 1990 to the English Department of Yale University for the degree of Doctor of Philosophy. Except where indicated, I have, for Shakespeare, used the *Riverside* edition, textual editor G. Blakemore Evans (Boston, 1974). For Nashe, I have relied upon *The Works of Thomas Nashe,* 5 vols., ed. R. B. McKerrow (1904–10; revised by F. P. Wilson, Oxford, 1966). I have modernized some of the more distracting features of older texts (*u* for *v* and vice versa, *i* for initial *j,* long *s,* heavy italicization, contractions) but have retained old spelling and punctuation where they are used. Unless otherwise specified, dates of composition and/or publication of texts are from Blakemore Evans's *Annals: 1552–1616* in *The Riverside Shakespeare.* References to the *OED* are to its first edition (1933 and supplements).

Acknowledgments

Many people have helped bring this project to conclusion. For advice, suggestions, criticisms, good conversation or moral support I warmly thank Ayşe Agiş, Tom Bishop, Otto Bohlmann, William Burgos, Hugh Craig, Ian Duncan, Dominique Favre, Susanne Fusso, Noel and Shirley Hickey, Tony and Amy Hirschel, Catriona Holyoake, Lewis Klausner, Susanne Liden, Wayne McKenna, Bill O'Reilly, Jahan Ramazani, Howard Stern, Peter Swan, and Gordon Turnbull. I am particularly grateful to Lars Engle for his encouragement and for generously reading the dissertation and making many helpful suggestions. I am also deeply indebted to Susanne Wofford and Mihoko Suzuki, both of whom also read the dissertation and had numerous helpful criticisms and suggestions. I benefited greatly from the reports of the Departmental readers, Cristina Malcolmson and Lawrence Manley. My principal scholarly debt is to the inspiring example of the supervisor of the dissertation, George K. Hunter, who was more generous of his time, patience, and thought than I care to recall. I am pleased to be able to thank the Research Management Committee of the University of Newcastle, Australia, for providing me with a grant for the completion of the project. Brian Gray kindly assisted with proofreading. For their encouragement and support, I am grateful to my parents, Frank and Margaret Holbrook. The greatest debt that I have incurred is to my wife, Annabel Hickey; it, however, is incalculable.

Literature and Degree
in Renaissance England

Introduction

Your high self,
The gracious mark o' th' land, you have obscur'd
With a swain's wearing, and me, poor lowly maid,
Most goddess-like prank'd up.
—Shakespeare, *The Winter's Tale*

One of the most reprinted of all Elizabethan and Jacobean plays, the anonymous *Mucedorus* (ca. 1590) was performed by Shakespeare's company at Whitehall before the king in 1610.[1] The play, drawing on an episode in Sidney's *Arcadia,* treats the prince of Valencia's love for Amadine, princess of Aragon. Mucedorus has learned that "blooming lilies never shone so gay" as the face of this "bright jewel" but, "lest report / Does mangle verity, boasting of what is not," he will proceed incognito to Aragon and see for himself. Mucedorus reveals the plan to his friend Anselmo, dismissing his objection that the mission is too perilous, "danger lurk[ing] each where": "Augment not then more answers; lock thy lips, / Unless thy wisdom suit me with disguise / According to my purpose" (1.17–39). Anselmo objects that "That action craves no counsel, / Since what you rightly are will more command / Than best usurpèd shape" (1.40–42)—disguise is unnecessary for Mucedorus's mission. But common sense is brushed aside by the ardent hero: "Thou still art opposite in disposition. / A more obscure, servile habiliment / Beseems this enterprise" (1.43–45). Disguise is not only required, it must be lowly, "obscure," "servile," as far removed from Mucedorus's station as possible. Anselmo helplessly suggests "a Florentine or mountebank": "'Tis much too tedious," complains Mucedorus, "I dislike thy judgement. / My mind is grafted on an humbler stock" (1.46–48). Anselmo hits upon a solution:

13

> Within my closet does there hang a cassock;
> Though base the weed is, 't was a shepherd's
> Which I presented in Lord Julio's masque.
>
> *Mucedorus:* That, my Anselmo, and none else but that,
> Mask Mucedorus from the vulgar view.
> That habit suits my mind; fetch me that weed.
> > *Exit Anselmo*
> Better than kings have not disdained that state,
> And much inferior, to obtain their mate.
>
> > (1.49–56)

For the rest of the play, until his self-disclosure to Amadine in scene 17, and except for the hermit's disguise adopted in scene 14, Mucedorus is known as a shepherd.

Mucedorus assumes the desirability of its hero's disguising without searching strenuously for a reason: if there is no obvious motive the play does not ask its audience to bother with one. (Later this disguise becomes an occasion for a display of Amadine's virtue, when she chooses the shepherd over the cowardly courtier Segasto; Mucedorus, however, does not anticipate that here.) The disguising, then, is to be justified in poetic terms. So the opening scene advertises pleasures in store: by the end of these sixty-odd lines we know this will be a play of adventure, noble love, and disguisings—in particular, a play about a prince in humble disguise. If the only necessity for disguise is poetic, we might ask what particular pleasure is at stake. (And we may note that the pleasurableness of disguise is hinted at by the mention of "Lord Julio's masque": donning shepherd's weeds is already associated with a theatrical pastime.)

This Introduction begins with *Mucedorus* because its popularity means that conclusions about it may be significant for what Elizabethan audiences enjoyed in plays generally: understanding this play may suggest approaches for interpreting the social meaning of other modes in dramatic or prose texts of the English Renaissance. All the texts considered in this book represent or articulate an interplay between social strata; and I shall argue that in many such texts we find writers exploring the nature and shape of the social system, subjecting hierarchy to the interimplication, play, and indeterminacy possible in fiction. Thus *Mucedorus* is a play about kings and courtiers, though it has an excellent clown, Mouse, and a wild man, Bremo. Nevertheless, even in a play more socially homogeneous than most works considered here, we may regard the convention of disguise as attractive to the dramatist precisely because it allows a certain social heterogeneity to be realized.[2] Mucedorus's metamorphosis into a shepherd can be seen as introducing this element of social interplay, his romance with Amadine being enriched by the tension natural to relations between princesses and shepherds. Mucedorus "becomes" a shepherd; and it is, I think, very likely that the pleasure offered by this change is the manipulation, through art, of hierarchical relations, which theoretically are unalterable. The play takes "degree" and hierarchy as in large part its subject matter: the hero will rescue Amadine by killing a bear (probably revived in *The Winter's Tale,* a play reminiscent of *Mucedorus* not only in bears and fantasticality but in its fascination with social interplay—for instance in the sheep-shearing and in Autolycus's fluent and parodic transformations from cowering "poor fellow" to "courtier cap-a-pe" [4.4.638, 736]), and his valor will incite the envy of the effete courtier and rival wooer Segasto, who engineers Mucedorus's banishment from Aragon's court:

> 'Tis well, Segasto, that thou hast thy will.
> Should such a shepherd, such a simple swain
> As he, eclipse thy credit famous through
> The court? No, ply, Segasto, ply.
> Let it not in Aragon be said
> A shepherd hath Segasto's honor won.
>
>   (10.1–6)

Segasto's envy shows how the play may through disguise explore specifically social tensions, along with other relations. *Mucedorus* entertains a reversal of hierarchy (a gentleman bested by a "shepherd") even while essentially preserving it. (Mucedorus is, after all, a prince.) It ventures a dramatization of the officially static social system, subjecting it to a certain variation and dynamism but without serious risk of offending fundamental social values. Mouse and the Messenger bring news of Mucedorus's banishment, which baffles him: why must "the shepherd" be expelled? (9.26). But the Messenger answers tellingly: "What should shepherds do amongst *us?* Have we not lords enough on *us* in the court?" (9.28–29; my emphasis). The Messenger's question is reasonable: what place indeed for shepherds in a court? (And what place, for that matter, for Mouse, marvelously superior now that "with weapons about him" [stage direction, scene 6] he may swagger like a courtier at "Mother Nip's house" and demand not what one supposes is his usual single drink but an extravagant "three pots of ale" [12.16–17].) *Muce-*

dorus poses such questions even if it doesn't answer them. Introducing a "shepherd" into the court renders hierarchy dramatic, complex, an object of interest: rather than being the play's given, it becomes itself play or theatrical raw material, raising the possibility of reflection upon the social categories foregrounded. A "social fact,"[3] hierarchy, may thus be supposed this romantic, fantastic play's subject, its fairy-tale quality enabling it to explore hierarchy by allaying the anxiety such exploration might arouse in a more realistic play: a certain convenient, not to say necessary, distance separates the actual hierarchy of sixteenth-century England from the play's. What does seem probable, in any case, is that the complication of social structure effected by introducing a "shepherd" into a court succeeds, however fleetingly, in representing, or explicitly articulating, that structure. The Messenger's worldly wisdom provokes a sentence from Mucedorus: "shepherds are men, and kings are no more" (9.30),[4] taking the suggestion of a reversal of degree as far as it will go in this play. "Criticism," however, is probably too blunt a characterization of this perspective, since it omits the vital ludic quality in the play's treatment of hierarchy. Mucedorus's sentiment is best understood within the context of an ostentatiously remote and fanciful toying with social distinctions. My object here, nonetheless, is to affirm that the text finds putting a nobleman in a shepherd's coat dramatic (as Segasto's envy implies). The play might in that case be supposed a kind of socio-dramatic experiment, raising difficult questions: What might happen if a prince were a shepherd? What should happen if a shepherd were worthier than a courtier, and a princess loved him? What differences obtain between shepherds and courtiers, and which are natural and which artificial? "What should shepherds do in a court?" This speculative dimension is important in the play, and the kind of pleasure offered the audience is bound up with it.

Mucedorus is, I suggest, highly aware of social distinctions, and it is correspondingly self-aware about literary mode, opening with a contest between "Envy" (that is, Tragedy) and "Comedy" over possession of the stage, a contest Comedy finally wins despite the play's two deaths.[5] This tension between tragic and comic perspectives seems to reveal a dramatist aware of the different possibilities manipulation of social distinctions has: it is a complication, after all, easily having a tragic aspect ("the harm of hem that stoode in heigh degree" [*Monk's Tale*] is the traditional matter of "Gothic tragedy"), and that awareness is to some extent made a part of the comedy. We are to be cognizant throughout of the potential for "tragic stuff" within "pleasant comedy" (induction, 70).[6]

That complications of social hierarchy have potential for "tragic stuff" is shown by numerous Elizabethan plays, but one with a concern comparable to *Mucedorus*'s in freeing up the system of social distinctions is the two-part *The Downfall* and *The Death of Robert Earl of Huntingdon* (1598; pub. 1601), probably by Anthony Munday with some contribution from Henry Chettle and tracing, among other matters, the earl of Huntingdon's transformation into Robin Hood. The first part of the play ends comically, with a reconciliation of Robin and his enemies and Richard and John. The second takes up "matters tragical."[7] Both parts equally exploit the dramatic potential of the hero's translation from one social level to another. In the *Death* Friar Tuck mischievously rebukes Richard when the king addresses Robin by his former title as "Earl Robert":

> *Friar:* A forfeit, a forfeit, my liege lord!
>   My master's laws are on record!
>   The court-roll here your grace may see.
> *King:*   I pray thee, Friar, read it me.
> *Friar:* One shall suffice, and this is he.
>   No man, that cometh in this wood
>   To feast or dwell with Robin Hood,
>   Shall call him earl, lord, knight, or squire:
>   He no such titles doth desire,
>   But Robin Hood, plain Robin Hood,
>   That honest yeoman stout and good,
>   On pain of forfeiting a mark
>   That must be paid to me his clerk.
>   My liege, my liege, this law you broke,
>   Almost in the last word you spoke:
>   That crime may not acquitted be,
>   Till Friar Tuck receive his fee.
> *King:*   There's more than twenty marks, mad Friar.
>   *[Casts him purse]*
>
>   (8.233–34)[8]

The earl's dispossession and death is tragic. But his decline to "simple yeoman" (8.123) seems to have interested Munday in the same way that the willed, deliberate (and so comic) translation of Mucedorus into a shepherd interested that play's author. Munday, I suggest, was intrigued by the hybrid noble-yeoman-outlaw. Certainly the change itself is underscored: Robert informs Little John of his "intent" to "lead an outlaw's life" in Sherwood Forest "till the king's return," and Little John's ready approval of his "honour's purpose" draws the protest "Nay, no more honour, I pray thee, Little John; / Henceforth I will be called Robin Hood. / Matilda shall be my maid Marian" (8.142). Somewhat as in *Mucedorus* (or in such achieved works as *As You Like It, The Winter's Tale,* or *The Tempest*), a removed perspective on social norms and structures becomes viable in a romantic, natural, or "outlaw" setting.[9] Given a society that publicly saw itself as a hierarchy of the strictest and most traditional kind, it is not impossible that the drama, and perhaps other forms of fiction, occasionally functioned as a field in which this stern hierarchical ideal might be playfully explored, even temporarily (and perhaps harmlessly) undone.[10] Robin is a socially complex figure generally: a nobleman who champions "the poor man . . . maids, widows, orphans, and distressed men" (8.154) and who is loved by his people (see the loathing of the Jailer and "goodwife Thompson" [8.188] for his oppressor Warman [8.186–89] as well as the servant who tells of the treacherous Prior's people cursing him: "Plague follow plague, they cry: he hath undone / The good Lord Robert, Earl of Huntingdon" [8.168–69]). Richard is likewise associated with common people, though without the kind of drastic social metamorphosis Huntingdon undergoes: Leicester paints a vivid picture of popular enthusiasm for the king's "holy war" (8.172). Just, then, as *Mucedorus* manipulates status through disguise, so in a tragic idiom do *The Downfall* and *The Death of Robert Earl of Huntingdon.*[11] In an order in which "the entire pattern of living enforced a rigid social identity from which there was little chance of escape," such literary rearrangements of hierarchy seem socially symbolic.[12]

Other plays offered pleasures similar to those of *Mucedorus* and Munday's. In the popular, high-spirited *George a' Greene, the Pinner of Wakefield* (ca. 1587–91; pub. 1599), probably by Robert Greene, the interaction of high and low groups is prominent, and disguise's usefulness in facilitating a less inhibited contact between individuals separated by degree is also obvious.[13] Despite the sketchy national-political matter (the conflict of Edward of England and James of Scotland, and the treachery of the earl of Kendal and other English nobles) the play is the "pleasant conceyted comedie" it says it is;[14] we only hear (and cursorily) of the battle in which James is defeated, where "of thirtie thousand men, / There scapt not full five thousand from the field" (738–39). The kings' reconciliation is effortless, and the last quarter of the play is devoted to a whimsical journey north to see the Pinner, whose monarchial zeal is famous:

> I sore doe long to see this George a Greene:
> And for because I never saw the North,
> I will forthwith goe see it;
> And for that to none I will be knowen,
> We will disguise our selves and steale down secretly,
> Thou and I, King James, Cuddie, and two or three,
> And make a merrie journey for a moneth.
>
> (825–31)

The play concludes with George winning Bettris, Edward commanding her status-anxious father to let her marry the humble Pinner. The final scene, in which George and the shoemakers of "merrie Bradford" (1018) drink with two kings is, one suspects, what the play is for: the spectacle of nobles and common people familiarly mixing pleases on its own account and as an image of national unity. Of course other divisions, besides that between an elite and populace, are important: metropolitan corruption, for example, is throughout compared with rustic virtue; and there is a significant regional contrast, which George expresses: "we Yorkshire men be blunt of speech, / And litle skild in court or such quaint fashions" (1088–89), a sentiment that underlies his decline of the proffered knighthood: "Then let me live and die a yeoman still: / So was my father, so must live his sonne" (1196–97).[15] George is not well described as a plebeian—"yeoman" was a rural status term[16]—yet the play is interested in dramatizing broadly nonelite and elite relations. George's prowess, his loyalty to and identification with Edward, his braving of the aristocratic traitor Kendal, whom he strikes ("A poore man that is true, is better then an Earle, if he be false" [473–74]), the kings' journey to the North—each of these aspects of the play highlights or complicates some specifically social, or hierarchical, relation.

Heywood will serve as another example of a significant playwright (working in a different genre and with, as he boasted, "an entire hand, or at the least a maine finger" in 220 plays)[17] whose work suggests that a principal interest of Elizabethan drama is the display and exploration of social distinctions—that social hierarchy, far from being inert "background," is one of the essential topics of comedy, tragedy, and history (or comical-history).

Though some of the plays' material is found in Hall and Holinshed, Heywood's involvement with the chronicles in the two-part *Edward IV* (ca. 1592–99; pub. 1600) is less apparent than his preoccupation with degree and its complication—his real subject, as the title page of the 1600 edition hints, advertising the king's "merie pastime with the Tanner of Tamworth, as also his love to faire Mistrisse Shore, her great promotion, fall and miserie. . . . Likewise the besieging of London, by the Bastard Falconbridge, and the valiant defence of the same by the Lord Maior and the Citizens."[18] The title captures the way traditional social relations are revised in the play, with a monarch consorting with commoners and citizens standing up to nobles. In addition to Edward's friendship (as "Ned," a butler to the court) with Hobs the Tanner ("such a merry mate, / So frolicke and so full of good conceite" [1.47]) and his seduction of Mistress Shore, there is the controversy over his marriage to the comparatively humbly born Elizabeth Grey, with which the play opens. As in the jovial adventure play *The Four Prentices of London* (ca. 1592–1600; pub. 1615) Heywood is in this supposed history preoccupied with social mingling. *The Four Prentices* is an unballasted fantasy of social unity. The dispossessed earl of Bulloigne has, of "bare necessity," been "forct to loose the name of Earle, / And live in London like a Cittizen" (36, 28–29); his sons have had to take up apprenticeships but, far from being cast down by their ignominious position, they are good-natured about their new vocations: "all high borne, / Yet of the Citty-trades they have no scorne" (34–35). After many adventures, including making "Pagans bleed" in Jerusalem's conquest, they "winne such glorious praise as never fades, / Unto themslves and honour of their Trades" (335, 332–33). The mixing of elite and common, chivalry and crafts, is even more developed, and more ridiculous, than in *George a' Greene*. But like that play it seems socially meaningful and marginally less absurd when considered as articulating aspirations for national unity. So in *If You Know Not Me, You Know No Body* (Part One, 1604, pub. 1605; Part Two, 1605, pub. 1606) a haughty Queen Mary is associated exclusively with the court while Princess Elizabeth enjoys an easy, affectionate rapport with the people, apparent in the sympathy shown her by common soldiers, the poor, countrymen, and townsmen (1.209–10, 221–23) and in the loyalty of nonaristocratic figures like Master Gage and the rich haberdasher Old Hobson (1.214–15, 318): she seems to encompass elite and common worlds. As in *George a' Greene*, it is not merely social differences that are at stake: the differences between Elizabeth and Mary cannot be collapsed into degree and both, of course, are princes. Nonetheless, social contrasts are suggested: Elizabeth's character is more inclusive than Mary's. Heywood's Edward IV (a more problematic monarch than Elizabeth) is likewise sympathetic in appearing closer to nonelite life than others in his court (a contrast established early on in the difference between the relaxed conversational prose given him and the verse spoken by his mother, the duchess of York [1.3–7]). Such formulations of the play's contrasts do risk collapsing a range of differences (of character or style, or between country and city) into "degree." Yet social differences are also often implied in these other discourses, for instance in that of character: Mary's haughtiness of manner connotes an alienation from common people, just as Elizabeth's amiability signifies empathy.[19]

This book explores the social symbolism of various English Renaissance texts that, like *Mucedorus* and Munday's Robin Hood plays, or those by Greene and Heywood, take social difference as their subject matter. All the texts discussed find social hierarchy interesting, and central to their exploration of it is the elaboration of various modes of social interplay. I am preoccupied, then, with the way they deliberately manipulate social relations, especially those between gentle and common life.[20]

It is not, however, simply that the texts discussed here complicate hierarchy in various ways. A shared characteristic of many of them, and bound up with their preoccupation with social distinctions, is a sensitivity toward, and self-consciousness about, the social meanings and functions of literary modes, or the ways in which literary form is social form. I suggest that the preoccupation with social structure in these texts (their interest in articulating the interaction of different social spheres) flows into an awareness of the role of literary modes within this structure, in reproducing, complicating, or undoing it. This approach implies a mingling of discourses (of aesthetics and poetics with politics and discourse about society), but then the entangling of discourses of poetics and society is a feature of English Renaissance culture, and perhaps characteristic of the whole tradition of classical literary theory. *Poetics* 1448a1–18, with its famous distinction between tragedy and comedy (the former representing *spoudaious* [fine, important] men, and comedy *phaulous* [low, paltry] types) is perhaps the originating instance of this discursive complication: for such terms, while ethical, referring to a quality of character, imply a social distinction—it is understood that a *spoudaios* will be from the elite. Much as in the conventional term for the city-state elites, *kaloi k'agathoi* (the beautiful and fine), ethical, social, and aesthetic categories are somewhat undifferentiated—a slippage that by the Renaissance has hardened into dogma.[21] When Puttenham defines tragedy and comedy in *The Arte of English Poesie* (pub. 1589), social criteria are as fundamental as didacticism. So traditionally in tragedies the infamous life and tyrannies [of princes] were layd open to all the world, their wickednes reproched, their follies and extreme insolencies derided, and their miserable ends painted out in playes and pageants, to shew the mutabilitie of fortune, and the just punishment of God in revenge of a vicious and evill life.[22]

Many of Puttenham's generic criteria are social as well as formal.[23] The interimplication of aesthetic and social discourse in English Renaissance poetics provides some justification for a study of the ways certain literary texts foreground the relations between particular discursive or literary modes and social life. Sensitive to social distinctions, many of these texts also set up, for a variety of reasons, a certain internal distance on modes, or adopt a critical attitude toward their social character.[24] Throughout, then, my topic is the interrelation of literary and social structures: how the former negotiate the latter.

"Negotiate," like the "symbol" in "social symbolism," is intended to emphasize that these texts do not merely "reflect" or "represent" the Elizabethan social system; it is precisely their fictionality that makes possible an exploration of social distinctions.[25] Nevertheless, confessing the difficulty any sociological reading of texts has in avoiding referential metaphors, I note that two assumptions about sixteenth-century English society inform my discussion of the following works:[26] first, that this was an extremely status-conscious society, and second, that the content of social distinctions was often ambiguous.[27] It may be, then, that in this status-obsessed society some works find literary possibilities in exploring degree. Equally, just as social distinctions in the world may have appeared arbitrary or indefinable, they are often obscure in literary works. On occasion I shall argue for the instability, the slipperiness, of such distinctions in texts.

A play useful for this discussion is Beaumont's *Knight of the Burning Pestle* (1607), which features a citizen and his wife at the theater.[28] Here literary self-consciousness is inseparable from a general consciousness of rank and social distinctions.

The Knight represents certain conventions of romantic comedy as opaque to spectators of a particular type. The Grocer and his wife cannot grasp the rules of this genre; or, with different implications for our understanding of the play's social relations, if they do, they do not respect them (thus the scenes where the actors of *The London Merchant* remonstrate with George and Nell and try to save the play from their directorial interventions). So the Boy actor vainly protests that George's wish to have his apprentice Rafe (playing the Knight of the Burning Pestle) fight the romantic hero Jasper Merrythought "lies contrary" to "the plot" and "'twill hazard the spoiling of our play" (2.271–72). George and Nell are then, in this context anyway, social outsiders: not only are they because of their social position incapable of responding appropriately to the conventions of the play before them (demanding, for instance, that Rafe "come away quickly and die," even though the Boy objects that a death "in a comedy" would "be very unfit" [5.284–87]), they are also innocent of an understanding of dramatic illusion itself, addressing the characters as if they were real people[29] and George even threatening to "bring half a dozen good fellows myself" to enforce the ludicrous Humphrey's claim to the Merchant's daughter (2.14–15). George and Nell can be counted upon to make the wrong interpretation within the play's terms: a base materialism ("Give me a penny i' th' purse while I live, George" [1.376]) guides their preference for Humphrey as Luce's husband (rather than the vivacious and engaging, but impecunious, apprentice Jasper Merrythought) and they disapprove of the latter's eccentric and thriftless father.[30] Elementary conventions elude Nell (she takes Jasper to be in earnest when he tries Luce's confidence by threatening her with death, calling George to "raise the watch at Ludgate" and the "gentlemen" in the house to "see the King's peace kept" [3.92, 94–95]), and neither she nor George are much concerned that their interventions "hazard the spoiling" (2.271) of the narrative: "Plot me no plots" (2.273) cries George. It is, however, not so much the satire on citizen tastelessness or *gaucherie* that makes this play significant for a discussion of socio-literary symbolism in the period, but its explicit thematization of such symbolism. Doubtless *The Knight* simplifies the relations between social rank and literary modes at this time.[31] Nonetheless, what is interesting about the play is precisely the difficulty of sorting out aesthetic and social allegiances in it: the conflict between the players' play, *The London Merchant,* and George and Nell's *Knight of the Burning Pestle* is neither a "formal" debate about better or worse modes of comedy, nor solely a question of "class loyalty" (or this is seen to involve aesthetic preferences). Instead, what we find—through the interaction of citizens, players, and mute gentlemen—are the conventions of chivalric romance and romantic comedy distanced and viewed as social symbolisms. *The Knight* understands particular discursive modes as socially specific, even exclusive, forms; and the "huffing part" (induction, 74) Rafe speaks for George and Nell (Hotspur's honor speech from *1 Henry IV*), translated to this incongruous social context and spoken by a Grocer's apprentice, is noticed as aristocratic form as much as poetic style.[32] More profoundly, the play presents a literary value, narrative coherence, as a social one: the Boy appeals to the "gentlemen" to "rule" the Citizen who "will not suffer us to go on with our plot" (3.297–99), asking their "pardon" if, the players yielding to George's wish for a passage of arms between Rafe and Jasper, "anything fall out of order" (2.276, 275). Although George and Nell's preference for shows and vigorous action over generic rationality is treated amusedly rather than harshly, the implications are clear: their apathy toward "art" speaks eloquently for the need that they be kept in tow by those who value "order," in art as in life.

Rather than simply assuming social relations, as a backdrop against which to explore other concerns, *The Knight* dramatizes them: the Wife's claim that she is "a gentlewoman born" (3.558) may or may not be absurd but is a subject of the play.[33] Nell's claim, however ridiculous, renders the ideal, traditional social hierarchy less static, giving some initiative to the citizens. Besides airing grievances (the players "have still girds at citizens," complains George [induction, 7–8]), the Grocer and his wife make their presence felt in the recreation of the "gentlemen." Yet the play affirms aesthetically their subordination. The artlessness of George and Nell's *Knight of the Burning Pestle* is finally politically meaningful.

I shall suggest, then, that the literary complexity of the works considered here is also a social complexity, and that such complexity accompanies an interest in the social character of discursive forms. In Thomas Nashe's prose, in some plays dealing with citizens or the lesser gentry, and in a few Shakespeare plays, certain discursive modes are apprehended as the cultural codes of social groups: tragedy particularly is seen as the cultural code of aristocratic privilege. The poetic self-consciousness of these texts is undetachable, it seems, from a social understanding: they register the possible social force of literary modes or, rather, they see them as cultural.

In Nashe the awareness of the social symbolism of forms seems to have its roots in unenviable social circumstances. Denied the life of power and prestige—unlike, say, the aristocrat-amateur Sidney—Nashe articulates this marginalization through a "knavish" irreverence toward the high discursive modes associated with elite milieux.[34] Assuming a persona virtually undecidable in social character (a mix of popular clown, humanist scholar and sophisticate, and would-be courtier), Nashe's texts articulate an ambiguous interplay between high and low social spheres—

an instability of tone and viewpoint that reflects and capitalizes upon the ambiguousness of his position as professional humanist author. Exploring the mingling of elite and common socio-literary styles in Nashe, I suggest that a certain social marginality underlies his view of high forms as cultural codes symbolizing the courtly, aristocratic world—a world that he belongs to by education but is otherwise excluded from. If a writer like Jonson manages to project himself as at home in this milieu—never mind his brushes with authority—Nashe's relation with it is less certain.[35]

The citizen, or minor gentry, plays discussed in chapter 2 present relatively humble or nonelite life as capable of tragic intensity and dignity, taking over many of the conventions of tragedy to do this. I have called them "bourgeois" tragedies, not because all their heroes are merchants or well-off craftsmen or otherwise members of the urban elite, but to stress that they diverge from aristocratic norms in at least one respect: the effort to write tragedies about "middling groups."[36] In them tragedy coexists uneasily with the "bourgeois" or nonaristocratic sphere evoked: if they use the tragic paradigm, they also seem to distance it (in one case critically) as elite, to identify it as an aristocratic cultural code (a literary mode thus being figured as a social one).

In the chapter on Shakespeare four plays are seen as highly self-aware regarding the social symbolism of form. *The Taming of the Shrew* and *A Midsummer Night's Dream* feature theatrical or quasi-theatrical occasions that involve (in a way reminiscent of *The Knight of the Burning Pestle*) social interplay; such occasions, moreover, are implicated in efforts to reaffirm conventional social order. Comedy (in the induction to the *Shrew*) and tragedy (in the Pyramus and Thisby playlet) are seen as forms with a social role in the play worlds. And both plays are interested in temporarily complicating, or confusing, socially hierarchical relations, though each resolves this complication differently. In *Coriolanus* and *The Two Noble Kinsmen*, tragedy, rather as in the nonelite "tragedies" of chapter 2, is understood culturally: not, that is, in narrowly formal, "literary" terms ("in Comedies, *turbulenta prima, tranquilla ultima;* in Tragedyes, *tranquilla prima, turbulenta ultima*"—Thomas Heywood invoking Donatus),[37] but as an aristocratic symbolic mode. The profound social interplay of both works constitutes the ground for this critical view of tragedy: in *Coriolanus* the plebeian perspective is a continuous, tense context for Caius Martius's actions, actually interrogating tragic values; in *The Two Noble Kinsmen*—that meditation on the ideal of nobility—the affecting underplot of the Jailer's Daughter moves tantalizingly close to tragedy and, stretching the boundaries of this form, foregrounds its traditional social identity. In all the plays, poetic self-consciousness shades into an awareness of the social-symbolic possibilities of poetic forms.

1

"Playing the Knave":
Social Symbolism and
Interplay in Thomas Nashe

Who's in, who's out

—Shakespeare, *King Lear*

Here let me triumph a while, and ruminate a line or two on the excellence of my wit: but I will not breath neither till I have disfraughted all my knaverie

—Nashe, *The Unfortunate Traveller*

These are but wild and whirling words, my lord

—Shakespeare, *Hamlet*

This chapter explores the complex social symbolism of some Nashe texts. My interest is in the socially restless and ambiguous nature of his work, the theme of a social "insider/outsider"[1] that runs through it, and its uncertain relation to elite culture and society. It is possible to see Nashe as drawing upon popular culture. I shall argue, though, that any assimilation of him to such a culture needs extensive qualification.[2] In considering what Nashe might have taken from this culture, I draw on Robert Weimann's well-known account of another Renaissance humanist's relation to "the popular tradition." The graduate Nashe's relation to this tradition, however, is overridingly ambivalent and anxious. More generally, I argue that an "oppositionalist" reading of Nashe, in which "popular culture" subverts high culture, is unhelpful for working out the social symbolism of his texts. This chapter, then, considers Nashe's work as articulating an ambiguous interplay of broadly low and high socio-rhetorical styles. We shall see that an interest in the literary possibilities of social interplay is central to his work. We shall also see that Nashe's

27

relative social marginality—of the elite generally, yet in important ways outside it—presented him with problems of self-presentation as well as possibilities: among the latter, the ironic manipulation of aristocratic symbolic modes. Some insight into the problems involved in formulating the social-political dimension of Nashe's style can be gained by examining, through a comparison with John Lyly, "variety" in the Nasheian text.

The Politics of Variety in Nashe and Lyly

> It is varietie that moveth the minde of all men. . . . The fayrest nosegay is made of many flowers, the finest picture of sundry colours, the wholesomest medicine of divers hearbs . . .
> —Lyly, *Euphues, The Anatomy of Wyt*

For many Elizabethans, the desirability of variety in literature seemed obvious. Title pages frequently advertise this preference: *Euphues and his England,* for example, one of the most popular books of the age, promises the reader Euphues' "voyage and adventures, myxed with sundry pretie discourses."[3] Even scholarly handbooks, such as Thomas Wilson's *Arte of Rhetorique* (pub. 1553), show themselves willing to accommodate the impulse running through much Elizabethan writing toward variety.[4] The convention seems so reasonable that Lyly merely appeals to common sense when he prefaces a digression by saying:

> And although some shall thinke it impertinent to the historie, they shall not find it repugnant, no more then in one nosegay to set two flowers, or in one counterfaite two coulours, which bringeth more delight, then disliking. (2.14)

A predilection for variety precedes the Renaissance and survives neoclassicism, no doubt partly because of the problem Shakespeare presented any unduly gallicizing theory; so Neander, in *An Essay of Dramatic Poesy,* wonders "why Lisideius and many others should cry up the barrenness of the French plots, above the variety and copiousness of the English. . . . our variety, if well ordered, will afford a greater pleasure to the audience."[5] Even the neoclassicist Jonson gave first place in composition to a fruitful, copious invention, notwithstanding that such invention often "riots out of plenty."[6] (Madeleine Doran notes that "Jonson loves variety as much as Shakespeare" as his "abundance of words, incidents, and characters" shows: "Rabelais, Ariosto, Cervantes, Spenser, and Shake-speare saw beauty in multiplicity of detail.")[7] The taste for variety, as Lisideius's remark suggests, was perhaps strongest in the drama, where the influence of academic theory was limited:[8] M. C. Bradbrook has remarked that the material of Elizabethan dramatists was "as heteroge-neous as that of a revue."[9] Yet Dryden's defense of "variety" specified that it be "well ordered," and to the classically minded of the sixteenth and seventeenth centuries delight in variety could appear as a degraded appetite for disorder. Thus C. S. Lewis observed that

> the great literature of the fifteen-eighties and nineties was something which humanism, with its unities and *Gorboducs* and English hexameters, would have prevented if it could, but failed to prevent because the high tide of native talent was then too strong for it.[10]

Lyly and Nashe exemplify the Elizabethan aesthetic of variety in strikingly different ways: a comparison of the place of it in each will make clearer some of the social implications of this mode in the period and provide a starting point for analyzing the social symbolism of Nashe's work. But let us first sketch how English Renaissance literary variety might be allegorized politically.

If the urge toward variety is an aspect of much Elizabethan writing, it exists alongside an "artistic" commitment to regularity and order, particularly generic order.[11] One could construct a literary history of the period 1500 to 1700 in England in which, pressured by an enlightened or progressive classical humanism, a naïve taste for variety gradually gives way to an inchoate ideal of formal order: such a history would trace a transition from a perceived formless or barbarous medieval literature toward a modern sense of generic order and consistency.[12] Whatever one makes of such a history, much Elizabethan literature does seem to display a tension between the theoretical ideal of generic coherency ("art") and a pretheoretical preference, most obvious in the drama but not exclusive-ly, for multiple (and not necessarily compatible) effects—effects that, when successful, can be bold and radical (the grotesque, for example), and, when not, inarticulate and obscure.[13]

A feature of this dialectic between order and variety in the literature of Renaissance England is that it is replicated in the political culture. We can argue, that is, that the key emphases of political and poetic theory loosely reflect or implicate each other or, more likely, that the normative values of neoclassic theory articulate in the aesthetic arena social-political ones. Such an interimplication of discourses should not surprise, since all neoclassical theories of poetry in the Renaissance accord it an unambiguous ethical function, thus implying a possible political role, as Nashe described: plays "shew the ill successe of treason, the fall of hastie climbers, the wretched end of usurpers, the miserie of civill dissention, and how just God is evermore in punishing of murther" (1.213).[14] The connection of reigning political goals with English neoclassicism is suggested, admittedly very abstractly, by the resonance the idea of aesthetic unity has when it is juxtaposed with the fundamental political difficulty of Elizabethan society: the problem of the Elizabethan settlement (which, as one historian remarks, "settled nothing"),[15] or that of securing unity in a country haunted, to greater or lesser degrees of intensity, by the specter of religious (and thus civil) conflict. Elizabeth's England, after all, was caught in a contradiction between the authoritarian desire for total uniformity and the practical need to tolerate a certain amount of variety in faith. The *Homily of Obedience,* from 1547 read by decree in all churches of the land, does indeed suggest that the keynote of Tudor political discourse is obedience (and its nightmarish antithesis, rebellion), and that the end of official discourse is always what the *Homily* calls "right order."[16] This stress on order seems to have had a simultaneous life in political, religious, and aesthetic discourses, which were themselves, probably, not as rigorously distinguishable then as now (the interests of authoritarian societies always lying, presumably, in repressing their autonomy). Orthodoxy in religion, national unity in politics, "degree" in social thought: all these ideals are part of a concern for order in the whole commonwealth, and an allegiance to art, aesthetic unity, and the kinds participates in this conservative commitment (the paradox being, of course, that neo"classicism" is both a conservative and an innovating aesthetic program). So aesthetic and social conservatism seem to run hand in hand:[17] the position of the stage in this context being especially complex, apparently as available to radical as to conservative constructions—alternately promoted as a mainstay of society or denounced as a breeding ground of sedition and disorder.[18] Possibly the empirical basis for firm judgments about the politics of the playhouses is inadequate; what cannot be doubted is the connection drawn between them and politics.[19] The discussion so far suggests that a concern for the right order of stage plays, from the demand that they not be seditious or scandalous to the concern that they observe canons of propriety, decorum, and generic coherency, was part of a larger preoccupation with the right ordering of society. Thus the scorn of a Jonson for popular romances (even *Pericles* being a "mouldy tale") might express the conservative's suspicion that the "artlessness" of such plays is both symptom and cause of a general disorder in the age.[20] In any case, it seems possible to identify neoclassic disapproval of formless, naïve, and supposedly popular poetic work with a certain official anxiety about social order generally, an anxiety doubtless having roots in the peculiar stresses that the Reformation and demographic and economic change had brought to England.[21] The concept of decorum is, after all, virtually a social one, as is clear from Sidney's famous attack: "all their plays be neither right tragedies, nor right comedies, mingling kings and clowns."[22] Sidney imputes the drama's mixedness to incompetence rather than to an interest in exploring hierarchical relations and social differences. Nevertheless, the important point is that his understanding of decorum is explicitly social, and that behind neoclassic hostility to the mixing of modes lurks a political regard for the good husbanding of society (the political import of the idea being captured in Shakespeare's line about the chaos in Vienna: "quite athwart / Goes all decorum" [*Measure for Measure,* 1.3.30–31]). Sidney's concern to regulate and modernize dramatic form may even be understandable as part of a general modernization of English society, so that the centralization of power in the state and the emergence of a national society would have equivalents in moves for the updating and improvement of culture.[23] However that may be, the interest in regulating the drama is relatable to a concern for "right order" *(Homily of Obedience)* generally. Occasionally an explicit connection is drawn between the state of the arts and the state. Thus a common humanist prejudice seems to have been that the refinement of language by the poets and art by the rules, the reformation of faith, and the achievement of relative political stability under Elizabeth and James constituted one grand modern civilizing movement away from the rudeness, strife, superstition, and "tyranny of ignorance" *(Nashe,* 3.322) of medieval life.[24] Ben Jonson, at least, is clear about the link between language, and by implication the arts of language, and social order: "Wheresoever manners and fashions are corrupted, language is. It imitates the public riot."[25] Jonson's remark indicates one approach to ascribing social meaning to the discursive modes of Thomas Nashe. For now, we may say that variety, if an aspect of Elizabethan art, is problematic for the way it threatens, from a neoclassic viewpoint, to turn into disorder or "riot": a corrupt society, from this perspective, producing a corrupt, undisciplined language and art, which in turn compound social corruption. Thus a concern for purity in language and unity in art might not be wholly academic: in a society largely without the means for enforcing obedience[26] and reliant on persuasion, ideology, and culture to keep the peace, this concern is probably connected with that for society in general.

Lyly, in a passage Robert Weimann has made prominent, grounds the variety of Elizabethan plays in social heterogeneity. The St. Paul's prologue to *Midas* (1589; pub. 1592) observes that every social group demands it own kind: "Souldiers call for Tragedies, their object is bloud: Courtiers for Commedies, their subject is love; Countriemen for Pastoralles, Shepheards are their Saintes." In satisfying each, the dramatist ends up with a "Gallimaufrey": "If wee present a mingle-mangle, our fault is to be excused, because the whole worlde is become an Hodge-podge."[27] Weimann accepts Lyly's notion of a literary "mingle-mangle" reflecting the social and economic "mingle-mangle" of Tudor England, that mix of social groups that finds its most sophisticated cultural expression in the interplay of popular and elite theatrical traditions in Shakespeare. For Weimann this expansive, turbulent social life is the historical precondition for Shakespeare's expansive and dynamically "complementary" art. For my purposes the interest of the passage lies in its presenting a "soft" version of a social disarray that receives more pessimistic expression by conservatives.[28] Plays, Lyly breezily tells us, lack order because society does, and the unruly variety of social life ("Trafficke and travell hath woven the nature of all Nations into ours, and made this land like Arras, full of devise, which was Broade-cloth, full of workmanshippe") instead of being disciplined by the genres, confounds them, for "all commeth to this passe, that what heretofore hath beene served in severall dishes for a feaste, is now minced in a charger for a Gallimaufrey." Yet what is remarkable about the passage is its balanced phrasing, imposing on this instability a rhetorical order. This transformation of social confusion into aesthetic symmetry provides the basis for a contrast with Nashe. Lyly's tone is relaxed and playful, and there is a confident recognition of the transformative power of art (the description of his own plays as "mingle-mangle" is the falsest humility) or its capacity to make over a perceived social disorderliness into an elegant, complex poetic abundance. And yet, despite its self-satisfaction, this passage speaks to the same concerns that underlie the lurid Tudor nightmares about "confusion," and the conservatives' fear that the center might not hold, that like the planets of Ulysses' speech in *Troilus and Cressida,* the vital social distinctions might "In evil mixture to disorder wander" (1.3.95).

It may be, then, that the division between order and variety in English

Renaissance literature has a politics as well as poetics—that this aesthetic tension is historically meaningful. Certainly much depends, in interpreting Elizabethan and Jacobean literature, whether one stresses genre, for instance, as a principle mode of order, or rhetorical and dramatic variety. If genre imposes unity on the materials offered by experience and the imagination, making sense by subordinating some elements of a text to others and disposing all into a coherent pattern, and if this commitment to genre is the primary commitment of Elizabethan literature, then that literature—and not inconceivably the society it might be taken to speak to and for—could be seen as characterized above all by order.[29] And if, following Stephen Greenblatt, those genres themselves are understood as quasi-official structures, "the aesthetically codified stock of social knowledge,"[30] then emphasizing them in Renaissance literature will have important consequences for understanding its politics. Interpreting variety as the fundamental impulse of Elizabethan literary art may, on the other hand, make available a picture of it and, possibly, of the period, characterized by difference and discontinuity—we will feel that the texts of this period in particular need to be understood dialectically, as an interplay of various elements, rather than univocally—and we may well judge that such a pluralistic, dynamic model is appropriate for the culture as a whole. These two pictures of the period (often seen as the products respectively of older or conservative and newer or radical historicisms in literary study) may thus be taken to emphasize distinct tendencies in the literature of the age.

I suggest that the different form variety assumes in Nashe and Lyly is capable of political allegorization, and it will be useful to outline this approach now if only to complicate it later. We shall see, indeed, that Nashe's ambiguous social position makes such complication unavoidable.

Taken as a whole, the preeminent quality of Nashe's writing is its difficulty: tone and viewpoint are often obscure, ironies are generated with a seeming lack of control, and the reader is left with the impression of a divided, incoherent energy. Nashe's editor spoke of the "utter want of unity and of definite plan" (5.18) in *Pierce Penilesse* (pub. 1592), the most commercially successful work, and G. R. Hibbard has argued persuasively that the obscurity and disconnectedness of *Pierce* is deliberate[31]—in effect that it is a sixteenth-century *Tristram Shandy*. Perhaps Nashe is reacting against the decorativeness of some Elizabethan writing. In one of the *Parnassus* plays (1598–1601; Part Two only pub. 1606) Ingenioso, possibly modeled on Nashe, has a foppish patron in love with the poems of "sweet Mr. Shakespeare": "Ile have his picture in my study at the courte."[32] Possibly, then, Nashe was thought to scorn the Ovidian fluency and, as Henry Chettle put it, "facetious grace in writing" of Shakespeare's narrative poems.[33] At any rate, the contrast between Nashe's style and Lyly's clarity and measure is startling, even though Lyly, apparently an influence (*"Euphues* I readd when I was a little ape in Cambridge, and then I thought it was *Ipse ille"* [1.319]) is present in the early *Anatomy of Absurdity* (pub. 1589):

> a payre of cardes better pleaseth her then a peece of cloth, her beades then her booke, a bowle full of wine then a handfull of wooll, delighting more in a daunce then in Davids Psalmes, to play with her dogge then to pray to her God. (1.18)

The more characteristic Nashe, though, is recognizable in this passage from *The Unfortunate Traveller* (pub. 1594; Jack Wilton "at Windsore or at Hampton Court"):

> For your instruction and godly consolation, bee informed, that at that time I was no common squire, no undertrodden torch-bearer; I had my feather in my cap as big as a flag in the fore-top; my French dublet gelte in the bellie as though (like a pig readie to be spitted) all my guts had bin pluckt out; a paire of side paned hose that hung downe like two scales filled with Holland cheeses; my long stock that sate close to my docke, and smoothered not a scab or a leacherous hairie sinew on the calfe of the legge; my rapier pendant like a round sticke fastned in the tacklings for skippers the better to climbe by; my cape cloake of blacke cloth, overspreading my backe like a thorne-backe, or an Elephantes eare, that hanges on his shoulders like a countrie huswives banskin, which she thirles hir spindle on, & in consummation of my curiositie, my hands without glooves, all a more French, and a blacke budge edging of a beard on the upper lip, and the like sable anglet of excrements in the rising of the anckle of my chinne. (2.227)

This illustrates the problem in much of Nashe's work: the extravagant "multiplicity of detail" (see above, p. 29) threatens to overwhelm the meaning (a description of Jack's dandified appearance). There is an overload of information. In Nashe, Gothic excess of detail teeters on the brink of disintegration (so C. S. Lewis and Jonathan Crewe have treated his texts as "pure" or themeless writing).[34] It is as if Nashe takes the old, naïve, decorative Elizabethan pleasure in variety (or *copia* or plenty) and redoes it in a disorienting and potentially disturbing form—potentially, because accompanying the disorder is the text's controlling, impish sense of play, complicating any attempt to read Nashe as radically criticizing order.[35] Indeed, Nashe's playfulness is as much of a problem for any radical interpretation of his work as the overt expressions of religious or social conservatism. The conservative pessimism of Nashe's interpretation of the age as one of a widespread moral decline ("this is an yron age, or rather no yron age, for swordes and bucklers goe to pawne a pace in Long-Lane: but a tinne age; for tinne and pewter are more esteemed than Latine" [1.182]) might legitimate rather than disallow a modernist understanding of his work, where that term connotes a despairing equation of modernity and disorder—Nashe's nostalgia then suggesting the distaste of another conservative and backward-looking modernist of this century for "the immense panorama of futility and anarchy which is contemporary history."[36] So Nashe's discontinuous, often bewildering form (or formlessness) might confront and express a late sixteenth-century awareness of this "panorama" of futile contemporaneity, might, that is (to recall the remark from Jonson's *Timber*), critically imitate a corruption in manners, the "public riot" of the late Elizabethan Iron Age (the "riot" Lyly articulates as abundance). This satirical, sharp-toothed Nashe is tempting as a way of formulating the social meaning of his style, particularly as it provides a rationale for his departure from humanist canons of decorum—and has, moreover, some historical authority in Greene's reference to him as a salty wit, "yong Juvenall, that byting Satyrist."[37] But the Nashe this picture provides is radical only in means: the ends are impeccably orthodox. An even more difficult obstacle for a radical reading of Nashe's style is that, in omitting the vital element of play, this "engaged" Nashe seems to distort the essential stance of the texts—for Nashe cultivates disorder with Puckish verve, and in this gleeful, mischievous attitude the satirist's tone, radical or conservative, is not easily discerned. The playfulness, then, of Nashe's disorder seems to preclude its description either as radical criticism or modernist despair. Play is, indeed, crucial to the social symbolism of Nashe's work. For the moment, however, and to return to our passage about Jack Wilton at court, we can say that Lyly is vestigially present even in this characteristic performance: Lyly, too, has detail and variety in the multitudinous *exempla* drawn from, for instance, mythological natural history and other such recondite lore. Yet one all-important difference is that in Lyly this lavish piling-up of instances has an obvious inner direction and discipline (converting "mingle-mangle" into art), with each detail obeying the strong logical scheme of the sentence. One never fears that the whole pile might come crashing down.

Lyly has variety, not only in the amount of "information" brought together in a Lylean sentence, but also structurally. But even this structural variety (the careful articulation of different social groups in the plays, for instance, or the layered levels of seriousness in the love relations of a play like *Endimion* [1588; pub. 1594]) tends to be hierarchically coordinated: structure, art, is foregrounded in Lyly's texts in a way unlike the more freewheeling modes of Nashe.[38] The different appearance variety takes in Nashe and Lyly can be better appreciated by looking at the function of wit in each.

Wit in both writers is a continuous concern. But in Lyly it is usually clearly circumscribed in range (it is rectified by wisdom in *Euphues*) while in Nashe it is a law unto itself: though it is very much the source of Jack Wilton's troubles in *The Unfortunate Traveller,* for example, (who is too clever for his own good), it is a question just how far wit is chastened by the end of that work. The contrast with Lyly is more obvious if we recall that in his plays the pages' riddling, fecund, logic-chopping wit is confined to specific scenes, at the margins of the play so to speak, and at its close they are brought into line. But instead of being subordinated to "serious" concerns, it is as if Nashe takes over Lyly's paradoxical wit-crackers and plumps them in the middle of his text; and the extraordinary abundance of imagery, incidents, and characters that are then generated are not harmonized by a clear controlling viewpoint or tone. Verbal wit is not, as in Lyly, an aspect of a carefully ordered variousness; it is an autonomous principle and the source of a prolific rhetorical variety. Partly this is the show-off in Nashe: the virtuoso extemporal Tarltonizing that is at the center of his texts as much as one of Lyly's naughty pages.[39] However that may be, the result is that Nashe's work is far less coherent than Lyly's: Elizabethan decorative variety (note the quaint, pretty imagery in the quotation from *Euphues* at the beginning of this section) turns into a kind of derangement and, as hinted at in the comparisons with Lyly's pages or with Tarlton, there is in this the appearance of a popular artlessness. May we impute to this literary Tarltonism, this cultivation of "popular" disorder and disregard of decorum and unity, a critical function? Robert Weimann's researches into the critical potential of popular culture in Shakespeare—relating Hamlet's "wild and whirling words," for example, to a tradition of popular topsy-turvydom, which drives "home a profoundly serious criticism of society"[40]—make this an inevitable question when considering Nashe's incoherence and extravagance. I hope to show the disadvantages of this "critical" reading even while granting its usefulness in key respects. For the moment, we may note that Nashe has more than a smack of the discontented scholar of Wittenberg about him, and that he may say with Hamlet, "Sir, I lack advancement" (Claudius's Elsinore is as "art-disgracing" a world as Ingenioso endures in the *Parnassus* plays),[41] and that Hamlet, with his supremely complex relation to both "popular" and "elite" cultures, epitomizes beautifully the ambiguous insider/outsider tension I will describe in Nashe. But to take up again the question of "criticism": Stephen Hilliard's recent judgment that Nashe's

> works would not necessarily be better if they were more reflective and better organized; rather, they acquire a special importance because . . . [they] reveal the contradictions of Elizabethan society rather than the idealized myth

while not in itself presupposing a critical edge to Nashe's style, does anticipate such an interpretation, especially when read in light of his later comment that "euphuism was in accord with the analogical and hierarchical cosmology that justified the social order."[42] Hilliard is interested in the paradox of Nashe's apparent conservatism and "radical" style,[43] and the contrast between a "unified" Lyly and "contradictory" Nashe is suggestive, as is the attempt to read these styles ideologically: it seems reasonable to suppose that in Nashe Elizabethan variety takes on, at times, a more serious aspect as the expression of social contradiction, possibly as a counterblast to the Lylean studied and harmonious, or artful, articulation of multiplicity. Lyly sees a social "hodge-podge" but evokes a serene, cool, elegant variety, where conflicts are resolved by "art" (in highly formal debates), and where inner conflict, for example, is seductively graceful:

> And canst thou Lucilla be so light of love in forsaking Philautus to flye to Euphues? canst thou prefer a straunger before thy countryman? A starter before thy companion? Why Euphues doth perhappes desyre my love, but Philautus hath deserved it. Why Euphues feature is worthy as good as I, But Philautus his fayth is worthy a better. I but the latter love is moste fervent. I but the firste ought to be most faythfull. I but Euphues hath greater perfection. I but Philautus hath deeper affection. (1.205)

Seldom does Nashe's prose attain, or seek, such poise.

Nevertheless, if Nashe's style pursues a stylistic disorder—finding its obvious antithesis in the work of Lyly (if Lyly sets a particular tone for the eighties, idealizing and "golden," if tinged with irony, Nashe supplies the next decade with its idiom)—providing a political allegory for this style is not easy: in particular, determining whether it counts as criticism of "right order" is difficult.[44] I shall argue that the radical language of contradiction is, finally, inappropriate for Nashe's work, and that we are safer emphasizing its social-rhetorical ambiguousness. Thus we cannot identify Nashe too readily with a so-called popular mode, especially where that is conceived as opposing an "aristocratic" style[45] (yielding a neat political-stylistic contrast with Lyly): for Nashe's relation to "popular" culture is as complicated and ambivalent as his relation to "elite" culture (while such a formulation probably inadequately describes the professional writer Lyly, even if he is taken as more closely related to the court than Nashe—for a time, perhaps, supplying it with a symbolic mode).

Yet it would be difficult to exaggerate the extent of Nashe's departure from humanist canons of eloquence, and the desire to read this departure as a political counterstyle (mistaking, perhaps, an artistic avant-garde for a political one) finds ironic support in the likelihood that Nashe's manner had its roots in the ebullient, scandalously irreverent style of Martin Marprelate, a style first appearing in the service of an oppositional religious cause.[46] Obviously the connection with Martin—and we recall that the Establishment's anti-Martin pamphlets of 1589–90 (some by Nashe and Lyly) aped their adversary's "plain and homely" but "railing" voice[47]—is suggestive in considering the potential radicalism of Nashe's style. Let us then conclude this introduction to the complexities involved in describing the social-political dimensions of Nashe's work by situating it in the context of Marprelatism and humanist controversial writing generally (taking Thomas More as our example). We continue here to outline possibilities for a radical reading of Nashe's aesthetic of variety.

C. S. Lewis's remark that More is the "literary ancestor of Martin Marprelate and Nashe" is debatable.[48] Perhaps there is nothing very novel in the varying of levels of seriousness or the alternation of socially marked discursive modes in Martin or Nashe. More peppers his texts with jokes and humor, proverbs and sarcasm, and an ironic wit: "A mery tale," as he tells the Messenger in the *Dialogue Concerning Heresies,* "commyth never amysse to me."[49] (Martin justifies humor in polemics in *Hay Any Worke for Cooper:* "The Lord being the author both of mirth and gravity, is it not lawful in itself, for the truth to use either of these ways, when the circumstances do make it lawful?") Perhaps the most significant continuity between More and Martin is the use of unlettered figures (Martin is one—probably the original is Piers Plowman) who debunk sham and humbug with realistic common sense: we shall see that

Nashe often exploits the deflationary potential of a putative popular idiom.[50] "You must then bear with my ingramness," says Martin: "I am plain; I must needs call a spade a spade; a pope a pope."[51] In *The Confutation of Tyndale's Answer,* More has the reader picture "some good honest merchauntes wyfe, a woman honest of her conversacyon," questioning the Protestant polemicist Robert Barnes.[52] Soon her mother wit scuppers Barnes's heretical subtleties: "Lo thus myght a wyse woman that coulde no more but rede englyshe, rebuke and confounde frere Barons uppon the syght of his owne ryall processe, in which he wold now teache us to know whyche is the very chyrche." (Barnes also comes to grief with the hostess of his inn, "a pore woman that coulde not rede.")[53] But the vital point about this mix of types of utterance in More—the urbane and learned, the "popular," the ironic and jocular—is, as Stephen Hilliard has argued, that they are integrated into a total meaning: they never disorient a reader as the rapid changes in register do in Martin and Nashe. "Humanistic irony," Hilliard points out,

> like that of Erasmus or More, has an elegant consistency: there may be some ambiguity, but there is no confusion, and the overall direction is clear. The later neoclassic ironists also controlled their ironic effects to serve their satiric or pathetic purposes. But Elizabethan irony . . . is often rough-hewn and confusing.[54]

So More is often pleasantly ironic in the *Dialogue Concerning Heresies,* but the Messenger exaggerates when he says: "ye use . . . to loke so sadly when ye mene merely that many tymes men doubte whyther ye speke in sporte when ye mene good ernest."[55] More's amiable ironies are never in doubt, unlike the multiple and seemingly undisciplined ironies released by the antic disposition of a Nashe (or a Martin). (One is reminded of Mann's Herr Settembrini, insisting that the only healthy irony is that which is "a direct and classic device of oratory.")[56] Irony in More clarifies rather than scandalizes (as Martin's irreverence did)[57] and there is a rational and traditional hierarchy of literary devices. By contrast, Martin and Nashe produce, as G. R. Hibbard has said, a "calculated indecorum" that in Nashe can be regarded as an unbounded *copia* or intensification of literary multiplicity.[58] The very unconventionalism of this discursive mode (what Hilliard dubs its "singularity") will suggest an aura of radicalism, literary nonconformism implying a general nonconformism or "scandal." The problem, then, is to determine the character in Nashe's hands of a style that in Martin's expresses a robust contempt for official institutions.

I have raised the possibility of reading Nashe's style as criticism and the question of its relation to a notion of popular culture. Subsequently, I shall emphasize against this "critical" interpretation the special pressures of Nashe's position: a position neither outside nor very satisfactorily inside the culture of the elite. Such a painfully ambiguous situation renders, I think, the idea of Nashe criticizing this culture and its modes unsustainable. Martin, at least, has helped raise the general problem of what it means to say that a style in this period is radical.

If we shall have to complicate the notion of criticism as applied to Nashe, we can say that More is a good example of the humanist discipline of variety into order (an order Lyly exaggerates into a highly self-conscious, ostentatiously artificial mode and which Nashe flamboyantly dispenses with)—and we can still identify in this contrast between Lyly and Nashe a significant social symbolism, two different mirrors held up to the age and body of the time. Lyly's elegant articulation of variety may be taken to symbolize a basic cultural optimism, a confidence in the possibilities for successfully managing difference and winning unity out of "hodge-podge": the foregrounded art of this style seeming to guarantee a social ideal of harmony and stability. By the time, however, of Falstaff's mockery of euphuism in the midnineties (*1 Henry IV,* 2.4.399–402), Lyly's idealizing, sanguine art, playfully reflecting society's best self-image, is beginning to look decidedly old hat, perhaps naïve; there is greater interest in a modern abrasiveness and bite (and this Nashe sought to satisfy) and, perhaps, less confidence in the social ideal itself.

Nashe, Contradiction, and Interplay: The Example of *Lenten Stuffe*

The politics of the Nasheian text appear complex. I have suggested that Nashe's revision of a traditional Elizabethan rhetorical variety into a disorienting multiplicity or apparently undisciplined formlessness can be read contrarily: as potential radical undermining and scandalous mockery of those canons of decorum that underpin social and aesthetic order; as the conservative's bitter indictment, through grotesque mimicry, of a chaotic, repulsive contemporary scene. In either case the contrast is with Lyly, where variety symbolizes a certain social beauty and stylistic order, a broader human harmony. In respect of the social symbolism of the two styles, we note how easily and completely, if briefly, euphuism became a court style and how Nashe's manner did not enjoy this dissemination as a social form. *Pierce Penilesse* had a certain vogue, and some imitators, but its success was nothing by comparison with *Euphues*'s: the Nasheian style seems not to have symbolized privilege as readily as the Lylean.[59] But euphuism discursively marked off for a time an elite social group, almost as surely as coats of arms or costly apparel—perhaps because of its full-blown ideological character: its appealing vision of a coherent natural and human reality. One searches vainly in Nashe for that intuition of the world as an ordered hierarchy, which informs Lyly's rhetoric. Nashe is the great antitotalizer of the period: thus where the "antithetic style" of euphuism has been well-described by Wilson Knight as a "balancing of contradictions,"[60] Nashe's writing seems consistently antigeneric and to pursue disharmony: if Lyly synthesizes, Nashe seems content with "mingle-mangle."

In exploring the social symbolism of Nashe's texts and their relation to traditional or socially endorsed modes, I suggest we begin with the difficulties and possibilities of his situation. Whereas Lyly's style epitomizes courtliness (and not least in that tone of cool, amused irony he adopts toward his courtiers), Nashe's texts project a certain crucial marginality. Thus his expressed conservatism (McKerrow described his social and religious opinions as "purely conventional" [*Nashe,* 5.130]) combines with what seems a sense of being on the outside of the powerful world. The notion that Nashe's texts should be read in the light of a social marginality is not original with me, but I do wish to argue with some inferences drawn from this view. In particular, I shall disagree with the idea that Nashe's texts are not only outside the dominant or authoritative culture, but opposed to it. In other words, I want to suggest that social marginality is not here to be read as contradiction. But at this point we must confront the question that asks how Nashe, a gentleman, can possibly be regarded as an outsider, and outside what?

Nashe was a gentleman, on the right side of that dividing line of Tudor and Stuart society that separated gentlemen from commoners. And he qualified as a gentleman on two counts, if we take as our criterion what Peter Laslett has called "the most celebrated Elizabethan definition of a gentleman," William Harrison's in his *Description of England* (pub. 1577):

> Whosoever studieth the laws of this realm, who so abideth in the university giving his mind to his books, or professeth physic and the liberal sciences, or beside his service in the room of captain in the wars, or good counsell given at home, whereby his common-wealth is benefitted, can live without

> manual labour, and thereto is able and will bear the port, charge and
> countenance of a gentleman, he shall . . . be called master . . . and reputed
> for a gentleman ever after.[61]

Nashe gave his mind to his books,[62] and could live without performing
manual labor. He was, then, a member of that group Anne Jennalie Cook
terms "the privileged."[63] That his father was a clergyman (rather than,
say, a tradesman, like Shakespeare's) was perhaps also fortunate—for the
clergy may have constituted a separate status group, if one uncertainly
related to the landed gentry.[64] Nashe was, then, by these standards,
essentially an "insider"—a member of that immensely favored, select, and
numerically tiny group that dominated society. Nonetheless, these facts
do not convey the complexity of his position. To begin with, if internal
differences among the gentry, particularly between peers and mere
gentlemen, were less important than the basic division between gentlemen
and the rest, they still counted; and Nashe was not an aristocrat. Thus it
makes sense to regard him as an outsider with respect to this elite, the
most powerful of all. Secondly, Nashe's claim to gentility was complicated by his vocation: a gentleman did not write for money—he did not
need to, of course, because ideally he lived off landed revenues.[65] As
Philip J. Finkelpearl points out, most of the literature written in what
Jonson called those "Nurseries of Humanity," the Inns of Court (a
considerable part of Elizabethan literature) was not written for publication: Donne, for instance, publishing only three poems in his lifetime.[66]
But Nashe appears to have supported himself directly from writing. Yet
few professional authors prospered: "with the notable exceptions of
Shakespeare and Spenser, the lives of Elizabethan authors comprise case-
histories of poverty." The predicament of "authors of humble origins"
was that "to attain gentlemanly status they had to avoid manual labour,
yet if they chose authorship as a profession, they lost caste in the eyes of
gentlemen."[67] Lack of riches, especially landed wealth, did not automatically disqualify one from gentility; yet Harrison makes it clear that a
certain minimum income was necessary to "bear the . . . charge" of a
gentleman, gentility being largely a matter of life-style.[68] A claim to
gentle status was not helped by poverty, especially in a period of
exceptional social mobility when many people were making such claims
and when, consequently, there prevailed some confusion as to who was
and was not entitled to style himself "gentleman."[69] Such a competitive,
status-conscious environment suggests a difficult situation for Nashe: his
own status cannot have felt as unassailable as he would have liked,

especially when persons less cultivated, but unfortunately richer, than he ("Carterly upstarts": see above, n. 36) gave themselves airs and perhaps believed themselves superior to impecunious scholars. I suggest Nashe's writing registers an anxiety about station, and that it attempts to wrest from the world a certain social distinction.

Obviously, then, Nashe was not outside the elite in the wretched way that "the people" were—those whom Sir Thomas Smith, in the 1560s, described as "the fourth sort of men which do not rule."[70] Nashe was a gentleman, though without as secure a claim upon gentility as those better bred or richer than he and, as a pamphleteer, he was stained, like the dyer, by a dubious occupation. It is important to stress Nashe's "insider-ship," because it complicates the tendency to assimilate his texts to an idea of the populace, often conceived of as having an essentially contestatory relation to the elite. Thus much seems implied by Robert Weimann, for example, in a book that, along with Bakhtin's writings, has done much to set the tone of contemporary formulations of the function of the popular in Renaissance literature.[71] "Nashe's satire and prose," Weimann observes, is "most effective when most intimately in contact with popular speech and jest book traditions"; but Weimann's interpretation of the nature of this "contact" is questionable. Arguing for "the common ground" shared by humanism and the "popular tradition," Weimann implies that Nashe's texts articulate a "social criticism which a popular audience might be expected to encourage." Thus *The Unfortunate Traveller* "attack[s]" both the "trading Puritan" and the "warring knight" (the tournament at Florence constituting an "ironic rejection of chivalry"), and his works generally, like those of humanists such as More and the University Wits of the nineties, suggest the possibility of "some ultimate concord between the humanist and popular points of view."[72] There are problems with this approach, which have to do with the theoretical assumptions of *Shakespeare and the Popular Tradition.* The most important of these is the tenability of the notion of a homogeneous, coherent, popular "worldview," almost always antithetical, it seems, to a ruling class "outlook."[73] For a historical critic, the underlying conception of elite and popular relations implicit in the book is strangely unhistorical, even essentialist.[74] The abstractness of the approach is more obvious when we consider what is intended by "point of view." The implication is of something akin to class or collective political consciousness, and yet it is not at all clear that such consciousness, or anything resembling it, was present among common people before the advent of industrialism and mass society (a consideration which, we should note, renders the term "the people," with its modern political connotations, problematic when used for this period).[75] There may not, in other words, have been a distinctively "popular" point of view, independent of and opposed to the elite's. (A related issue is whether the forms of speech Weimann identifies as popular, for example proverbs, are properly defined as such when the elite also used them.)[76] How best to describe social and social-literary relations in this period, and the limitations for cultural analysis of a strictly oppositional understanding of elite-popular relations, are major concerns of this study. The issue here is the nature of the association observed between "the people" and Nashe, the way contact with "popular speech" and literary forms enjoyed by the people is construed as indicating a potential solidarity of "outlook" between Nashe and them. It is the suggestion of affinity with those outside the political nation I think misleading, in that a relative sense of social insecurity, of being on the margins of elite life, is confused with a positive form of social solidarity. This is not to deny that Nashe was "in contact with" popular forms or, insofar as it existed, a popular point of view. But I shall argue that such contact does not entail solidarity: Nashe's outsiderness is a complicated affair, and seems not to have issued in a feeling of identification with those further down the social ladder, doing without a Cambridge degree. On the other hand, Nashe's sense of distance from the influential fostered a certain ironic or "realistic" perspective on elite culture, which at times strategically exploits, without identifying with, a style of irreverence that the texts mark as popular (whether justifiably or not). Nashe uses an interpretation or idea of popular culture, but in such a way as to distinguish himself from his inferiors.

Weimann has not been the only writer to link Nashe with a popular, contestatory perspective. Perhaps more common, though, has been the tendency to see Nashe if not as a popular writer then as in some other way oppositional or radical, possibly unintendedly. We have come a long way from McKerrow's twitting of Nashe for his conventionalism. He now attracts a more aggressive critical language: "destabilizing," "subversive," "transgressive." Thus Stephen Hilliard, contrasting Nashe with Lyly, views Nashe's texts as essentially contradictory, expressing the "social discontents" of "the displaced young men of the city," and his career as showing an "increasing estrangement from his own society."[77] However, when it comes to the social relations of and in Nashe's texts, contradiction is a less helpful notion than the broader, more flexible one of interplay. I shall argue that Nashe's relation to high modes is not really describable as contradiction and that his texts are not radically alienated.

Equally, Hilliard's stress on Nashe's "singularity," where it implies a stylistic radicalism at odds with social-rhetorical norms, needs reformulation: I would see these as playfully, ironically distanced or manipulated rather than undermined (the ironization of elite modes not preventing some identification with them, as the insider/outsider model used here is intended to suggest).[78] Again, Weimann's recent description of *The Unfortunate Traveller* as "modernist" is not a casual reference to Nashe's pride in his idiosyncrasy and novelty.[79] What is invoked is a twentieth-century modernism, assaulting and undermining traditional mainstream culture.[80] But the analogy of this radical anti-institutional modernism is finally as inappropriate for Nashe as it is for the citizen or nongentle tragedies, discussed in chapter 2 of this study, which ironically distance elite modes even as they affirm them. Two final examples of the kind of approach that draws on the conflictual social model I hope to complicate. Michael D. Bristol offers a Bakhtinian reading of *Nashes Lenten Stuffe* in terms of a "popular-festive . . . politics of uncrowning," in which Nashe "identifies with . . . disadvantaged and struggling groups" to present an "oppositional and subversive position . . . vis-à-vis . . . entrenched power and authority."[81] And Jonathan Crewe's conception of the problematic, subversive relation of Nashe's scandalous rhetoric to decorum (see above, n. 35) has been equally influential. Yet just as the view which assimilates Nashe too readily to popular culture turns marginality into solidarity, so such approaches may mistake it for alienation. Nashe occupied a border, insecure, and anxious social position (his texts are full of concern about status), but I cannot see him as alienated from the authoritative aristocratic culture or disposed to adopt a radical stance toward it. I must disagree, then, with Stephen Hilliard's ambitious attempt to read Nashe's work as that of an "alienated intellectual," participating in currents of thought that would play a role in the crisis of Stuart society.[82] Nashe's works reveal discontent, but this does not issue in a fundamental, subversive alienation. Instead, they attempt to articulate a more secure and rewarding social persona. Interpreting Nashe's outsiderness as alienation is to reduce the complexity of his situation and to overlook the extent to which Nashe is very much an insider, that is, a gentleman.[83]

Reading Nashe in the light of a supposed social marginality has concentrated on *The Unfortunate Traveller* and begins with Richard Lanham's notion that Jack Wilton's "outsider" position, occupying "an ambivalent, indeterminate space . . . neither . . . commoner, nor . . . gentleman," may articulate the "frustrations," (or sense of disenfranchisement), "of a whole group of Elizabethan writers." The idea that outsider-ness maintains an aggressive or combative stance toward authority (Lanham speaks of Jack's "anger" and "aggressiveness" as lacking the control of satire and of his "persistent attack on authority") emerges in Lanham's essay and has been influential in Nashe criticism since.[84] It has been developed by Ann Rosalind Jones in an important essay on *The Unfortunate Traveller,* in many respects similar to my approach, and which I shall discuss now—before getting to Wilton—because of its ramifications for understanding Nashe generally.

The importance of Ann Jones's approach lies in her appreciation that Wilton "inhabits a series of inside-outside positions," a "marginal status" matching "the nonalignment of many sixteenth-century writers." She sees Wilton as a "socio-psychological . . . projection of Nashe's understand-able frustrations and wishful thinking onto a freer and more powerful narrator/hero"; Wilton's tale, therefore, is basically a "success story," or "rise to wealth and security."[85] The emphasis upon the doubleness of Wilton's (Nashe's) position is important: Nashe is not simply an estranged "outsider." So Jones speaks of Nashe having a "double relation-ship to reigning discourses": this, too, seems a helpful conclusion to be drawn from the insider/outsider status of Nashe's work. Moreover Jones, interested in Nashe's relation to high forms, sees *The Unfortunate Traveller* as developing a certain "critical distance" on literary modes, a distance interpretable in the light of Nashe's own marginality.[86] However, Jones's interest in the radical potential of *The Unfortunate Traveller* leads her to liken it to the Bakhtinian or Kristevan "anarchic" or polyphonic text, which, exposing "conflicts among . . . literary and social practices," is potentially "transgressive" of "official" or monological discourses.[87] Notable is the use of a language of contradiction to formulate Nashe's relation to elite culture: the text "challenges the ideologies implicit" in the "genres" it distances.[88] But is this the best way to describe the interrela-tions among discourses in Nashe?[89] We should note that Nashe's "double relationship" to elite discourses is insufficiently described by the notion of parody, even an aggressive, agonistic parody demystifying high modes, if that means merely that as parodist he "cannot do without" them.[90] This probably underestimates the significance of such modes for Nashe: he could not do without them, but not only in the weak sense that he is parasitically dependent upon them for literary guerilla warfare. We must attend to Nashe's investment in such forms and the elite culture they symbolize—forms that may reinforce a claim to gentility and even kinship with aristocracy.[91] Ultimately, Nashe's relation to the high symbolic modes is ill-described in polemical metaphors: to play ironically with "official" forms is not necessarily to undermine them. Rather than reading the texts through this oppositional paradigm (and it is hard to see what opposition of this kind could offer Nashe) I will read them as attempts to develop, in a socially difficult position, a viable, productive, alternative persona.

Nashe, then, is to be understood in the context of the University Wits: and here we recall that while sixteenth-century humanism regarded state service as its prerogative, "opportunities of service . . . do not seem to have been particularly great."[92] But if Nashe, like many others, is out in the cold, we need not understand the ironic realism he occasionally turns upon elite culture as antagonistic, outsiderness just as easily inspiring ingenious strategies for successful identification with insiders. Marginality might well, however, foster a complicated relation to the culture of the powerful: in Nashe it seems to underlie an ironic complication and "critical distancing" of elite literary modes. While this approach raises again the question of Nashe's "radicalism," we must resist collapsing critical distance into radical subversion. Since my topic is Nashe's manipulation of socio-rhetorical distinctions, it is necessary to revisit Robert Weimann's powerful account of the relation between "popular" and "elite" elements in Renaissance texts and, distancing myself from his approach, clarify what *critical* distance means in Nashe.

It does not mean a radical rejection of elite cultural modes and life. At least since Weimann's study, it is this sense of criticism that has formulated the social dialectics of Renaissance texts, and which has of course in certain contexts been profoundly illuminating—no less a play than *King Lear* has benefited from this approach.[93] But the problems in it also need to be addressed. A serious shortcoming of Weimann's book is its ultimate reliance on contradiction as a way of conceiving hierarchy relations, or the reduction of such relations to a paradigm of class-conflict.[94] In other words, behind Weimann's vision of English Renaissance plays as articulating different social outlooks and class-specific communicative modes lies a contestatory theory of their interrelations. Weimann, of course, does not treat Shakespeare's texts as radically contradictory in the way that Ann Jones, invoking a poetics of "heteroglossia," does Nashe's: his point is that Shakespearean drama achieves a new artistic synthesis of elite and popular traditions, based on a social and cultural unity to be lost in the supposed century of revolution. Yet this national unity is essentially a unity in contradiction, a tense synthesis, and popular culture challenges elite conceptions.[95] This conflictual understanding of the relations between high and low social strata and their cultural modes has been applicable in some texts studied here, and, obviously, recent ways of talking about Renaissance culture are in its debt. But "the notion of contradiction," which, as Fredric Jameson writes, "is central to any Marxist cultural analysis," is not universally applicable in the period and risks flattening out the complexity of social relations in Renaissance texts.[96] The following analysis relies heavily, both for global approaches and local insights, on Weimann's work, which remains the most exhaustive study of social heterogeneity in a humanist author. I am "Weimannian" in feeling that Nashe cannot be understood without invoking a relation between modes nominated by him as "popular" and "elite" and that their interplay is as central as in many Shakespeare plays. Nashe often uses "popular" modes to assert an individual power and his own marginality means he is open to a "popular realism" that critically frames elite modes as fantasy or unworldly idealism. But this use of apparently nonelite modes does not involve a polemical identification with the popular (on the contrary, if aware of his marginality, Nashe is anxious to have known what separates him from the vulgar). Yet such ironic distancing is "critical" in a limited but important sense: through this process particular modes are foregrounded as specifically elite symbolisms, the texts showing an awareness of the cultural meaning of literary modes. By this defamiliarizing, critical point of view, Nashe is disengaged somewhat from the dominant group.

Let us attempt, then, to understand this distancing in Nashe's texts, in which discursive modes are viewed ironically, from "outside," as the cultural codes of an aristocratic elite, by focusing on the tense dual character of Nashe's insider/outsider position. For it is clear that Nashe is emphatically associated with the culture of power, or has its culture, humanism, if not its power (the problem being how to exchange that culture for the hard currency of power). This culture links him, tenuously, to the elite and distinguishes him from the populace. Thus his ironic, realistic attitude to it, grounded in the fact that he cannot identify with this milieu and its modes with the full, unself-conscious ease of an aristocrat like Sidney or the naïve charm of Henry Howard, earl of Surrey, in *The Unfortunate Traveller,* is itself likely to be problematic.[97] For what is at stake in Nashe's writing is his social identity. The problem is alarmingly simple: if not obviously of the elite then of the populace or uncomfortably close to it. The writing, then, improvises some workable alternative social space. And it may be in knavish play ("play[ing] the knave," as Will Summers puts it in *Summers Last Will and Testament* [*Nashe*, 3.233]), in the impudent, bold manipulation of social-rhetorical modes that we call social interplay, that Nashe constructs such a space, circumventing the oppressive division between elite and popular. Wittily manipulating elite and "popular" modes, Nashe turns the passivity of outsiderness into the activity of power, redefining marginality as opportunity and privilege. We must read the knavishness of Nashe's texts as the attempt to turn unconventionality to account. The knave, the central figure of Nashe's texts, is not easily placed, but this unplaceability suggests freedom. Still, Nashe's knavishness combines with allegiance to an elite which he is by training deeply associated with. While tracing Nashe's defamiliarization of establishment forms, we must also note his investment in them.

Our sense of Nashe living this curious but, given the predicament of Elizabethan authors, probably representative double life of insider/outsider will be heightened if we look again at two literary characters. I have alluded to Nashe's Puckish playfulness, and the analogy is intended seriously. For Puck is one of Shakespeare's most socially ambiguous figures, "as familiar in a palace as in a cottage with his broom,"[98] his playfulness being an essential part of his ambiguousness: play is what makes Puck too fluid a figure to fix his social character (the very notion of "social character," when applied to him, seeming hopelessly clumsy). Puck is in some sense a member of Oberon's court, but knows intimately the ways of the "villagery" (2.1.35). His humorous relish of this common scene reminds us of Nashe's zest for the seamier, baser sides of life. But what of Puck's relations with the populace? As with Nashe's relations with popular culture, they are not easily defined. He does not merely condescend to the "hempen home-spuns" or to "the wisest aunt telling the saddest tale" in her cottage (3.1.77; 2.1.51), at least not much more than he does to the aristocratic lovers, and he enjoys the quotidian, mundane milieu of humble folk. Yet if Puck is at home in this ordinary world, we don't think of him as a part of it, and so with Nashe. Both Puck and Nashe play with the popular—moving in it, understanding it, never completely removed from it, ridiculing it—never, though, identifiable with it. And yet the Puck who sweeps the house at the end of the play is not quite to be identified with an elite milieu, either. Like Puck, Nashe is a marginal figure. (Note too Puck's relation to Oberon: it is not equality, but there is no antagonism—it is not Caliban and Prospero. The knave is not necessarily a subversive figure.) Puck is a "knavish sprite"

(2.1.33), and this spirit of wanton, mischievous play is Nasheian, and detaches both figures from an elite/plebeian dichotomy, the knave being neither high nor low but eluding the status-structure altogether.

One hesitates before advancing again the parallel of Hamlet, but the Hamlet in question is not the prince sung by flights of angels to his rest but the modern student, who, like Nashe, "lack[s] advancement," Hamlet who is both inside and outside the court. Weimann's brilliant reading of Hamlet as a figure articulating a "popular outlook" is not completely satisfactory.[99] He is better described more tentatively: it is the social ambiguousness of Hamlet that is essential. Hamlet raises the problem of the politics of marginality, whether it is "popular" and oppositional. Doubtless Hamlet is more alienated from the court than Nashe from the elite: England is not a prison to Nashe. And Hamlet, even as "our chiefest courtier" (1.2.117), is loved of the "general gender" (4.7.18), and closer to the play's plebeians than, say, Claudius or the fop Osric (though these characters remind us of the central importance of distinctions among the play's ruling class as against those between it and the people). Does relative closeness, however, require identifying Hamlet with this humble scene of life? If, in "inky cloak" (1.2.77), he is separated from the court, he has a strongly ironic sense of popular life: the First Clown is a "knave" (5.1.76, 137), a "mad knave" (5.1.101) and an "ass" (5.1.78), and he observes with bemused dismay that the Clown's repartee shows how "the age is grown so pick'd that the toe of the peasant comes so near the heel of the courtier, he galls his kibe" (5.1.140–41). Such expressions of a clear sense of social superiority (rather underestimated by sentimental interpretations of Hamlet) remind us of Hamlet's distance from nonelite life, sympathy with the grave diggers necessarily implying separation.[100] Overall it is the lack of social solidarity, excepting friendship, that characterizes Hamlet. Puck highlights Nashe's playfulness and marginality. Hamlet's sardonic, knavish wit reveals a serious side to play: the madcap "antic disposition" (1.5.172) is strategic (even if its goal is notoriously obscure); it is anxiously defensive and originates in a certain vulnerability; it attempts to reserve a certain free expression in a constricting situation; it is elusive, refusing to be pinned down ("Hide fox, and all after" [4.2.30–31]). Hamlet's flippant yet taut "wild and whirling words" (1.5.133) are oblique, the point being evasion. This sense of play as survival strategy helps us understand the madcap, knavish, antic writing of another insider/outsider, who also won't be pinned down and who attempts to secure a certain social power.[101] Nashe's anxiously assertive play is more like Hamlet's tense maneuvering than easygoing aristocratic *sprezzatura*. The anxiety is intrinsic to the situation: if one cannot be totally inside, one can claim a certain power by mocking the pretensions of those who are (ironizing, for example, the idealism of high, heroic, or romantic cultural modes). Yet at the same time one does not want to be mistaken for one of those hopelessly outside: there must be the disclaimer, "But really, I am not like *them!*"

The account of Nashe's writing omitting its playful character distorts it, and Nashe is open to the playful perspectives on elite culture of supposed nonelite modes because he is not himself completely identified with that culture. Thus his critical perspective on literary modes often involves an irresponsible disregard for decorum, a ridiculing of high discourse. This irresponsibility will often seem popular, though its affinities are equally with humanist traditions of learned folly, playful paradox, and mock encomium in Erasmus, More, and Cornelius Agrippa.[102] It is not wrong to see a Tarltonizing spirit of popular irreverence in Nashe, even if *Strange Newes, Of the Intercepting Certaine Letters* denies specific influence: "the vaine which I have . . . is of my owne begetting, and cals no man father in England but my selfe, neyther Euphues, nor Tarlton, nor Greene" (1.319), but we must remember the social heterogeneity of this mocking spirit.[103] When we recall the satire directed at plebeian or citizen life (which probably asserts kinship with aristocratic society), it is clear that Nashe's writing has no more a simple relation to "popular" than to "elite" culture. "Knavish," then, better captures the stance of the Nasheian text than "popular," because it implies a strategic social undecidability. The trickster can feel equal to or superior to anybody. But "knave" also has lower-class associations (it is traditionally opposed to "knight")[104] and can suggest what we have called the popular strain in Nashe's writing. The knave, such as Puck, is linked with humble life—Autolycus "is" a tinker—but isn't to be confused with it: Autolycus is "constant" to his "profession" of "knavery" (4.4.682–83) and isn't equatable with the Shepherd and his son; Greene's wily conny-catchers swindle simple husbandmen visiting the city.[105] The distinction is between low and lower-class life, or virtuous simplicity and disreputable savvy:[106] it's not an absolute one, but it is central to Nashe's works.

In any case, it is in knaves like Wilton, Summers, or Pierce Penilesse, insignificant figures at the margins of gentility, that Nashe finds bohemian freedom from decorum. We meet this idea of a nonelite freedom in *The Unfortunate Traveller,* when Surrey changes roles with his servant Wilton to enjoy "more liberty of behaviour" (2.253). Just as Wilton does not inherit Surrey's morality with his clothes, neither has he internalized humanism—true of all of Nashe's knavish personae, and making possible a discursive "liberty of behaviour." Nashe's knavishness is often a disenchanting, demystifying realism, experience, in Weimann's formulation, contrasting with idealism.[107] But the aggressively popular character of Weimann's conception of this realism (like Bakhtin's "popular laughter" debunking "official" seriousness) makes it less useful in analyzing Nashe's realism.[108] Realism of sentiment in Nashe is not a mode of solidarity, though it does obliquely assert an unconventional distinction. We must allow, then, for the links between his realism and nonelite life (elite cultural modes are seen "from below," from the apparent perspective of common life),[109] but we must resist treating this realistic perspective as exclusively low or as confronting high culture. Nashe's admiration for Aretino ("one of the wittiest knaves that ever God made") underscores the point that realism in Nashe is not necessarily political in the Weimannian or Bakhtinian sense. Aretino is the poet of the real, *Il veritiero:* "His pen was sharp pointed lyke a poinyard; no leafe he wrote on but was lyke a burning glasse to set on fire all his readers. . . . His sight pearst like lightning into the entrailes of all abuses" (2.264, 265). In Aretino (to whom Nashe was likened)[110] Nashe celebrates wit and prestigious Juvenalian satire rather than a lower-class, oppositional viewpoint.[111] Still, Nashe's knaves ironize high forms by low life and upset polite discursive conventions, and in isolating and manipulating elite cultural symbolisms Nashe aims at an individual social-literary power. This playful attitude toward authoritative modes is clear in the jokey, brilliant retelling of the Hero and Leander story in *Lenten Stuffe.*

Because it, in Horatio's words, "consider[s] too curiously," *Nashes Lenten Stuffe* (pub. 1599) recalls Hamlet's demythologization of "the noble dust of Alexander," till he finds it "stopping a bunghole" (5.1.203). The deidealizing wit of *Lenten Stuffe* is almost as charged as Hamlet's in the graveyard: there is a sense of distance from noble life, issuing in a strange relish for anti-Ovidian, degrading itineraries (Leander ["sodden to haddocks meate" (3.198)] is turned into Ling, and Hero into Red Herring), and there is also a certain realism, a sense of having seen through it all. In Nashe this is a seeing through form, a knavish undoing of tragedy. I begin with *Lenten Stuffe* because, purporting to have been written away from London "in the countrey" (3.176) and in praise of the fishing town of Yarmouth, which harbored Nashe after the suppression of the play *The Isle of Dogs* (performed 1597), it literalizes some of the questions about social-literary insiders and outsiders I have been asking. These circumstances also raise starkly the issue of the relation of Nashe's writing to elite society and authority. I want to argue that although the work seems to aggressively travesty a high literary mode, we need a more nuanced conception of the relation between elite mode and Nashe than words like *estrangement* and *travesty* suggest.

The argument that *Nashes Lenten Stuffe* aligns itself with popular culture against elite culture has been forcefully made by Michael Bristol. Yarmouth, famous for herring fisheries, is described topographically and "historically" and extravagantly eulogized. It is the affecting to see tragedy as "tragedizing," or the contradiction posed between popular truth and elite fabulation, which suggests Nashe's "alienation" from courtly culture. If tragedy, the falsifications of "divine Musaeus" and "Kit Marlow" (3.195), is attacked, the idealizing Sidneian poetic may be challenged by the polemical valorization of truth over art. These categories are not neutral: implied is a contradiction between proletarian reality and upper-class mystification. In chapter 2 we will see a similar contrast at work in "bourgeois" tragedies that seem to reject the "glozing stuff" of the traditional form for the "simple truth" of humble life.[112] Certainly it is present in this version of Hero and Leander, "a brilliant use of indecorum," as Sandra Clark puts it:[113] the implication of Nashe's retelling is that, seen from the social space of a fisherman's town, tragedy seems a contrivance. By invoking this undistinguished "real" to criticize tragic idealization, Nashe may seem to cast himself as radical-popular demystifier. Much depends on how we picture the relation between the high formality of tragedy and the low, ignoble content—Hero's bawd-nurse, for example, "a cowring on the backe side whiles these things were a tragedizing" (3.200)—that is, while Hero laments over Leander's corpse (the Nurse is subsequently translated into mustard). One can see how the standardized rhetoric, dramaturgy and stagecraft of the Elizabethan playhouse might draw such irony,[114] but it is the social symbolism of form that is emphasized.

In "degrading" tragic representation (to recall Bakhtin's formulation about Renaissance art)[115] Nashe frames or distances it, opening up a certain gap between its aristocratic idealization and plebeian "experience." Social interplay ironizes what is seen as social form. This detached perspective on the prestigious idealizing modes of representation is reinforced by the insistence on novelty: "I am the first that ever sette quill to paper in prayse of any fish or fisherman" (3.224). Championing singularity, Nashe takes an individualistic stance toward generic norms. Robert Weimann has said that "out of the constraints of a socially most precarious position, Nashe snatched a modicum of freedom and experiment," a freedom that for Weimann, like Crewe, subverts decorum.[116] Thus the flamboyant play Nashe makes with hierarchical order—Hero and Leander exchanged into Herring and Ling, and red herrings glorified ("but to thinke on a red Herring, such a hot stirring meate it is, is enough to make the cravenest dastard proclaime fire and sword against Spaine" [3.191])—will appear as "subversion." Moreover, if we accept the work's conspicuous self-identification with Yarmouth and with plebeian culture (the title page of the 1599 edition recommends it as "fitte of all Clearkes of Noblemens Kitchins to be read: and not unnecessary by all Serving men that have short boord-wages, to be remembred" [3.141]),[117] such overturning of decorum will seem indebted less to learned paradox than to popular carnival and radical topsy-turvy, unmasking elite pretension. What I have sketched is the possibility of reading this part of *Nashes Lenten Stuffe* as identifying with nonelite life and contesting quasi-official neoclassical institutions (seen as contradicted by "truth"). But Nashe's disengagement from and irresponsibility toward aristocratic symbolism in *Lenten Stuffe* requires a less aggressive characterization.

What I want to stress about this (in some ways self-consciously "popular") work is the delicacy of its rhetorical task. Rather than simply drawing on popular culture, it deploys it. The circumstances of composition give some clue here: having crossed the line between permissible and impermissible satire in *The Isle of Dogs*, Nashe humorously deflects suspicion by associating himself with the unpretentious culture of fisher folk, the implication being that it is malicious, "selfe-conceited misinterpreters," with their "peevish moralizing and anatomizing" (3.216), who have got him into trouble: far from meddling in important matters, Nashe's preoccupations are as lowly as those of fishermen.[118] Associating himself with this virtuous simplicity, Nashe gives the lie to the accusation that his interests tend to subjects they would be wiser not to ("deepe politique state meaning" [3.214]). If popular culture has this tactical importance, as an impish gesture of humility, it is wrong to speak of real identification. The piece distances elite cultural modes as idealizing, but not to privilege plebeian "reality." The Puck analogy is again useful. The image of the old nurse ("mother Mampudding . . . a shrewish snappish bawd" [3.200]) on her backside is relished for the sheer actuality of the scene and its deidealizing possibilities, and yet the author's distance from it is stressed: he laughs with the Nurse, using this scene to bring out the pretensions of tragedy, and at her, in the same way that Puck can express amused detachment and understanding of the "villagery" (2.1.35) and mechanicals. The work does not, then, except ironically, proclaim itself popular: it is "a light friskin of my witte . . . wherein I follow the trace of the famousest schollers of all ages, whom a wantonizing humour once in their life time hath possest to play with strawes, and turne mole-hils into mountaines" (3.151). It emulates "Phylosophers . . . with their paradoxes [i.e., praises] of povertie, imprisonment, death, sicknesse, banishment, and baldnesse" (3.176) and strenuously asserts its scholarship, invoking "Polidore Virgill" and "Camdens *Britannia*" (3.172; Nashe also stresses his "seven yere" at "S. Johns" [3.181]). Most importantly, its witty triviality distinguishes its author as a virtuoso.[119] The demythologizing of tragedy asserts a confident familiarity or kinship with this tradition. It is manipulated or overturned rather than simply being presented as alien to a popular viewpoint. Nashe exploits a social-rhetorical tension between high and low discourse, but it is not easy to situate his work within this tension. A passing allusion to chronicle

> To recount *ab ovo*, or from the church-booke of his birth, howe the Herring first came to be a fish, and then how he came to be king of fishes, and gradationately how from white to red he changed, would require as massie a toombe as Hollinshead; but in halfe a penniworth of paper I will epitomize them. (3.195)

expresses a flippant irresponsibility toward the genre by someone seemingly outside its social assumptions (the low pamphlet cheekily promises entertainment rather than the "massie" history of kings)[120] but also confers upon Nashe its authority (he is familiar with it). Irony allows Nashe to have his cake and eat it: the pretensions of a symbolic tradition he is partly outside can be mocked and its power over him neutralized, but its prestige can be invoked, and its power for him activated. That *Nashes Lenten Stuffe* presents itself as, in some ways, an outsider's text, written not at court but at Yarmouth, is important for a social-rhetorical reading of Nashe's outsiderness, which has a real social basis; but the pointed assertion of being inside elite modes, of a knavish independent power over them, is also significant.

The discussion of *Lenten Stuffe* suggests some general features of Nashe's works:

1. *Degradation/Idealization.* Nashe's works articulate the central Sidneian contrast between "brazen" and "golden" worlds[121] as a social interplay between "popular" and "aristocratic." But two qualifications are

necessary. First, the "brazen" in Nashe is not always reducible to the popular in the same way that "golden" is to the aristocratic: Nashe's knavish realism is not equatable with the viewpoint of simple fishermen. Second, the texts do not necessarily privilege a socially commonplace reality: though it may be invoked to distance elite poetic conventions, this need not mean that the text embraces a "popular sense of reality."[122]

2. *Separation/Identification.* Nashe often playfully and individualistically separates himself from sanctioned modes (Weimann calls this "modernism" and Stephen Hilliard "singularity"). Yet this separation includes identification, or the tapping of the prestige of modes, the appropriation of their value by a virtuoso handling. This sense of separation, we may add, is ultimately rooted in Nashe's circumstances. The ambiguousness of the relation to high modes requires avoiding constructions of it which, like those stressing modernism or an alienated, scandalizing singularity, reduce complexity to radical contradiction.

3. *Irresponsibility/Responsibility.* Exploiting a broadly nonelite or knavish perspective, Nashe converts marginality into a playful assertion of independence from symbolic modes (which otherwise express an order of life to which he cannot entirely belong). But if Nashe's handling of elite modes is irresponsible, with irony compensating for outsiderness, there is nonetheless the attempt to assert, through their sophisticated and accomplished manipulation, a fundamental responsibility for such modes. Irresponsibility is the ironic mask of the knowing insider.

4. *Interplay between High and Low:* Hero and Leander/Herring and Ling. All the Nashe works treated here manipulate social contrasts, and ethical and aesthetic contrasts in them have social content. The emphasis, however, is on "manipulate": it is in playing with this division that Nashe as knavish, elusive author writes himself as unplaceable in it—which is the alternative to an impossible identification with high culture. These points amount to a single claim: Nashe's writing is not reducible to one social perspective and its essence lies in a complicated social interplay. Having sketched an account of social symbolism in Nashe, we may now turn to the exasperatingly socially undecidable *Pierce Penilesse.*

Pierce Penilesse

Pierce Penilesse His Supplication to the Divell explicitly foregrounds outsiderness:

Having spent many yeeres in studying how to live, and liv'de a long time without mony: having tired my youth with follie, and surfetted my minde with vanitie, I began to length to looke backe to repentaunce, & addresse my endevors to prosperitie: But all in vaine, I sate up late, and rose earely, contended with the colde, and conversed with scarcitie: for all my labours turned to losse, my vulgar Muse was despised and neglected, my paines not regarded, or slightly rewarded, and I my selfe (in prime of my best wit) laid open to povertie. Whereupon (in a malecontent humor) I accused my fortune, raild on my patrones, bit my pen, rent my papers, and ragde in all points like a mad man. In which agony tormenting my selfe a long time, I grew by degrees to a milder discontent: and pausing a while over my standish, I resolved in verse to paint forth my passion: which best agreeing with the vaine of my unrest, I began to complaine in this sort. . . .

These Rymes thus abruptly set downe, I tost my imaginations a thousand waies, to see if I could finde any meanes to relieve my estate: But all my thoughts consorted to this conclusion, that the world was uncharitable, & I ordained to be miserable. Thereby I grew to consider how many base men that wanted those parts which I had, enjoyed content at will, and had wealth at commaund: I cald to minde a Cobler, that was worth five hundred pound, an Hostler that had built a goodly Inne, & might dispende fortie pounde yerely by his Land, a Carre-man in a lether pilche, that had whipt out a thousand pound out of his horse taile: and have I more wit than all these (thought I to my selfe)? am I better borne? am I better brought up? yea, and better favored? and yet am I a begger? What is the cause? how am I crost? or whence is this curse? (1.157–58)

The theme is traditional (the neglect of learning) but vents the specific frustrations of the Elizabethan humanist, vainly hoping for prestigious government service or generous patronage.[123] Pierce is the slightest mask for Nashe himself.[124] The paradox of Nashe's predicament is greatest when he is most conformist—in his riposte to City attacks on plays, for example, when he rebukes those who care less for Talbot's glorious deeds (in *1 Henry VI*) than for "execrable luker, and filthie unquenchable avarice" (1.213). Contempt for citizen base-mindedness is one way for Nashe to identify with the influential (note, for example, the self-distancing, in the passage above, from "base men" like the "Hostler" or "Carre-man"). To use the terms developed so far, Nashe champions an aristocratic-chivalric idealism against a bourgeois-materialistic realism; we see the necessity of not assuming that because Nashe's texts often strike a cynical pose he is to be identified with a popular debunking of aristocratic high-mindedness. But aside from the hit at "Vintners, Alewives, and Victuallers," who would restrict the players because they offer competition

(1.214), and notwithstanding his defense of the stage as a pastime (better playgoing than "gameing, following of harlots, drinking" or sitting "melancholie in [a] Chamber, devising upon felonie or treason" [1.212, 214]), Nashe's line on plays is standard ethical-humanist: they are "sower pills of reprehension, wrapt up in sweete words" (1.213). The only remarkable feature of this apology is that it doesn't tally with his practice in *Pierce Penilesse*. As I have suggested, humanist precepts are not more important for understanding Nashe's work than his experimentation with an apparently unlettered mode of writing. *Pierce* is one of the most socially ambiguous of Nashe's works. It experiments with a bold discursive licentiousness in the attempt to turn outsiderness to advantage, reinterpreting this outsiderness as the social exceptionalism of the knave, yet it also insinuates that, pennilessness notwithstanding, the author "belongs."

Because of its inconsequential, seemingly formless, absurdist manner, *Pierce* defies description. Nashe calls it a "Paper-monster" (1.161): even in an age when, as Madeleine Doran points out, "structure" in literary works "is relatively weak,"[125] *Pierce Penilesse* is self-consciously, flamboyantly structureless. One thought is tacked onto another, and the work concludes with a gratuitous, lengthy, and plagiarized speculation on devils. Actually it stops rather than concludes, typically advertising the arbitrariness: "And so I break off this endlesse argument of speech abruptlie" (1.245). The emphasis on variety in the first edition title page *(Pierce Penilesse His Supplication to the Divell: . . . Pleasantly interlac'd with variable delights: and pathetically intermixt with conceipted reproofes* [1.137]) hardly prepares us for the work's bewildering eccentricity. The printer in his epistle to the "Gentlemen Readers" acknowledges that *Pierce* "may seeme strange and in it selfe somewhat preposterous," but asserts that with persistence the puzzled "shall finde reason"—which hints at a tension in the work between a "gentle," humanistic ideal of reason, and a nonelite, "monstrous" disorderliness. The printer admits the "Authors uncouth nomination," and apologizes for his "unwonted beginning without Epistle, Proeme, or Dedication . . . which he hath inserted conceitedly in the matter"; if readers "bestow the looking" they shall find them (1.150). Nashe stresses the topsy-turvy, "extemporall veine" (3.312), which he above all Elizabethans mastered: "*Deus bone*, what a vaine am I fallen into? what, an Epistle to the Readers in the end of thy booke? Out uppon thee for an arrent blocke, where learndst thou that wit?" (1.240–41). He acknowledges the "uncouth" title: "Whilst I am thus talking, me thinks I heare one say, What a fop is this, he entitles his booke *A Supplication to the Divell,* and doth nothing but raile on ideots, and tels a storie of the nature of Spirits" (1.240). Nashe's underscoring of formal incoherence, however, covertly lays claim to the humanist conventions he affects ignorance of: by foregrounding "monstrousness" Pierce indicates sophistication. Nashe plays at popular incoherence, the import of which is not that he is a popular writer or that he "draws on" popular culture, least of all that he subverts decorum. Social-rhetorical play demonstrates an ability to manipulate social categories and thus power. The work asserts its own independence, the purpose of playing at an "uncouth" mode being precisely to be seen playing at it, and so not to be identified with it. Turning a weakness into strength, pennilessness becomes a vantage-point from which to survey society. Nashe's popular stance is conspicuously an ironic role. Yet it also allows a playing with, and so signification of independence from, aristocratic decorum. Knavishly manipulating social-rhetorical modes asserts a wit that comprehends and rises above all social groups.

The Knight of the Post, who will convey Pierce's letter to the devil, exclaims that it is "the maddest Supplication that ever I sawe. . . . It is well done to practise thy witte, but (I beleeve) our Lord will cun thee little thanks for it" (1.217). The implication that the *Supplication*'s "madness" is a witty exercise is complicated by the suggestion of naïveté before polite conventions, or of popular undiscipline. The reader's exasperation is caught in a double-edged aside: "I dare say thou hast cald me a hundred times dolt for this senseles discourse" (1.239). If the work feigns "senselessness" the important thing is the feigning: by admitting to senselessness Pierce claims sense. Acknowledging decorum, however, is not only ironically to identify with it: a rhetorical clownishness signifies a certain distance from elite cultural standards, their authority over Pierce (and Nashe) being subtly diminished, even while an affinity with them is insinuated (the implication is something like: "Since they are mine, I am free to play with these elite standards too"—though putting it so baldly is to expose Nashe to the ridicule he avoids). *Pierce* flaunts its *sui generis* character, as a text outside "official" conventions. Like *Lenten Stuffe,* it abandons humanist priorities, discarding discursive canons, eschewing clarity, and cultivating obscurity in a freewheeling "literary clowning."[126] This stylistic individualism may seem Nashe's scandalous repudiation of a philistine society (so the apparently estranged figure of Pierce would imply), but this misinterprets as agonistic the very different rhetoric of marginality. Nashe invokes the prestige of aristocratic conventions, but the key thing is to signify control over them.

As a graduate, Pierce is not as associated with popular life as other Nashe heroes—the jester Will Summers, for instance, or even the page Wilton—and yet the resemblance between the text's discursive impropriety and the "liberty of behaviour" (see above, p. 51) conventionally attributed to the humble in Elizabethan literature is there. Pierce's irresponsibility recalls that carefreeness Henry V, burdened with kingly responsibilities, imagines the solace of "the wretched slave" (*Henry V*, 4.1.268).[127] Pierce's playfulness is that "natural" to the unprivileged (note, for example, the way clown episodes in Elizabethan plays are often holidays from the plot), and displays the freedom of popular ignorance— his senseless, idle, preposterous text participates in the popular back-to-front logic of the stage:

> *Don Pedro:* Officers, what offense have these men done?
>
> *Dogberry:* Marry, sir, they have committed false report; moreover, they have spoken untruths; secondarily, they are slanders; sixt and lastly, they have belied a lady; thirdly, they have verified unjust things; and to conclude, they are lying knaves.
>
> *Don Pedro:* First, I ask thee what they have done; thirdly, I ask thee what's their offense; sixt and lastly, why they are committed; and to conclude, what you lay to their charge.
>
> *Claudio:* Rightly reason'd, and in his own division . . .
>
> (*Much Ado*, 5.1.213–24)

Of course, where Dogberry's unintended manglings of right reason affirm his low status, Pierce's resemble Don Pedro's playful, superior mimicking of the constable's blunders. Nonetheless, the social-rhetorical positions of Pierce and Don Pedro are not quite equivalent. It is true that the humanist Pierce's formal preposterousness is not ignorant and that it signifies an ironic separation from the popular. So we might suppose that Don Pedro's easy complacency—he is merely aping Dogberry, there is no possibility of confusion of social positions (a fact recognized by the rather smug Claudio)—is also Nashe's: Pierce is playing at clownishness, with Don Pedro's unambiguousness. Certainly Nashe's playfulness aims to underscore, by parodic imitation, his difference from the thing parodied—but has it Don Pedro's poise and assurance? Pierce lacks the nobleman's solid social authority, and consequently there is that assiduity in assimilating himself to elite, as well as distancing himself from vulgar, life. The text's witty play is more frenetic than Don Pedro's easy jesting, in which nothing is at stake. We notice this strenuousness in the satire on nonelite life and in Nashe's care in positioning himself with regard to such life, using its ironic potential as a perspective on elite culture but foregrounding his brilliance so as to differentiate himself from it. Pierce's unconventionalism is socially intricate. If he does not commit Dogberry's blunders, he is not as distant from Dogberry's world as Don Pedro. Beneath the assertiveness of wit lies insecurity.

Pierce's relation to popular culture is anxious yet articulates a social position preferable to that of the court hanger-on. The ironic use of a conventionally defined nonelite culture "realistically" frames a "golden" elite rhetoric and highlights its monological, limited character.

Nashe's exploitation of socially symbolic discourses is most obvious in the discrepancy between Pierce's quasi-popular style and his humanist self-image. The theoretical affirmation of humanism links Nashe with elite culture, while its violation asserts an independence from the social system. Certainly Pierce drastically departs from humanist ideals of elegance and perspicuity, even while fervently championing them. He praises the poets for having "cleansed our language from barbarisme," and for encouraging "the vulgar sort . . . to aspire to a richer puritie of speach" (1.193), and finds this modern, antimedieval, refined eloquence in the preaching of "Silver tongu'd Smith," whose "well tun'd" and "melodious" style pierces "deep to the heart" (1.192, 193). Sweetness, melody, smoothness, transparency, are the virtues hailed in Smith which are contrasted with the language of a less sophisticated era. Yet if these are the virtues of More, Sidney, and Bacon ("chiefe pillers of our english speech" [1.194]), they are not Pierce's. Far from being rational and mellifluous, *Pierce Penilesse* is flamboyantly wayward, its style rough and opaque: to adopt the ethical vocabulary of Elizabethan rhetoric, its language is corrupt. In Spenser, Nashe hails a courtly, pure poetry ("The Fairy Singers stately tuned verse" [1.244]), but this ideal is sacrificed to an ostensibly popular clowning, airily eccentric and contrary, and obvious in the fun had with conventional titles when Pierce coins some for the devil: "your sinfulnes," "your honourable infernalship," "your helhood," "Signior Cornuto Diabolo" (1.165, 162). The perspective here recalls the idea of the popular that sees it as typically irreverent, as "uncrowning" authority. The devil as grandee is subjected to a pert familiarity: "Clim of the clough" (1.206), "Laurence Lucifer" (1.181), "Bedle of the Blacksmithes," "Timothy Temper" (1.189); his face is black because he has been "a great Tobacco taker" in his youth (1.181); he has the gout (1.163). It is the reduction to a workaday world that justifies the description of these nicknames as popular: the servant scenes in *Dr. Faustus* (1592; pub. 1604; 1616) or in Greene's *Friar Bacon and Friar Bungay* (1589–92; pub. 1594) are parallels, where coarse simplicity deflates Satanic pretension (the clowns' point of view in *Faustus,* for example, being in some ways more reliable than their master's, in that where Faustus sees Mephistopheles' power as divine, they see tricks). Pierce's mockery of the devil is "popular" because the viewpoint is not coincident with power and because this disengaged perspective fastens upon power's ridiculousness. Yet just as assimilating the marginalized scholar-student Hamlet to a popular perspective is mistaken, so it is mistaken with Pierce. If Hamlet's relation to Claudius's court is complicated and ambiguous, so is Nashe's to elite culture—a little more than kin, and less than kind—and it is this ambiguity, rather than a popular exclusion from power, that needs emphasizing. *Pierce* indeed shows a Hamlet-like regard for the contemporary neglect of degree, where the toe of the peasant galls the courtier's kibe: "ther is not that strict observation of honour, which hath been heretofore" (1.159). It is true that Nashe's writing seems not to defer to social-literary norms, yet this is neither subversion nor an affirmation of the popular but an ingenious, if desperate, effort at positioning.

The "monstrousness" of *Pierce Penilesse,* its anti-eloquence, thus has a more complicated social basis than "popular" implies. The interplay between an outsider's mode and an identification with humanism is central, and clear from the defense of plays ("a rare exercise of vertue" [1.212]). Pierce's moralism here surprises in a work in which wit justifies itself. For while wit may be partially corrected by experience in *The Unfortunate Traveller* (with Jack Wilton fleeing iniquitous Italy for England), in *Pierce* wit licenses monstrous incongruity, paradox, and grotesquerie, and there is little room in this for humanist ethical-didacticism. And although *Pierce* uses a traditional ethical rhetoric (the morality scheme of the Seven Sins), this bespeaks less the public-minded corrector of abuses than one pursuing private ends, with moral satire being the weapon with which discontent seeks satisfaction. We are aware of feelings—envy, disappointment, frustration—not conformable with the satirist's disinterested indignation. So moral rhetoric is picked up and used amorally, in a work whose pretext is a very personal pennilessness. Nashe's relation to conventional moral rhetoric is an example of the double social symbolism of his work, whereby official, elite forms are critically distanced while their social value is appropriated.

Nashe's writing has a theatrical, performative aspect, Hibbard, for instance, speaking of his "literary showmanship."[128] In Pierce's handling of the Seven Sins, exposing abuses at home and abroad, there is a distance between performer and literary mode performed. The sharply modern feel Nashe brings to this relatively archaic form problematizes it. We notice the dissonance between the ironic, fully contemporary portraits Nashe offers of each sin (and the brilliant, modern wit offering them), and the crude generality of the old-fashioned allegory.[129] Thus Pierce is differentiated from the form, just as an actor can be from his role. Weimann has seen in *The Unfortunate Traveller* a conflict between a universalizing and an empirical poetics,[130] and this insight is relevant to *Pierce*'s use of allegory, the bland, traditional universalism of the scheme contrasting with the pointed, concrete, topical contemporaneity:

From Gluttony in meates, let me discend to superfluitie in drinke: a sinne, that ever since we have mixt our selves with the Low-countries, is counted honourable: but before we knew their lingring warres, was held in the highest degree of hatred that might be. Then, if we had seene a man goe wallowing in the streetes, or line sleeping under the boord, we would have spet at him as a toade, and cald him foule drunken swine, and warnd al our friends out of his company: now, he is no body that cannot drinke *super nagulum,* carouse the Hunters hoop, quaffe *upsey freze crosse,* with healthes, gloves, mumpes, frolickes, and a thousand such dominiering inventions. He is reputed a pesaunt and a boore that wil not take his licour profoundly. And you shall heare a Cavalier of the first feather, a princockes that was but a Page the other day in the Court, and now is all to be frenchified in his Souldiers sute, stand uppon termes with, Gods wounds, you dishonour me sir, you do me the disgrace if you do not pledge me as much as I drunke to you: and, in the midst of his cups, stand vaunting his manhood, beginning everie sentence with When I first bore Armes, when he never bare anything but his Lords rapier after him in his life. If he have beene over and visited a towne of Garrison, as a travailer or passenger, he hath as great experience as the greatest Commander and chiefe Leader in England. A mightie deformer of mens manners and features, is this unnecessary vice of all other. Let him bee indued with never so many vertues, and have as much goodly proportion and favour as nature can bestow uppon a man: yet if hee be thirstie after his owne destruction, and hath no joy nor comfort, but when he is drowning his soule in a gallon pot, that one beastly imperfection will utterlie obscure all that is commendable in him; and all his good qualities sinke like lead down to the bottome of his carrowsing cups, where they will lie, like lees and dregges, dead and unregarded of any man. (1.204–5)

The passage's sense of the present (the allusions to a less effeminate, less luxurious past, to novel drinking games and the wars, to the stereotypical rapier-bearing traveler) subtly distances the narrator from the archaic abstractions ("Gluttony," "Drunkenness") of the allegory. Pierce's separation from the rhetorical simplicities of what Sidney called that "misty time" before humanism is conveyed:[131] Pierce writes in the rich complexity of a present irreducible to such abstractions. The accretion of detail, combined with a realistic, knowing, sophisticated wit, is modern, and unharmonized with the nonempirical, medieval moralism. Again it is Nashe's intellectual, independent relation to a mode, the ability to playfully remake it, that is on show. And the virtuosity of the passage, the impression of outdoing a traditional mode, projects confidence: this is a speaker in control, rather than a casualty, of the contemporary scene.

As in most Nashe texts, the world of *Pierce* is material, abounding in common, everyday things and experiences seen in extraordinary, seemingly unselective, detail. "Material reality"—base, sordid, ignoble—is Nashe's subject.[132] The grotesque, ludicrous, or deidealizing in Nashe expresses this material perspective, for instance the aside that the devil "doth not use to weare a night-cap, for his hornes will not let him" (1.162) or the attack on English gluttony: "wee make our greedie paunches powdring tubs of beefe" (1.200). This materialism has two consequences for the social character of *Pierce*. It relates it to a nonelite milieu (not exactly popular, unless that term can encompass base, disreputable scenes such as Shakespeare's Boar's Head tavern, or the scenes of Greene's low-life pamphlets, as well as the worlds of artisan, citizen, and husbandman). It also casts a critical, often humorous perspective on discursive modes symbolizing the Establishment, which appear insipid and conventional when set beside this richly realized, seemingly indiscriminate material context—a rhetoric of "the real" ironizing aristocratic artificiality (thus the effect in the passage on Drunkenness of a solid, detailed actuality highlighting the old-fashioned, abstract selectivity of allegory). But the outcome of this social interplay between the material and low, and the ideal and aristocratic, is not the simple valuation of the former over the latter but the making visible of an elite symbolism. In *The Unfortunate Traveller* such critical defamiliarization features prominently. For the present, what needs recognition is that this interplay between material and ideal has a social character. The difficulty, though, is that Nashe's materialism is ironic: it symbolizes a nonelite milieu, even expressing its empirical authority over elite idealism. Yet this material, socially undistinguished reality is also the effect of a showy wit self-consciously displaying the linguistic inventiveness that articulates this abundant materiality.[133] Moreover, apart from formal deference toward Sidney's idealism ("what age will not praise immortal Sir Phillip Sidney" [1.193]), Nashe combines zest for this base scene with scorn for it. What is prized is not the scene itself but Nashe's brilliance. It is too simple to see Pierce as adopting the perspective on the official world of a low, unprivileged milieu. Rather he conspicuously exploits putative popular modes. Weimann has said that in Shakespeare, "Tarlton's heritage" is inseparable from "the literary legacy of Terence." Tarltonizing in Nashe, however, is not a "source" but an aspect of a complex "self-fashioning."[134] *Pierce* is important among Nashe's works because it dramatizes his predicament, which is that of Elizabethan humanism, and because its basic social contrast of abstraction and materialism is central to other works by him. It is a key work because of the importance (but also radical ambiguousness) of the popular in it. We cannot describe Pierce without reference to an idea of nonelite culture, but neither can we situate him in it.

Summers Last Will and Testament

Will Summers, Henry VIII's jester, presents *Summers Last Will and Testament*, thus literalizing the knavishness of *Lenten Stuffe* and *Pierce Penilesse.* The play was probably performed at Archbishop Whitgift's Croydon palace in 1592. Here too the work's perspective subtly distances a courtly mode, revealing its social character. As presenter, Will views the play from the margins, as an outsider. Yet his social position is actually more complicated than this description suggests.

This stately, solemn play represents the passing of Summer and the choosing of his heir. The mood is autumnal and elegiac, with festive, rustic notes introduced by Ver, Harvest, and Bacchus. To this decorous atmosphere Will Summers brings a marked informality: the opening stage direction has him "enter . . . in his fooles coate but halfe on"; he confesses that, "what with turmoyle of getting my fooles apparell, and care of being perfit, I am sure I have not yet supt to night" (3.233). Chatting inconsequentially with the audience, he notices "my Lord" in the audience and resolves to "set a good face on it, as though what I had talkt idly all this while were my part" (3.233). Nashe emphasizes, then, Will's engagingly "idle," irresponsible casualness, and, as with Pierce, this preposterousness is ambiguous. There is the element of playing with rules, suggesting knowledge and preservation of them (such "play" depends upon their existence), and, on the other hand, it is suggested that Will is a social outsider and that this freedom from rules is the freedom of one without responsibility for them, one who does not inherit them.[135] The knave's attitude is explicit: "There is no such fine time to play the knave in as the night," Will declares; he will "sit as a Chorus, and flowte the Actors and [the author] at the end of every Sceane . . . looke to your cues, my masters; for I intend to play the knave in cue, and put you besides all your parts" (3.233, 236). Ridiculing the author ("Ile shewe you what a scurvy Prologue he had made me, in an old vayne of similitudes"), he appeals to the audience: "How say you, my masters, doe you not laugh at him for a Coxcombe?" (3.234, 235). The bookish, euphuistic prologue contrasts with Will's colloquialism, the author's rhetoric contrasting with Will's "natural" idiom, which is closer to what we suppose popular speech than to the court's. Nashe, then, distances the "old," artificial Lylean mode as elite social style or aristocratic symbolism. Certainly the contrast is not merely formal: however difficult it is to ascribe to Will's speech a definite social identity, the interplay between his apparently spontaneous discourse and the studied, artful symmetries of the Lylean prologue seems intended to contrast socially specific modes. The interest of *Summers Last Will and Testament* is in this interplay of socially and rhetorically high and low discourses. Thus Will's banter, framing the prologue, presents it as social form, as an elite language, and contextualized in this way it indeed seems strange. Yet, as often in Nashe, distantiation has a complex effect: the audience is invited to laugh at the unreality of this mode, contrasted as it is with a "truer," "more natural" one, yet it is also invited to acknowledge it as once having been its own. What is involved is not a lowly outsider's alienation of a high mode, but the more shaded effect of insiders laughing at their own defunct fashions (a point more obvious when we consider that original audience and its probable elite character). Rather than the play bluntly debunking an elite style, it co-opts a "popular" outlook to achieve an internal distance within a mode (with obvious pleasures for its audience: enjoyment of a sense of sophisticated self-irony, the gratifying awareness that one is not naïve about one's tastes, a feeling of up-to-dateness). Rather than opposing courtly fabulation, Will's "realism" is a socially specific perspective made available to a privileged audience.

What is certain is the presence of an unanswerable realism: "What can be made of Summers last will & Testament? Such another thing as Gyllian of Braynfords will, where shee bequeathed a score of farts amongst her friends" (3.235). Such humor brings the mythmaking down to earth, but it is too simple to see the play as correcting elite idealism by a popular, realistic, unillusioned outlook: indeed, we need to revise the idea that "popular culture" in Renaissance works invariably challenges, subverts, or demystifies upper-class fictions. The play does suggest such a conflict, so that popular experience can be seen as humorously undermining high-flown elite symbolization and implying its falsehood ("Heigh ho . . . I promise you truely, I was almost asleep; I thought I had bene at a Sermon" [3.244]). Will Summers can be seen as the play's adversary, harrying, exposing its idealization with "popular laughter": in Bakhtin's terms, carnivalizing Summer's court. So might we understand Will's remarks after the departure of Solstitium, who embodies "moderation," and who carries "a payre of ballances, with an houre-glasse in eyther of them" (3.245, 244):

> What cheere, what cheere, my hearts? are not you thirsty with listening to this dry sport? What have we to doe with scales and hower-glasses, except we were Bakers or Clock-keepers? I cannot tell how other men are addicted, but it is against my profession to use any scales but such as we play at with a boule, or keepe any howers but dinner or supper. It is a pedanticall thing to respect times and seasons: if a man be drinking with good fellowes late, he must come home, for feare the gates be shut: when I am in my warme bed, I must rise to prayers, because the bell rings. I like no such foolish customes. Actors, bring now a black Jack, and a rundlet of Renish wine, disputing of the antiquity of red noses. . . . but let us have no more of these grave matters. (3.246–47)

Will is "an open enemy to Inke and paper" (3.279): "Hang copies; flye out, phrase books; let pennes be turnd to picktooths: bowles, cards, & dice, you are the true liberal sciences; Ile ne're be Goosequil, gentlemen, while I live" (3.280). A critical anti-elite perspective would be located in him rather than Bacchus, Ver, or Harvest, whose disruptions of the play's decorous mood seem merely conventional, mythic, and typical. It is Summers who breaks with this universal, transhistorical mode, in a discourse gravitating to the local and particular, the here and now. Thus his response to Ver's morris-dance:

> O brave Hall! O, well sayd, butcher. Now for the credit of Wostershire. The finest set of Morris-dauncers that is betweene this and Stretham: mary, me thinks there is one of them daunceth like a Clothyers horse, with a wool-pack on his backe. You, friend with the Hobby-horse, goe not too fast, for feare of wearing out my Lords tyle-stones with your hob-nayles. (3.240)

He stands for the everyday: "Watling street" (3.235), "Newgate" and "London" (3.286), "Dick Huntley" (apparently the stage manager) crying "Begin, begin," the household's "Lawndry" (3.233). In Weimann's sociology of medieval and Renaissance theater, Will speaks from *platea* rather than *locus,* familiar performance area rather than illusionistic place.[136] The use of real names, the allusions to the players' Worcestershire background and "my Lords tyle-stones," the common place-name— all this introduces a consciousness of the theatrical and social present and an actuality missing in the poetic, golden transcendence of the play proper. The play may well imply that there are aspects of humble experience untreatable in a noble symbolic mode (with Will reminding us of the blind spots in this aesthetic). Yet framing this courtly mode in this way need not highlight its limitations so much as suggest its sophisticated capacity to include its social-rhetorical outside. To point out the social specificity of a mode is not to show its deficiency. Summers, indeed, is outside and inside the play he presents, functioning as go-between for social realms seen as separate rather than in contradiction. It is true the audience is not allowed an unmediated access to the play's myths. Yet we need not argue that in distancing this mythical realm the play criticizes it as closure, negatively comparing it with "nonelite" life. Clearly, we must look more closely at Will, who in many ways helps us understand Nashe.

The point is that, as jester, Will is crucially related to this court mode. The complexity of his relation to the mythical is not well captured in the aggressive vocabulary used so far ("harrying," "debunking," etc.). True, such terms rehearse the text's: "The great foole Toy hath marde the play" (3.294). But Will is seen to manage rather than "mar" it when we acknowledge what links him to the court. The notion of the "knave," which captures the creative indeterminacy of Nashe's social-literary self-presentation, is again apposite. For Will is not distanced from courtly life if that means profound alienation. We notice the easy self-confidence in the court of this uncourtly figure, his comfortable appearance of "belonging."[137] Will has almost the social range of Falstaff—he is at home in court or tavern, as ready with a humanist allusion as a tale or jest. His discursive facility suggests a social facility. Will, then, is another Nashe figure who projects a particular social power, a power involving a gratifying measure of solidarity with aristocratic life. The irony directed at the "Coxcombe" (3.235) of an author (Nashe) and the mockery of "squitter-booke[s]" (3.279) bespeaks a gentlemanly disdain for professionals like Harvey or the German academics we meet in *The Unfortunate*

Traveller. Such sallies allow Nashe to take over the norms of a group that, strictly speaking, excludes him. Yet elsewhere learning distinguishes Nashe from the vulgar, the bourgeois (the Usurer in *Pierce,* for instance [1.162]) or from ignorant upstarts—like the "Arts-man," Holofernes, he is to "be singuled from the barbarous" (*Love's Labor's Lost,* 5.1.81–82). Like "popular" discourse, humanism is expediently deployed, and is best understood in the context of Nashe's attempt to contrive, from a "socially most precarious position" (Weimann; see above, p. 53), an original social power.

Nashe's expression through Will of a fundamental or potential solidarity with court culture is subtle and acute. There is no unsustainable claiming of an identity between himself and that milieu. What is imagined is someone neither simply outside nor inside it, and rather than this uncertain situation being presented as painful, which it must have been in real life, Nashe presents it as Puckish social fluidity. Rather than Will being set against the fictions of the play, courtly culture is through him attributed a mature, attractive self-irony: the awareness generated is self-congratulatory rather than demythologizing (the court does not suppose its artistic bushes bears, to invoke Theseus in *A Midsummer Night's Dream*). And even as he distances it, Will responds to this mode's poetic power. He is not unmoved by the great haunting song of the play ("Lord, have mercy on us, how lamentable 'tis!" [3.284]), and his function is not to hardheadedly mar its mythmaking by exposing, in the light of common life, the limits of fiction, but to suggest the connection between these polarities. In the end, the myth that includes Will's ironies is a stronger, more compelling, and authoritative myth.

The Unfortunate Traveller

In *Lenten Stuffe, Pierce,* and *Summers Last Will and Testament,* Nashe distances noble symbolic modes, articulating a contrast between a supposedly "nonelite," "artless," "true" realism and high artifice. Manipulating this contrast, he manages to imply a knavish independence from it. In *Pierce* and *Summers Last Will,* this nonelite perspective takes the form of an unconventional, idiosyncratic speech and demeanor that asserts a relative freedom from quasi-official modes. This "discursive licentiousness," or lack of art, signifies the popular, but the emphasis really falls on the archly sophisticated author using this mode to play with the conventions of aristocratic culture. As one of those humanists whose career was "an unavailing search for a suitable patron,"[138] Nashe's texts surely articulate a "schollers discontent" in an "art-disgracing" world.[139] But the ambiguousness of the insider/outsider theme in the texts also problematizes construals of "distance" as alienation. Nashe's stylistic eccentricity and framing of elite modes does not, after all, seem to harbor a radical politics or even a profound disenchantment with the court, and Mark Curtis's theory of "alienated" Jacobean or Elizabethan intellectuals sowing the seeds for the coming crisis does not seem to describe Nashe.[140] Given Nashe's professed conservatism, it is certainly, as Stephen Hilliard stresses, one of the strangest aspects of his work that it attracts epithets like "modernist" and "scandalous." Yet radicalism need not follow hard upon discontent. And there is no doubt that Nashe's dislike of heterodoxy is intense:

> An other misery of Pride it is, when men that have good parts, and beare the name of deepe scholers, cannot be content to participate one faith with all Christendome, but, because they will get a name to their vaineglory they will set their selfe-love to studie to invent new sects of singularitie, thinking to live when they are dead, by having theyr sects called after their names, as Donatists of Donatus, Arrians of Arrius, and a number more new faith-founders, that have made England the exchange of Innovations, and almost as much confusion of Religion in every Quarter, as there was of tongues at the building of the Tower of Babell. (1.171–72)

In Nashe, humanist disaffection is expressed in shrewd attempts at association with a governing elite. Orthodoxy plays a part in this strategy.

In *The Unfortunate Traveller,* Nashe's ambiguous relation to elite modes is at its most playful: various aspects of high culture are defamiliarized from a viewpoint socially very hard to define. Neither simply popular nor elite, nor even "middling," the page Jack Wilton, as David Kaula has observed, "moves with equal facility in two spheres, the elite and the plebeian."[141] Certain generic modes, in particular tragedy, are distanced, and their elite character emphasized; knavish preposterousness merges with allegiance to them.

The book concerns Wilton's Continental adventures, but he remains slight and shadowy, his irrepressibility making him more a rhetorical attitude than a character. This vagueness has a social aspect. If Wilton lacks the presence of naturalistic characters, he is also not as socially fixed as they, but ranges through and across social levels and modalities. He has a richly skeptical function too, placing elite cultural modes in perspective. But treating such critical irony as oppositional is finally inadequate,[142] the key to the text being its social complexity.

Like *Pierce* and *Summers Last Will*, Wilton preposterously inverts established literary values. But this antic disposition is strategic, affecting an outsider's naïveté but conveying the *savoir faire* of one whose marginality comes to seem a kind of privilege. The mingling of social modes is striking, as in the opening paragraph's exploitation of the incongruity between the stories that might be told and Wilton's:

> About that time that the terror of the world and feaver quartane of the French, Henrie the eight (the onely true subject of Chronicles), advanced his standard against the two hundred and fifty towers of Turney and Turwin, and had the Emperour and all the nobilitie of Flanders, Holand, and Brabant as mercenarie attendants on his ful-sayld fortune, I, Jack Wilton, (a Gentleman at least), was a certain kind of an appendix or page, belonging or appertaining in or unto the confines of the English court; where what my credit was, a number of my creditors that I cosned can testifie: *Coelum petimus stultitia*, which of us al is not a sinner? Bee it knowen to as many as will paie mony inough to peruse my storie, that I folowed the court or the camp, or the campe and the court, when Turwin lost her maidenhead, and opened her gates to more than Jane Trosse did. There did I (soft, let me drinke before I go anie further) raigne sole king of the cans and blacke jackes, prince of the pigmeis, countie palatine of cleane straw and provant, and, to conclude, Lord high regent of rashers of the coles and red herring cobs. *Paulo maiora canamus.* Well, to the purpose. What stratagemicall acts and monuments doo you thinke an ingenious infant of my yeeres might enact? (2.209)

The wit lies in the interplay between affairs of state and the jest-book exploits of "a certain kind of an appendix or page," and the contrast is as stark as possible. Yet the passage does not exactly establish a contradiction between these spheres. The marvelous impudence with which Jack runs together his own and Henry's affairs is saved from being ridiculous by a self-conscious, intelligent irony. Throughout, Wilton suggests his insiderness humorously and tactfully: thus the flippant applications of the Latin convey an ease with "the tradition" as well as a jocular distance from it. The reference to his adventures as "stratagemicall acts and monuments" slyly recalls Foxe, and the lofty, public-historical note of the opening might almost introduce some dignified chronicle-history (the delayed placement of "I, Jack Wilton . . . " in the first sentence, thus letting us down with a jolt). But history we do not get; instead, that heroic, Henrician, idealizing narrative is inverted: "There did I (soft, let me drinke before I go anie further) raigne sole king of the cans and blacke jackes . . . and . . . Lord high regent of rashers of the coles and red herring cobs." If life in camps is matter for epic, tragedy, and chronicle, Nashe's switch to Wilton's adventures (the duping of a cider merchant, exposure of a braggart, and fleecing of some court dandies) seems perversely to prefer the trivial and sordid. Yet this reduction does not quite travesty elite categories: instead, the play with titles, like that with elite modes generally, tends to neutralize problematic social distinctions. An aristocratic narrative of martial Acts and Monuments is invoked only to deliver a quasi-popular jest-book: "This was one of my famous atchievements [tricking the cider-seller] . . . but I have done a thousand better jests, if they had been bookt in order as they were begotten" (2.217). The realistic attitude is bound up with a certain social perspective: not only is feudal culture seen from a modern, unillusioned point of view, but this detachment is the prerogative of an unimportant "certain kind of an appendix or page." It is not a "popular" viewpoint (Wilton's intimate knowledge of elite life excludes that), but one involving an interplay of inside and outside perspectives. Implied is a point of view not identical with elite power and yet related to it. (Wilton claims he is "a Gentleman at least.") The social ambiguousness of this passage is captured in the first tale about the gulling of a would-be noble cider and cheese merchant, the "armes" of whose "ancestors" are "drawen verie amiably in chalke on the in side of his tent dore" (2.210–11). The victualler's chalk-drawn arms neatly exemplify the text's interest in playing with elite symbolism. This play is a form of social power; to Wilton it offers a sense of superiority to such absurd pretension.

The opening passage of *The Unfortunate Traveller* relates itself to nonelite life even though Wilton can pass for a gentleman. And its realistic, cynical viewpoint is meaningfully spoken of as nonelite (rather than, say, as the advanced outlook of sophisticated milieux like the Inns of Court) because the work equates idealism with aristocracy. Yet in making his protagonist a page, Nashe gives him a social mobility, which, combined with the superciliousness of Will Summers or Pierce (which takes almost every social group or type as its butt), allows Wilton to convince us that he is not merely subjected to the elite. Thus Wilton is more associated with common life than his master Surrey, but only in the sense that, for example, Autolycus is closer to it than Florizel.[143] Shuttling between nonelite and gentle culture, Wilton stands for the madcap ironizing of elite fabulation and conventions. This realism is not a matter of mimesis but of social viewpoint, or the examination of elite fictionality from a socially commonplace "real." But because Wilton is marginalized ("belonging or appertaining in or unto the confines of the English court"), there is no privileging of a popular, jest-book realism, and upper-class high-mindedness is ironized and esteemed.

The text is a network of social-rhetorical contrasts. At its opening Wilton gulls an "ugly mechanicall Captain" (2.217), persuading him to kill the French king by feigning desertion. He disdains his victim, who lacks his wit and culture, yet who is, alas, his superior. He commends the glory of spies:

> howe many of the Romaine worthies were there that have gone as Spialls into their Enemies Campe? Ulysses, Nestor, Diomed went as spies together in the night into the Tents of Rhaesus, and intercepted Dolon, the spie of the Trojans; never any discredited the trade of Intelligencers but Judas, and he hanged himselfe. (2.220)

This "silver-sounding tale" (2.222), with its classical patina, is another strategic use of humanism: the French expose and humiliate the arrogant "intelligencer," as Wilton had hoped. At the same time there is an ambiguousness about Wilton's facility with the classics. The classical tradition is in some sense his own, as it isn't the upstart Captain's, and yet there is implied a distance between speaker and tradition: there seems a difference between its politic manipulation here and more naïve identifications with it, such as Surrey's. Besides flattering the Captain, these "silver-sounding" allusions to Greek and Roman worthies contrast with the leaden reality of the rest of the passage, in which Wilton sends off "Captain gogs wounds" (2.223) with a "Gone he is; God send him good shipping to Wapping" (2.222),[144] and recounts the French hilarity at his confession:

> This confession could not choose but moove them all to laughter, in that he made it as light a matter to kill their King and come backe, as to goe to Islington and eate a messe of Creame and come home againe . . . (2.224)

Nashe's writing cultivates this sort of inharmonious juxtaposition (classical heroes and a Sunday outing spot), and the mischievous confidence in manipulating social-rhetorical contrasts along with the free handling of decorum convey a certain "liberty of behaviour." The gap between speaker and mode suggests someone at home in, and enjoying some perspective on, the tradition, striking a holiday attitude of nonelite irresponsibility. And the complementarity between classical and modern is an example of the encoding, in Renaissance texts, of social contrasts. However, though everyday and classical here imply social differences, Wilton does not simply endorse the former.

The description of the massacre of the Anabaptist rebels is an instance of this encoding of social contrasts. Nashe ridicules these "illuminate botchers" (2.241) in the way that Jonson mocks Zeal-of-the-Land Busy ("he was a baker . . . but he does dream now, and see visions; he has given over his trade").[145] Following the massacre Wilton meets Surrey, who recounts his love for "statelie Geraldine" (2.243). In juxtaposing the courtly love tradition with popular experience, Nashe highlights the conventional idealism of the elite mode. Yet there is no valorization of plebeian actuality over elite fiction, and Wilton's ironies do not "expose" Surrey.

From the rebels' grisly defeat to Surrey's account of the "more than celestiall" Geraldine (2.244), we pass from a "tragicall catastrophe" (2.241) to the Court of Love.[146] We also leave a plebeian scene (the Anabaptists are "base handicrafts" [2.232]) for an aristocratic one, which is conveyed ethically. Surrey's "spirites" are "airie," "firie" (2.242); "he entertained no grosse earthly spirite of avarice" (2.242), and his etheriality counterpoises the rebels' coarseness. He is himself a perfect poem, and moral purity underlies his pure verse; his mistresses are Geraldine and poetry. Throughout this introduction to Surrey, high-mindedness is isolated as elite, and Wilton stands apart from it in an attitude of sincere yet ironic admiration. If the Anabaptists are derided, Surrey 's naïveté and innocence are regarded amusedly, his romanticism being framed as a mode of elite self-congratulation. Wilton, then, is not identifiable with the "illuminate botchers," but neither is he identifiable with Surrey. Perceiving it from below highlights the cultural significance of this romantic mode, since it is contrasted with the horrible fate of the Anabaptist "coblers and curriers and tinkers" (2.232). The contrast heightens the ideality of Surrey's discourse, and though the text's bracketing it off as an aristocratic mode does not diminish its charm, it places it in a realistic context. Thus Wilton's comment:

> Not a little was I delighted with this unexpected love storie, especially from a mouth out of which was nought wont to march but sterne precepts of gravetie & modestie. I sweare unto you I thought his companie the better by

a thousand crownes, because hee had discarded those nice tearmes of chastitie and continencie. Now I beseech God love me so well as I love a plaine dealing man; earth is earth, flesh is flesh, earth wil to earth, and flesh unto flesh; fraile earth, fraile flesh, who can keepe you from the worke of your creation? (2.245)

Why can we not say that this anti-Petrarchan, worldly realism is socially neutral, from "outside" rather than from "below"? Given the scorn for the rebels we cannot, of course, suppose a straightforwardly popular viewpoint; and criticizing idealism need not depend on some "practical" attitude of "popular culture." Nonetheless, Wilton's attitude is enabled by his not enjoying Surrey's rank: the text assumes a connection between courtliness and idealism. Like Nashe, Wilton assimilates himself to the elite. But he does not naturally belong to this world, and views it "objectively."

The transition from the Anabaptist massacre to Surrey's Petrarchism takes us from a "particular" to "general" or generic discourse.[147] The contrast is between two socially meaningful representational modes: Wilton's, dealing with tinkers and tailors and indiscriminately inclusive, the only limitation being wit, and Surrey's, which has the selectivity of a highly codified genre. The contrast between "artlessness" and "artifice" has a social dimension.[148] Wilton's account aims at an "anti-generic," "anti-rhetorical" effect: like *Pierce,* it cultivates a random appearance, as if unindebted to social-stylistic canons. Surrey's manner, on the other hand, is "correct," has a clear generic identity, and reflects an ideal of decorum.

Surrey's account seems blandly conventional and universal by comparison with Wilton's tale. It is unparticularized, unengaged with the "real" world, and like the allegory of love everywhere. His allegiances are to a discursive mode rather than to a particular woman,[149] and it is clear that this love is a mode of social definition when, after the leaden reality of the Anabaptists, he boasts that it is not felt by "leaden braines" (2.243). This love is a sign of nobility (again ethical and social distinctions are inseparable) and Wilton is a stranger to it. Surrey's discourse cashes places, people, events, and feelings into the international currency of the mythology of love: Hampton Court is "Cupids inchaunted Castle," Surrey is "Metamorphozed" by "a little God called Love," Elizabeth Fitzgerald ("celestiall Geraldine") walks with her ladies in "paradice," Surrey's wish to visit Italy suggests Dido and Aeneas: "I, pete Italiam" (2.243–44). We note the socially symbolic character of the language of love:

> Her high exalted sunne beames have set the Phenix neast of my breast on fire, and I my selfe have brought Arabian spiceries of sweet passions and praises to furnish out the funerall flame of my follie. Those who were condemned to be smothered to death by sincking downe into the softe bottome of an high built bedde of Roses, never dide so sweet a death as I shoulde die, if hir Rose coloured disdaine were my deathes-man. (2.243)

The unreality of this is highlighted by coming after the slaughter of the Anabaptists:

> The Emperialls themselves that were their Executioners (like a father that weepes when he beates his childe, yet still weepes and stil beates) not without much ruth and sorrow prosecuted that lamentable massacre; yet drums and trumpets sounding nothing but stearne revenge in their eares, made them so eager that their handes had no leasure to aske counsell of their effeminate eyes; their swordes, theyr pikes, their bills, their bowes, their caleevers slew, empierced, knockt downe, shot through, and overthrew as manie men everie minute of the battell as there falls eares of corne before the sythe at one blow: yet all their weapons so slaying, empiercing, knocking downe, shooting through, over-throwing, dissoule-joyned not halfe so manie as the hailing thunder of the great Ordinance: so ordinarie at everie foot-step was the imbrument of yron in bloud, that one could hardly discern heads from bullets, or clottred haire from mangled flesh hung with goare. (2.240–41)

The exhaustive detail, and aggressive rhetoric of fact, of such passages foreground the automatic conventionalism of Surrey's discourse, or its appearance of being drawn on the universal pattern of courtly love. Obviously, the Anabaptist passage is rhetorical: we note "dissoule-joyned," as well as "their swordes, theyr pikes, their bills, their bowes, their caleevers slew, empierced, knockt downe, shot through, and overthrew . . ." Nonetheless, the passage displays an energetic, eccentric, uninhibited wit. And there is a sense in which one can describe its mode as comparatively "artless": where Surrey's discourse appears rational, discriminating and governed by a deliberate, formal code of representation, Wilton's seems empirical rather than idealistic, dedicated to the disordered actuality of the world. The difference, then, is between a "truth" unmindful of neoclassic commitments (that is, the true as the fitting), and a self-conscious observance of elite canons. Yet if Wilton deploys an empirical, popular truth, he also distances himself from his plebeian heretics. Again, we face a text that cultivates through its roguish hero a mode antithetical to elite discursive standards, but which stops short of identification with the populace.

Stylistic concreteness or its absence is, then, socially symbolic. Wilton's tale proliferates in base details, eschewing Surrey's stylistic rationalism:

> That day come, flourishing entred John Leiden the Botcher into the field, with a scarffe made of lysts like a bow-case, a crosse on hys breast like a thred bottome, a round twilted Taylors cushion buckled like a Tankard-bearers device to his shoulders for a target, the pyke whereof was a pack-needle, a tough prentises club for his spear, a great Bruers cow on his backe for a corslet, and on his head for a helmet a huge high shooe with the bottome turnd upwards, embossed as full of hob-nayles as ever it might sticke: his men were all base handicrafts, as coblers and curriers and tinkers, whereof some had barres of yron, some hatchets, some coole-staves, some dung-forkes, some spades, some mattockes, some wood-knives, some addises for their weapons: he that was best provided had but a peece of a rustie browne bill bravely fringed with cop-webs to fight for him. Perchance here and there you might see a felow that had a canker-eaten scull on his head, which served him and his ancestors for a chamber pot two hundred yeeres, and another that had bent a couple of yron dripping pans armour-wise, to fence his backe and his belly; another that had thrust a paire of drie olde bootes as a breast-plate before his belly of his dublet, because he would not be dangerously hurt; an other that had twilted all his trusse full of counters, thinking, if the Enemie should take him, he would mistake them for gold, and so save his life for his money. Verie devout Asses they were . . . (2.232–33)

This passage is "empirical" in offering a defined, particularized scene, and generates grotesque incongruities from the spectacle of the rabble playing at soldiers: "a tough prentises club for his spear." It exemplifies antidecorum, articulating a ludicrous disorder from which Wilton distances himself: "Verie devout Asses they were." Yet in evoking them it also relishes these absurdities. Wilton acknowledges that describing matters the elegant Surrey would not descend to is to risk contamination: "what with talking of coblers, tinkers, roape-makers, botchers, and durt-daubers, the mark is clean out of my Muses mouth" (2.241). This expresses the anxiety that the use of nonelite modes associates one with them, and Nashe wants to disavow kinship with the vulgar. Yet the passage's rhetorical verve also indicates a desire to play with the possibilities of "popular culture": what is displayed is Nashe's ability to manipulate what is taken to be the culture of the populace in the same way that he manipulates the elite's. To call this passage popular, then, simplifies: what we have is a self-advertising use of the popular rather than simple indebtedness to it. It has strategic value, suggesting independence from Surrey's polite manner and an author traversing social distinctions. Using a popular mode, however, raises problems of self-presentation. Thus the disdain for "base handicrafts," and the passage's participation in a so-called popular mode (the mark is out of the Muse's mouth) while snobbishly straining to distinguish itself from that mode.

What is necessary to note is that while this passage pursues the effect of a fuller engagement with reality than the earl's overstylized discourse, it does not privilege an unaristocratic "realism."[150] A discourse spurning the real for poetry is contrasted with a nonelite "anti-style" that comprehends matters (like chamber pots) that Surrey cannot. Wilton's discursive practice imitates the casual randomness of his adventures: its accidental, unreflective appearance contrasts with the courtier's orderly, generic manner. The important point, though, is that if such "artless" realism pokes fun at Surrey, this is part of Wilton's self-empowering rhetorical strategy, which is imperiled by any hint of solidarity with "illuminate botchers."

Surrey's passion gives rise to another episode critically distancing elite symbolism: the tournament at Florence, which he calls to champion Geraldine's beauty, and in which the elaborate symbolism of each knight's armor is decoded. Here again Nashe provides a perspective on courtly discourse. Rather than seeing this episode as radically ironizing the court, though, I wish to stress its ambiguous framing and validating of aristocratic symbolism.

> The right honorable and ever renowmed Lord Henrie Howard, earle of Surrie, my singular good Lord and master, entered the lists after this order. His armour was all intermixed with lillyes and roses, and the bases thereof bordered with nettles and weeds, signifieng stings, crosses, and overgrowing incumberances in his love; his helmet round proportioned lyke a gardners water-pot, from which seemed to issue forth small thrids of water, like citterne strings, that not onely did moisten the lyllyes and roses, but did fructifie as well the nettles and weeds, and made them overgrow theyr liege Lords. Whereby he did import thus much, that the teares that issued from his braines, as those arteficiall distillations issued from the well counterfeit water-pot on his head, watered and gave lyfe as well to his mistres disdaine (resembled to nettles and weeds) as increase of glorie to her care-causing beauty (comprehended under the lillies and roses). The simbole thereto

annexed was this, *Ex lachrimis lachrimae.* The trappings of his horse were pounced and bolstered out with rough plumed silver plush, in full proportion and shape of an Estrich. . . .

The worde to this device was *Aculeo alatus,* I spread my wings onely spurd with her eyes. The morall of the whole is this, that as the estrich, the most burning sighted bird of all others, insomuch as the female of them hatcheth not her egs by covering them, but by the effectuall rayes of her eyes, as he, I say, outstrippeth the nimblest trippers of his feathered condition in footmanship, onely spurd on with the needle quickning goad under his side, so he, no lesse burning sighted than the estrich, spurde on to the race of honor by the sweet rayes of his mistres eyes, perswaded himselfe he should outstrip all other in running to the goale of glorie, onely animated and incited by hir excellence. And as the estrich will eate yron, swallow anie hard mettall whatsoever, so woulde he refuse no iron adventure, no hard taske whatsoever, to sit in the grace of so fayre a commander. (2.271–73)

Clearly, this methodical chivalric symbolizing contrasts radically with Wilton's "extemporall" mode. The even more ludicrously elaborate arms of the other eight knights are likewise faithfully detailed and explained, and Wilton's comment that "I wil rehearse no more [of these "discontented or amorous devises" (2.277)], but I have an hundred other" (2.278) reinforces the impression of an absurdly overcultivated symbolism.[151] There is a distance between the speaker and the bizarre courtly symbolism, seen from outside in all its dead, artificial formalism. Nevertheless, Wilton's relation to the tournament is not one-sided.

If this spectacle seems ridiculous, Wilton does not attack it. His attitude is remarkably inscrutable as he lavishly describes and decodes these ceremonies. Of course, the foolishness of the knights is apparent, especially in their incompetence in combat against Surrey, who alone "observed the true measures of honour" (2.278). Their awkward symbolism and ineffectuality underscores Wilton's resourceful, worldly assurance. Yet none of this implies a rejection of the aristocratic. The stance is wry, indulgent: that of someone enjoying a distance on these solemnities, but not of one subverting them with radical irony. As conspicuous as the ludicrousness of the knights' ceremonial is Wilton's sympathetic entering into "shewes . . . the admirablest that ever Florence yelded" (2.278). What is on display is a facility with a socially symbolic mode: the detailed explications of this arcane discourse demonstrate a complete familiarity with it and its milieu, as well as an ability to appreciate its absurdity.

As observed above, *The Unfortunate Traveller* exploits the difference between a noble narrative of glorious "Acts and Monuments" and the insignificant adventures of "a certain kind of an appendix or page." Thus the contrast between "volume" and "pamphlet": *The Unfortunate Traveller* is a "Chronicle" at the end of the book and there are ambiguous references to the work as a "historie," meaning "tale" but potentially also the record of "famous atchievements" (2.217; see 234, 242). Nashe humorously stresses this social contrast in his "Induction to the dapper Mounsier Pages of the Court" (2.207–8). Addressing them with mock solemnity and courtesy, and exploiting again a contrast between particular social forms and milieux, Wilton exhorts them "to be true to [their] puisant order" and to honor "this Chronicle of the king of Pages" (2.207–8): "Everie Stationers stall they passe by, whether by daie or by night, they shall put off theyr hats too, and make a low legge, in regard their grand printed Capitano is there entombd" (2.208). Simultaneously, however, the worthlessness of this tale of marginal misadventures is noticed: "pages" (the pun is Wilton's) are here "wast paper"; the book, with obvious innuendo, a "privie token of his good will" (2.207). Nashe reminds his audience how negatively this story compares with an elite narrative dealing with significant material of a high, universal nature, and so describable within the serious forms of tragedy, epic, and history: "I must not place a volume in the precincts of a pamphlet . . . " (2.227). Nashe's field, the particular experiences of a page, lies outside elite forms, and the text flaunts this outsiderness. So with Wilton's arrival in Rome. Here too we might anticipate an account of "Acts and Monuments," for Rome is of universal proportions, "Queen of the world & metropolitane mistres of all other cities" (2.279). Instead heroic or chronicle tradition is trivialized:

> Johannes de Imola, a Roman cavaliero. . . . shewed us all the monumentes that were to bee seene, which are as manye as there have beene Emperours, Consulles, Oratours, Conquerours, famous painters or plaiers in Rome. Tyll this daie not a Romane (if he be a right Romane indeed) will kill a rat, but he will have some registred remembraunce of it. (2.279)

"I was at Pontius Pilates house and pist against it," he adds, finally confessing his lack of interest in such grand material: anyone who has "but once dronke with a traveller" has heard of "Pompeies theater. . . . Gregory the sixths tombe, Priscillas grate. . . . Let me be a historiographer of my owne misfortunes, and not meddle with the continued

Trophees of so olde a triumphing Citie" (2.280–81—"historiographer" underscoring the irony). After this the narrative returns to the sordid, dangerous contemporary Italian scene, relating the rape of Heraclide by the "notable Bandetto" Esdras of Granado (2.287). Pointedly disdaining the public tradition of "Acts and Monuments," Nashe asserts an ability to play with the forms of the great, framing these by the modern, low, and particular. The effect is less a contestation of elite forms, pitting nonelite experience against elite tradition, than an appearance of autonomy. By writing in a mode self-consciously outside such forms, and emphasizing contingent, ephemeral actions unaccommodated in them, Nashe projects an independence from the social order they underwrite: the "irrationality" of *The Unfortunate Traveller* contrasts with the formalism of high modes. There is a sense in which Wilton writes outside the symbolic, or, in more specifically "literary" terms—a distinction being complicated in this study—outside the generic system. Yet this rhetorical fiction should not be formulated oppositionally: the knave wants not to undermine the system but to manipulate it advantageously. Nashe emphasizes his playing with this system, his ability to control it, and his ironic ease within it. It is the social value of the high forms that counts for him.

The Unfortunate Traveller projects an ironist's ascendancy over literary or discursive modes. The rest of this chapter treats Wilton's handling of the social meaning of tragedy: the rape of Heraclide by Esdras and the gallows confession of his murderer Cutwolfe—events sufficiently shocking to convince even the hardened Wilton that he is out of his depth in Italy and would fare better in the shallower waters of England.

In his theory of "novelization," Bakhtin suggests that the high genres of epic and tragedy are inimical to contemporaneity and rely upon a distant and "valorized past."[152] English tragedy in the sixteenth and seventeenth centuries seems to confirm this, with native or Roman history providing the matter.[153] Even if Shakespeare introduces a modern atmosphere into tragedy (the sense of lateness in *Lear* or of contemporaneity in *Hamlet*), it is usually significantly related to an archaic time.[154] This importance of the past in high modes contrasts with its treatment in *The Unfortunate Traveller,* in which the perspective, far from being that of a distant, "valorized past," is flippantly, iconoclastically contemporary: "I was at Pontius Pilates house and pist against it. . . . Let me be a historiographer of my owne misfortunes . . . " As we have seen, the text plays with the whole mode of "Acts and Monuments," stressing awareness of and yet departing from it. There is a certain bravado about

Nashe's self-conscious preoccupation with incidents rather than Acts. Their accidental nature is emphasized: they are not instances of some master narrative or genre. Wilton's experience does not signify within a cultural system (in, for example, the way that Surrey's love for Geraldine does, with its sighs and tears or wind and rain [see 2.245]).[155] Nashe wants to be seen as venturing outside elite generic structures into aspects of experience invisible within them, and thus an ironic relation between system and experience is suggested. Just as Summers seems to stand outside the play proper, framing its universal myth with a here-and-now reality, so Wilton presents his adventures as if they were "experience" rather than literary mode. A rhetorical contrast obtains between elite modes of symbolizing reality and a nonelite experience realistically framing them.

Wilton calls the story of Esdras's rape of Heraclide and her death a "tragicall tale" and "eligiacall historie" (2.292). The work's modernity, however, complicates this so-called tragedy. The sophisticated contemporaneity of the scene, modern-day Rome, sits incongruously with the classical texture of the stiffly formal speeches in which Heraclide remonstrates with Esdras and then laments her rape:

> Having passioned thus awhile, she hastely ran and lookt hir selfe in hir glasse, to see if her sin were not written on her forhead: with looking shee blusht, though none lookt upon her but her owne reflected image.
> Then began she againe. *Heu quam difficile est crimen non prodere vultu;* How hard is it not to bewray a mans falt by his forhead. My selfe doo but behold my selfe, and yet I blush: then, God beholding me, shall not I be ten times more ashamed? The Angels shall hisse at me, the Saints and Martyrs flye from me; yea, God himselfe shall adde to the divels damnation, because he suffered such a wicked creature to come before him. Agamemnon, thou wert an infidell, yet when thou wentst to the Trojan warre, thou leftst a musitian at home with thy Wife, who by playing the foote Spondaeus till thy retourne, might keepe her in chastitie. My husband going to warre with the divell and his enticements, when hee surrendred, left no musition with me, but mourning and melancholy: had he left anie, as Aegistus kild Agamemnons Musitian ere he could be successfull, so surely would hee have been kild ere this Aegistus surceased. My distressed heart, as the Hart when as hee looseth his hornes is astonied, and sorrowfullie runneth to hide himselfe, so be thou afflicted and distressed; hide thy selfe under the Almighties wings of mercie: sue, plead, intreate; grace is never denied to them that aske. It may be denied; I maie be a vessell ordained to dishonor.
> The onely repeale we have from Gods undefinite chastisement is to

chastise our selves in this world: and I will; nought but death be my pennance, gracious and acceptable maie it be: my hand and my knife shall manumit mee out of the horrour of minde I endure. Fare-well, life, that hast lent me nothing but sorrowe. Fare-well, sinne-sowed flesh, that hast more weedes than flowers, more woes than joies. Point, pierce, edge, enwiden, I patiently affoorde thee a sheath: spurre forth my soule to mount poste to heaven. Jesu, forgive me, Jesu, receive me. (2.294–95)

Wilton compares Heraclide to Hecuba, and her grief on seeing her murdered husband's corpse (which, like Demetrius and Chiron in *Titus Andronicus*, Esdras makes "a pillow to his abhomination" [2.292]) to that of "Cephalus when he . . . kild Procris unwittingly, or Oedipus when ignorantly he had slaine his father, & known his mother incestuously" (2.293). The comparison overall is with Lucrece, "chastities first martyr" (2.255). But the depth and richness of such allusions, and the dignity of Heraclide's rhetoric, rings strangely in the contemporary bourgeois setting; with Wilton as our guide we have got used to a peculiarly unideal notion of contemporaneity. That this heroic and passionate scene is witnessed by him ("I, thorough a crannie of my upper chamber unseeled, had beheld all this sad spectacle" [2.295]) reinforces its estrangement: for while there is no irony in Wilton's account, it is difficult not to register the extreme disjunction between his realistically modern, low, skeptical outlook and this highly artificial, elevated, and apparently aristocratic "spectacle."[156] Wilton's word captures the fustian conventionalism of the scene—it is treated as if it were a scene in a play, as fiction, and this distancing is in line with the way we have seen elite conventions and modes presented ironically in the light of a "reality" with a broader social character.[157] Once again social distinctions are conveyed through an ethical rhetoric, the high-mindedness of Heraclide's speech signifying nobility just as Wilton's deidealizing rhetoric throughout *The Unfortunate Traveller* implies ignobility. Thus foregrounded, a reader notices this speech as tragic form, or as a discursive mode that is not merely stylistically heightened (somewhere above the "everyday" register of the work in the manner, say, that the First Player's speech in *Hamlet* is removed from the relatively familiar world of Elsinore).[158] The reader also notices the speech as denoting social distinction, and has a critical awareness of it as a socially symbolic mode. Such awareness is available precisely because of the social interplay between rhetorical and cultural modes that is such a central strategy of Nashe's works.

Perhaps, though, the critical perspective on tragedy in *The Unfortu-*

nate Traveller goes further than translating some rhetorical features of tragedy into an unfamiliar setting. The key here is the concept of fortune in the text, Wilton's narrative ironically invoking tragic mutability. Among the ups and downs of his progress through the Continent we may discern, stripped of its portentousness, the traditional matter of tragedy, the role of fortune in the lives of the great.[159] Yet the chief feature of this theme is the frivolity with which it is addressed. Here is Wilton at his most desperate pass (about to be hanged after being wrongly convicted of Heraclide's murder):

> Uppon this was I laide in prison, should have been hanged, was brought to the ladder, had made a Ballad for my Farewell in a readines, called *Wiltons wantonnes,* and yet for all that scapde dauncing in a hempen circle. . . . I had the knot under my eare, there was faire plaie, the hangman had one halter, another about my necke was fastned to the gallowes, the riding device was almost thrust home, and his foote on my shoulder to presse me downe, when I made my saint-like confession as you have heard before, that such and such men at such an howre brake into the house . . . took my Curtizan, lockt me into my chamber, ravisht Heraclide, and finallie how she slew her selfe. (2.295–96)

But "present at the execution" is "a banisht English Earle," with evidence corroborating Wilton's story (2.296). Fortune is handled here with insouciant levity: it is not just that the thrusting hero of this text, in his arbitrary manipulations of narrative, implicitly acknowledges no power except his own, but that the flip, audacious, irresponsible tone of *The Unfortunate Traveller* belittles Fortune. There is about this passage a derisory impertinence toward a traditionally august concept that is fitting for one on whom tragedy has no compelling cultural claim. (Wilton does not understand his life story in this way—Surrey would have spoken differently.) Thus Wilton can be thought of as the unfortunate traveler in a sense indicating not merely greater than average bad luck: his adventures distance, by virtue of their social incongruity with, a narrative concept conventional to an elite mode. (A comparable defamiliarization of literary mode, based, that is, on a gap between form and social content, is considered in the "bourgeois" tragedies of the next chapter.) Again, however, this reduction of a tragic idea does not mean we face an unproblematically "popular" work, one placing itself simply outside the tradition, for Wilton's speech and his misadventures ironically set in play its august associations, the high forms thus having a spectral presence throughout the text.

If *The Unfortunate Traveller* ironically invokes a tragic mutability by translating it into the disreputable setting of Wilton's Italy, we have to formulate carefully our estimation of this work as pursuing an artless effect. We must at least repudiate the notion that *The Unfortunate Traveller* simply draws on popular culture. We have to say instead that, in playing with the potential of a "senseless," formless text, Nashe wants his reader to notice his informed, fully aware, ironic handling of an elite tradition: thus to characterize the text as antigeneric, or popular in an oppositional sense, is only half-true—*Fortuna* shadows Wilton's adventures throughout. The narrative finishes abruptly: after listening to Cutwolfe's horrifying description of his murder of Esdras (tricked just before his death into uttering the most damnable blasphemies), Wilton, appalled and contrite, marries his courtesan, gives alms, and abandons Italy for Henry VIII's army. We are free to wonder about his reformation (there is a hint that more "Chronicles" might appear), and the book's sudden close confirms the general impression it gives of flagrant arbitrariness,[160] an arbitrariness communicating, as we have seen, an arch social-literary confidence. Reading Nashe involves a continual adjustment to different, apparently socially specific points of view, and the effect of this social interplay is a certain bracketing off of elite or "artificial" modes, so that their exclusive social character is foregrounded. But Nashe does not produce radical texts, and they are not really "popular" in any meaningful sense. What Nashe does produce are impish, knavish works, playing with high and low social modes and attempting through their manipulation to construct a unique form of authorial social power.

2

"No Glorious State":
The Social Interplay of
Bourgeois Tragedy

Arden of Faversham (pub. 1592), *A Warning for Fair Women* (pub. 1599), Robert Yarington's *Two Lamentable Tragedies* (pub. 1601), *A Yorkshire Tragedy* (pub. 1608), and *A Woman Killed with Kindness* (pub. 1607) are among the plays making up the Elizabethan minigenre "domestic tragedy."[1] The solidity of that label is something of an anachronism, given the fluid, vague character of the theory and practice of literary genres in the English Renaissance,[2] but singling out these plays as a special type seems justified where they indicate a conviction that they are deviating from "conventional" tragedy, and negatively: "Look for no glorious state," declares the prologue to *A Woman Killed with Kindness,* "our Muse is bent / Upon a barren subject, a bare scene." Quite as blunt is the epilogue to *Arden:*

> Gentlemen, we hope you'll pardon this naked tragedy
> Wherein no filèd points are foisted in
> To make it gracious to the ear or eye;
> For simple truth is gracious enough
> And needs no other points of glozing stuff.

The epilogue to *A Warning for Fair Women* declares itself a "true and home-borne Tragedie." These plays, then, present themselves as reductions of tragedy, from bloody stories set in far-off or long-ago courts and camps (Marlowe's "stately tent of war")[3] to bloody or serious stories set in the homes of well-to-do, nonaristocratic, modern English, a "sceane . . . native and your owne" *(A Warning for Fair Women,* induction, 95). Tragedy in the English Renaissance is, of course, more various than the monotonous tradition these plays conjure up to define their own innovations against.[4] But that is perhaps less important for understanding them than the negative rhetoric itself: that is, the deliberate reduction of, or self-distancing from, an established form.

That point seems worth making because of an understandable tendency to assimilate these plays to some all-encompassing notion of Elizabethan tragedy or, more generally still, to "the tragic"; and this despite those gestures in which the plays distinguish themselves from "tragedy."[5] Not that this comparison with tragedy has always been odious to the plays concerned: witness the critical enthusiasm over the "bourgeois Clytemnestra," Alice Arden.[6] (Conversely, the measuring yard "tragedy," defined without much regard to Elizabethan practice, may become a stick to beat the plays with—their didacticism, moralism, and so on—if, that is, it is assumed that their authors are simply writing tragedy rather than responding to tragic traditions.) Even the conventional genre name, Elizabethan domestic tragedy, encourages us to see the plays as a subset of some larger totality, thus emphasizing affinities rather than differences—yet it is upon these differences that the plays insist. In the end it is the plays themselves, and not just modern interpreters, that invoke this spirit of tragedy: their invocation of the conventions of tragic representation is one of their crucial characteristics, and my subject here. I shall argue, however, that such invocation is not a matter of passively applying the repertoire of tragedy to a citizen or bourgeois (or minor gentry) setting.[7] Rather, what we find in these plays is a complex investment in "the tradition" as well as distance from it. (Thus that pattern traced in Nashe's work—distancing of, yet commitment to elite modes—is discoverable in these texts too.) These plays seem sharply aware of the social symbolism of tragic form, and it is tempting to see their interest in areas of social life traditionally ignored by tragedy as a modification, perhaps a rejection, of an aristocratic mode. Of at least one of the plays treated here I believe this can be said; but for the most part we shall see not an oppositional orientation toward tragedy but an ambiguous, shifting pattern in which the plays move in and out of this high mode, which is regarded as usually taking for granted aristocratic norms. *Arden*'s "naked tragedy," Heywood's "bare scene," imply that the tradition is present in a changed sense, perhaps only in a diminished way, and if we do not see a conscious break with tradition, we do find some significant reflection upon it.

From one point of view it is unsurprising that such reflection should involve social categories. For the Elizabethan theater was, of course, as an institution, necessarily sensitive to differences of rank and to the structure of society, and survived precariously through a strategic alignment with an aristocratic elite, noble and royal patronage frustrating City opposition. In other words, the theater was itself a factor in the complex relations of City, Court, and populace.[8] An acute awareness of rank can hardly have been strange to the players, occupying as they did a dubious position in the Tudor scheme of things and never, not even in later and better years, quite shaking off the taint of vagabondage (Greene's animadversion on the "upstart Crow," for instance, showing a University man's contempt for those "rude grooms," the players).[9] The English Renaissance theater was mixed in other ways, not least in the character of its social relations, which were nominally feudal (the players being the liveried servants of a noble or royalty) but actually capitalist (by 1600 the theaters were developed profitable concerns).[10] And the audience was mixed (though there were probably not as many lower-class spectators at the public theaters as was once supposed), including courtiers and students, merchants and shopkeepers, artisans and apprentices.[11] The controversies that gathered around the theater, its dual precapitalist and entrepreneurial character, the players' ambiguous status, possibly the need to satisfy a fairly heterogeneous audience—such factors suggest a theater as aware of itself as a social phenomenon as it was aware of its obligation to entertain. And they suggest an institution inevitably—often, perhaps, painfully—aware of rank because of the way this social fact impinged upon its work.

Among the plays considered here, *A Warning for Fair Women* stands out for its explicitness in presenting dramatic genres in terms of their social affiliations: it contains the most schematic social representation of genre. The play, based on a case reported in Stow and Holinshed and also in an account by Arthur Golding, concerns the seduction of the wife of a London businessman, George Sanders, by a gallant, Captain Browne, the subsequent murder of Sanders, and the discovery and execution of Browne, Anne Sanders, and their aiders and abettors, Mistress Drury and her servant, Trusty Roger.[12] The play opens rambunctiously, with a quarrel between Tragedy, History, and Comedy for possession of the stage. History is accoutered "with Drum and Ensigne," Tragedy with "a whip, [and] in the other hand a knife." Such paraphernalia suggest some obvious broad contrasts: thus History appears as the inclusive national form (the drum being the normal metonym for war,[13] and implying, perhaps, patriotism), while Tragedy's concerns are less national than elitist, showing us, taunts Comedy, "How some damnd tyrant, to obtaine a crown, / Stabs, hangs, impoysons, smothers, cutteth throats" (50–51).

In the manner of tyrants, Tragedy is ludicrously irascible: "Downe with that Ensigne," she rails, "which disturbs our stage / Out with this luggage, with this fopperie" (6–7). But the bombast of

> I must have passions that must move the soule,
> Make the heart heave, and throb within the bosome,
> Extorting teares out of the strictest eyes,
> To racke a thought and straine it to his forme,
> Untill I rap the sences from their course,
> This is my office . . .
>
> (44–49)

is promptly undercut by Comedy's irreverent interpretation of the tragic stage:

> . . . a filthie whining ghost
> Lapt in some fowle sheete, or a leather pelch,
> Comes skreaming like a pigge halfe stickt,
> And cries *Vindicta,* revenge, revenge:
> With that a little Rosen flasheth forth,
> Like smoke out of a Tabacco pipe, or a boyes squib . . .
>
> (54–60)

Nonetheless, this playful scene has some far-reaching implications, notably that which presents Tragedy as a less socially comprehensive, more exclusionistic form than either History or Comedy: these two have monopolized the theaters so long, complains Tragedy, "That I am scorned of the multitude, / My name prophande" (76–77). It is implied that her appeal is to judicious (that is, upper-class) spectators when she allows that Comedy can, indeed, "tickle shallow injudiciall eares" with "odde ends of old jeasts scrap't up togither," but that her "filthie fidling trickes, / . . . poyson any noble wit" (40–41; 23–24). What is contrasted is, from Tragedy's perspective, art with entertainment. Tragedy's Machiavellian matter ("some damnd tyrant" poisoning and cutting throats) contrasts strongly, as an altogether more ambitious and weighty form, with Comedy's honest, harmless, native fare ("odde ends of old jeasts"), and History's drum and trumpet themes. It is Tragedy's day, however, and the other contenders are hustled off the stage.

The induction cannot really be spoken of separately from the rest of the play, with which it must be associated in terms of generic self-consciousness.[14] Not being a conventional tragedy with aristocratic subjects, the play takes some pains to signal its tragic pedigree—or at least to relate itself to a tragic tradition. So History observes, "Looke Comedie, I markt it not till now, / The stage is hung with blacke; and I perceive / The Auditors preparde for Tragedie" (81–83). But the play's attitude toward this high tragic tradition is in some ways obscure: while Tragedy presents herself as art, concerned not with jests but with extreme and important emotions, Comedy sees her as purveying crude entertainment, and indeed Tragedy is, with her huffing, melodramatic style, not a little ridiculous. In the epilogue, however, she seems to apologize for departing from convention:

> Perhaps it may seeme strange unto you al,
> That one hath not revengde anothers death,
> After the observation of such course:
> The reason is, that now of truth I sing,
> And should I adde, or else diminish aught,
> Many of these spectators then could say,
> I have comitted error in my play.
>
> (2722–28)

This posits a potential gap between truth and the artifice of tragedy, and at the same time announces a commitment to truth even at the expense of form. The spectators are invited to compare what they see with what they "know," a rhetoric of truth being played against an idea of tragic convention.[15] The truth in question differs from Jonson's in the preface to *Sejanus* (1603; pub. 1605), where "truth of argument" is one of the chief "offices of a tragic writer."[16] For Jonson, truth, by definition, cannot contradict art—but such a conflict is precisely what the induction and epilogue to *A Warning* hint at. The self-consciousness of *A Warning* about truth and art inevitably recalls Hamlet and the players, where, too, tragedy is identified in the first place with high and stormy emotion: "Come give us a taste of your quality, come, a passionate speech," asks Hamlet of the First Player (2.2.431–32); and the Pyrrhus speech does indeed "racke a thought," "straine it to his forme" and "rap the sences from their course." But Hamlet also demands that the player "give it smoothness" (3.2.8), and this requirement of control or "temperance" (3.2.7) marks the prince out as a connoisseur of drama. Hamlet's condescension to unlearned Tarltonizing comedy is not very unlike that which Tragedy expresses—she, too, deplores ignorant clowns thrust in by head and shoulders to play a part in majestical matters, whose only concern is "to set on some quantity of barren spectators to laugh" (*Hamlet,* 3.2.41–42).[17] The analogy with Hamlet's views, however, can only be taken so far, since the playful induction to *A Warning* means that Tragedy emphatically does not have it all her own way: we are aware of an ironic perspective on the tradition more or less absent in Hamlet's self-identification with "art." Yet if *A Warning* can present all tragedy as out-Heroding Herod, there is, as we shall see, a thoroughgoing commitment to this mode. In other words, if the play does not actually present the ghastly revenge tragedy alluded to in the epilogue, there is little squeamishness about the large, horrendous emotions, the tragic "overdo-ing"[18] mocked in the induction—evident particularly in the egregiously overblown (to a modern audience) dumb shows (especially the first, where tragedy appears with bowl of blood, mazers made of dead men's skulls, black tapers, etc.).[19] This apparent dividedness in what the play is up to suggests that the contrast initially drawn here between "truth" and "art"—an art which, for the irreverent, entertainment-oriented Comedy and History is merely tedious and ridiculous—inadequately describes the play, which has a more complicated relation to the conventions it foregrounds than its rhetoric of opposition implies. It is along these lines that I wish to discuss five plays here, in which tragedy is explored and in some cases problematized on social grounds, but in which we also find a full, though not unself-conscious, allegiance to the mode. As with Nashe, describing the social-literary character of these works requires in most cases exchanging a critical discourse of opposition for one of interplay. If, therefore, tragedy in *A Warning* is represented ironically, as a conventional tradition potentially at odds with truth, even, Comedy turning the tables, as trivial and absurd, the three dumb shows tend to modify this simple opposition: the truth of the seduction of Mistress Sanders and the murder of Master Sanders is disclosed in terms of a universal, heightened allegory, featuring figures like the Furies, Lust, Chastity, Justice, and Mercy. And there is no ambiguity in the claim that, in these shows, the true meaning of the events in Billingsgate, Shooters Hill, Rochester, and Newgate is unfolded, with a lurid and frightening, and utterly serious, moralism: it is implied that these familiar elements of tragedy are actually "in" the events portrayed.

More than likely the assumptions about the social character of certain genres in this induction (tragedy as appealing mainly to the cultivated, history and comedy to the masses) are not historical: they need not be, of course, for the piece to have its fun. But the induction also suggests a theater used to thinking about literary modes in terms of social distinctions. Tragedy claims to be an upper-class mode, not only because of its subject matter but in its appeal to a specific kind of spectator. The induction, too, with its representation of genres, implies a stage capable of reflection upon dramatic kinds. This confirms the suspicion aired above, that the play's pronounced self-consciousness about the social symbolism of tragedy renders its genre description (Elizabethan domestic tragedy) unhelpful, the stage of the induction exploring tragedy rather than unreflectively assuming it. Moreover, as we have also seen, the play does set up a suggestive, highly ambiguous contrast between tragedy and truth, in which, on the one hand, tragedy is reduced to a matter of rudimentary, even distorting, conventions, a set of feeble, awkward devices, and, on the other hand, is seen as uncovering the profounder truth behind the murders of the play, showing that what appeared only random, meaningless fact is divine pattern. We must, I think, suppose the play to be working with this double, incompatible sense of the tradition. In other words, while it opens with what appears a criticism of tragic representation, targeted as grotesquely inadequate to the real-life events it is to be concerned with, and, insofar as there is a gap between its usual princely subject matter and merchant life, irrelevant to lower-class or nonelite milieux, the play goes on to explore the ways in which such life is conformable to the tragic paradigm after all. The point that needs emphasizing is the play's exploratory stance: a distance is opened up between form and content, and the play proper presents not bloody tyrants or vengeful ghosts but a "true and home-borne Tragedie" (epilogue) about adultery and murder in citizen London. The play stimulates attention to tragedy as a formal tradition to be separated from the actuality of ignoble life yet in certain respects adequate to it. We see the playwright working both in and outside of a tradition apprehended as limited to aristocrats. Thus *A Warning for Fair Women* has some important parallels with *Arden of Faversham,* which also (though not, to be sure, as explicitly) produces an awareness of tragedy rather than merely assumes it, tragic form appearing as something alienable from, yet intrinsic to, the story's social reality.

Like *Arden, A Warning* is highly attuned to social distinctions and self-aware about literary mode. Ordinary unaristocratic life and the idea of tragedy are compared, with the induction posing this relation as a simple contrast but the rest of the play suggesting possibilities of interimplication. The rank-consciousness is oppressive, conveying a narrow, anxious, materialistic world: it is after all one of the factors in

Sanders's murder, because Drury, Anne Sanders's neighbor and Browne's hired go-between, can play upon Anne's insecurity about Sanders's status. At the beginning of his pursuit of her, Browne offers himself as a useful contact for her husband, and Anne's defensiveness before the self-confident courtier is notable: "I thanke ye sir, but if he have such cause, / I hope hees not so voide of friends in Court, / But he may speede and never trouble you . . . " (384–86). Sanders is many times referred to as a gentleman: Anne says that "My George is gentle . . . / And I have even as good a husband of him, / As anie wench in London hath beside" (701–3) but, as Drury deviously observes, "True, he is good, . . . / Yet better's better . . . " (704, 709). It does not take long to batter down Anne's scruples with images of her in a "gowne of silke," riding in a "coach," attended by a "dozen men all in a liverie" (711–13). The social anxiety in the play, then, is as palpable as in *Arden,* and there is a sense in which its story can be thought of as translating aristocratic or tragic conventions into a bourgeois context, for this is both a tragedy of love and of ambition, of "heate of love and hasty climbing" (1780). To the extent that the play is about "the Ladder of Promotion" (699; Drury reading Anne Sanders's palm), we get a double-take on aristocratic conventions: they are exoticized by being brought into contact with an ordinary sphere of life, yet their pertinence to this sphere is also suggested, as if to show that the same motives leading to the falls of princes are at work in the lives of humbler folk.

Much of the play has a quasi-documentary feel. If the dumb shows give us grandiose and moralistic allegory, there is in the rest of the play an opposite tendency toward the impression of a bald reporting of fact: hence the stress on actual, familiar places, as well as the long latter half of the play devoted to Browne's capture and the trial of the guilty parties, where the mimetic impression is most pronounced, as legal ceremony and language are reproduced with an effect of detailed verisimilitude. Here too the play manipulates a contrast between a commonplace, realistic environment and high, romantic rhetoric, a rhetoric more properly "tragic" by the induction's simple criterion of inflated emotion. Thus Browne's speech on spying Anne Sanders at her door:

> Yonder she sits to light this obscure streete,
> Like a bright diamond worne in some darke place,
> Or like the moone in a blacke winters night,
> To comfort wandring travellers in their waie,

> But so demure, so modest are her lookes,
> So chaste her eies, so vertuous her aspect,
> As do repulse loves false Artilerie;
> Yet must I speake though checkt with scornful nay,
> Desire drawes on, but Reason bids me staie . . .

(343–51)

Probably our natural supposition about this extremely self-aware play is that its realistic mode is in tension with, perhaps undercuts, tragedy; such a tension would be the formal equivalent of class contradiction, as a nonaristocratic "reality" exposed the artificiality of upper-class mythologizing (a type of contrast whose role in Nashe's work we have addressed). But a more complicated relation exists between writer and genre, and the ability to see this mode, with clear-eyed, Hamlet-like critical detachment, as both that of a ranting "scould" (induction, 66) "tear[ing] a passion to totters" (*Hamlet*, 3.2.9–10), and as having a truth of its own, is notable. Thus the characters repeatedly acknowledge some wider meaning in experiences rooted in everyday London: "fatal destinie" (1251) is continually intuited and invoked in the whole tragic apparatus of omens, premonitory dreams, unmistakable tokens of God's guiding hand, and, not least, passionate speech:

> *Enter Anne Sanders, Anne Drewry, and Roger: Drewry having the bloudy handkercher in her hand.*
>
> *A. San.* Oh shew not me that ensigne of despaire,
> But hide it, burne it, bury it in the earth,
> It is a kalender of bloody letters,
> Containing his, and yours, and all our shames.
>
> *Dru.* Good mistris Sanders, be not so outragious.
>
> *A. San.* What tell you me? is not my husband slaine?
> Are not we guiltie of his cruel death?
> Oh my deare husband I wil follow thee:
> Give me a knife, a sword, or any thing,
> Wherewith I may do justice on my selfe.
> Justice for murther, justice for the death
> Of my deare husband, my betrothed love.

(1535–46)

Drury begs her to be silent, lest "Your servants, or some neighbours else will heare" (1550): on stage this was a speech fit to cleave the general ear and drown the stage with tears. This, then, is a play in which tragedy is vigorously ridiculed as a high mode, as flagrantly out of touch with real life as lived by most people (who are not engaged in cutting throats to get kingdoms), but one in which it is also reaffirmed, or seen as a genre customarily separate from this sphere yet relevant to it. We need a critical language that can describe a text offering the advantages of irony that an outsider (that is, nonaristocratic) perspective can provide on a socially exclusive mode, but which also taps this mode's theatrical potential. Against the contingency of modern London life is posed the spiritual, fundamental order unfolded in the dumb shows and by Tragedy.[20]

What is the "truth" of *Arden of Faversham?* "Thus have you seen the truth of Arden's death," the epilogue says, asserting that "simple truth is gracious enough," in need of no "glozing stuff." Such a claim to fact is redundant if one assumes general knowledge of that convention which held that tragedy was based on history, while the comic writer might invent his tale.[21] (The author of this play follows Holinshed closely, describing the murder of Master Arden, a gentleman of Kent, by his adulterous wife Alice and her lover, the tailor Mosby.) But the epilogue's truth-claim may involve more than literal veracity. The play distinguishes itself from other true tragedies based on history or pseudohistory, claiming an unadorned, realistic style. Again, the commitment to "truth" raises questions about the nature of tragedy, so that the title of the 1592 edition *(The Lamentable and True Tragedy of M. Arden of Feversham in Kent . . .)* might mark a tension between the play's empirical truth, yielding a complex, inconsistent, detailed representation of society, and the tragic formalization (and simplification?) of those diverse, particular materials.

For Robert Weimann medieval theater, like medieval philosophic realism, looks essentially to the universal or general, while the drive of a modernizing Renaissance theater is toward a new empiricism, fore-grounding "concrete experience" and exhibiting "a new sense of the interdependence of character and society."[22] *Arden of Faversham* has an empirical understanding of its story, its rich social detail and emphasis on concrete social experience contrasting strikingly with the kind of selectivity and abstraction we associate with generic modes. Arden is an obscure, perplexing figure. Should we accept Greene's evaluation? He casts him as one of the "great ones" that "eat up the little ones" (*Pericles,* 2.1.28–29), asserting that

> Desire of wealth is endless in his mind,
> And he is greedy-gaping still for gain;
> Nor cares he though young gentlemen do beg,
> So he may scrape and hoard up in his pouch.
>
> (1.474–77)

Or should we trust our own impression of him, which is surely not that of the shabby grasping predator Greene portrays? Arden's false servant confesses his master's "kindness" (4.62), Alice his affection (8.61); there is his friend Franklin's evident respect. The poor sailor Dick Reede eloquently curses Arden for depriving him of some land, a curse the epilogue, which Franklin speaks, bears out, telling us that the imprint of Arden's corpse lay two years "in that plot of ground / Which he by force and violence held from Reede." But this scene still leaves us in the dark: Franklin apparently agrees that Reede is "the railingest knave in Christendom" (13.54), and Arden's sincerity seems compelling: "I assure you I ne'er did him wrong"; "I think so, Master Arden," replies his friend (57–58), whose judgment we have no reason to disparage. M. L. Wine rightly says that Arden is "altogether ambivalent."[23] Which of the incompatible impressions of him derived from the play should we accept?

"Inconsistencies cannot both be right, but, imputed to man, they may both be true" (Rasselas). The point is that all of these conflicting impressions are acceptable: the play presents social experience in all its complexity, in which people are different in different social relations. The inconsistency is the effect of an open, unselective method as against the interpretive concentration of genre. Where genre tends to provide an exclusive viewpoint, Arden keeps in play a variety of perspectives, all true for the individuals holding them yet incompatible together. Genre abstracts from experience and clarifies; Arden is remarkably concrete, and, indeed, courts radical confusion by disclosing the contradictions of social life. Concreteness attaches to the word tragedy in the play, and its dual signification (meaning simply violent death but also a formal tradition) brings to the fore a central problem. The hit man Black Will vows that "the forlorn traveller / Whose lips are glued with summer's parching heat / Ne'er longed so much to see a running brook / As I to finish Arden's tragedy" (3.100–103), and tells Michael that "Thy office is but to appoint the place / And train thy master to his tragedy" (3.164–65).[24] The meaning of tragedy seems utterly literal and specific, drained of that abstraction or interpretation of death normally supposed indispensable to tragic tradition.

This empirical focus is evident in the play's rich social detail. From the beginning Arden is implicated in a total social-economic process. Having acquired the abbey lands he is one of those for whom, as J. E. Neale put it, the Reformation constituted a "great vested interest."[25] Arden's melancholy, of course, arises from his suspicion of Alice's affair with Mosby. But there is another kind of melancholy suffusing the play, conspicuous in the troubled, ominous atmosphere of scene 1, and with its roots in the premonition that an entire epoch is passing away, and that traditional social ties are as soluble as the old abbey. This sense of "social disintegration"[26] looms over the play: it is an untrusting, mean world that is depicted, characterized, as Catherine Belsey has pointed out, by a ruthless "economic individualism."[27] It is also gossipy and malicious: Alice speaks of her blabbing, "narrow-prying neighbours" and of "the biting speech of men" (1.135, 139), and Arden of how men "mangle credit with their wounding words" (4.4). In warning off Mosby he alleges that "all the knights and gentlemen of Kent / Make common table-talk of her and thee" (1.343–44). Such allusions to a larger community are no more "background," inert "setting," than are the hints of profound social transformation: they are central to the play, showing the principals as radically shaped by the pressures of a particular society. One of these pressures is status, which critically affects even intimate relations. M. L. Wine remarks the aggressive class-consciousness of the play,[28] and Alice and Mosby's liaison, at times attaining a heroic distinction,[29] warps under anxiety over rank, Alice taunting Mosby with his "low-born name" (8.77): "Even in my forehead is thy name engraven, / A mean artificer" (8.76–77). Later, spurning her blandishments, he retorts

> O, no, I am a base artificer;
> My wings are feathered for a lowly flight.
> Mosby? Fie, no! not for a thousand pound.
> Make love to you? Why, 'tis unpardonable;
> We beggars must not breathe where gentles are.
>
> (8.135–39)

Differences of degree impinge upon the action from the outset: Arden is appalled that Alice should link herself with "a velvet druge, / A cheating steward, and base-minded peasant" (1.322–23). He seizes Mosby's sword, since "The statute makes against artificers. . . . / Now use your bodkin, / Your Spanish needle, and your pressing iron" (1.311–13). (The stress is on Mosby's lowly trade: in Holinshed he kills Arden with a pressing iron.)

As if to the side of this particular, concretely social emphasis are those "classical" set-pieces that abstract from the actuality of the story a metaphysical order, simplifying its relative "solidity of specification"[30] into a universal shape. But these "tragic" aspects—some of Black Will's rhetoric, for example ("I am the very man, / Marked in my birth-hour by the Destinies, / To give an end to Arden's life on earth" [3.159–61]), or the classical-mythological redolence of much of the language and action (Arden's prophetic dream in scene 6, or the jokey ominousness of the ferryman in scenes 11 and 12)—although they contrast starkly with the rest of the play, ought not to be treated as quotations from a tradition fundamentally removed from the play's world. Instead, the play explores how far conventions drawn from a mode traditionally identified with aristocracy fit a less elevated sphere of life. We may also assume that the dramatist has tried to dignify such material by reinterpreting it through some recognizable conventions or reminiscences of high tragedy, the effect of which is to render those conventions visible. Thus tragedy in this play may appear as a framing of material in itself inconsistent and uneven, without necessary shape, and which is endowed with meaning through tragedy. We become aware, that is, of tragedy as a mode not entirely aligned with the matter of the story. And there is a sense in which the play rehearses or tests the tradition, measuring it against an idea of empirical truth. A rhetoric of actuality plays against form or interpretation (that is, tragedy) so that the mode is defamiliarized: we become aware of it as a perspective associated with an order of life not identical to that evoked before us. This internal distantiation of tragedy is an important feature of the play. But its relation to its genre is, finally, more ambiguous than this formulation, with its oppositional implications, suggests. If tragedy emerges as a perspective applied to incongruous material, it also seems to inhabit the events themselves: like *A Warning for Fair Women,* this play sets up a potential gap between truth and tragedy but declines pressing this split—it is finally undecided as to whether truth and tragedy are in a relation of contradiction. What is clear is the interest, less overt than in *A Warning,* in reflecting upon tragedy as a social fact and in appropriating for the story its special prestige, raising in the process the question of the relations between this tradition and realms of social life.

A similarly complicated division between truth and tragedy appears in a play by Robert Yarington: *Two Lamentable Tragedies. The one, of the Murther of Maister Beech A Chaundler in Thames-streete, and his boye, done by Thomas Merry. The other of a Young childe murthered in a Wood by two Ruffins, with the consent of his Unckle.* This uncontroversially lamentable play is perhaps chiefly memorable for the speech in which a neighbor mourns Beech's boy, Thomas Winchester, whom Merry has beaten to death with a hammer:

> What cruell hand hath done so foule a deede,
> Thus to bemangle a distressed youth
> Without all pittie or a due remorse!
> See how the hammer sticketh in his head,
> Wherewith this honest youth is done to death!
> Speak, honest Thomas, if any speach remaine:
> What cruell hand hath done this villanie?
> He cannot speake, his senses are bereft.

(31)

Considerable time elapses before Winchester dies, and before he does he is brought out once more, still with the hammer in his head and eliciting proper sympathy. Notwithstanding its ridiculousness, though, this work interests because its literary self-consciousness seems closely related to the social experiment undertaken in making a tragedy about a tavern keeper and chandler. The play opens with Homicide complaining of underemployment in "this happie towne," whose inhabitants "are bent with vertuous gainefull trade" (induction, 7). Homicide prefers "the sad exploites of fearefull tragedies" (induction, 7) to this upright industry and, joining forces with Avarice (an old companion, the stage direction having them "kisse, imbrace" [induction, 8]), declares that they "will make a bloodie feastivall . . . a two-folde Tragedie" (induction, 9). Truth enters and, with some hand-wringing, outlines the two stories to be told, which are kept separate throughout. The kind of these stories is indicated: "Our Stage doth weare habilliments of woe" (induction, 9). There is no mention of the low social identity of the English story. Instead there is again an emphasis on fact, actuality, and truth ("The most here present, know this to be true: / Would Truth were false, so this were but a tale!" [induction, 9]), and the audience is again invited to compare its knowledge of the events with what it sees on stage: when Merry and his sister Rachel are to be hanged, Truth observes that "Your eyes shall witnesse of their shaded tipes, / Which many heere did see perform'd indeed" (close of act 4, 86). "Truth will not faine," it is claimed, "but yet doth grieve to show, / This deed of ruthe and miserable woe" (induction, 10). Once more the interesting question is the nature of the truth insisted upon and its relation to tragic art. The dramatist does not exactly *oppose* truth to tragedy: the high Italian story and the low London one do not contradict but confirm one another. In both Avarice leads to Murder and the criminal suffers the punishment not only of his own death but of the execution of one dear to him (Merry his sister; Fallerio—the wicked uncle of the story set "neere Padua" [induction, 9]—his virtuous son Allenso). Implied is a universal pattern of crime and punishment, common to high and low society. Truth is both the truth of God's hand bringing criminals to justice and the truth of the genre Tragedy, overseeing this particular kind of play. There is no tension between a lower-class reality and high tragedy; rather, elite and common spheres of life converge, equally exemplifying tragic truth. Yet, despite this convergence, the audience's being encouraged to test the "shaded tipes" of the representation against its knowledge of events establishes, one would guess, an appreciable detachment toward the genre: the audience is accorded a certain authority over the performance, sitting in judgment upon its veracity or falsehood. Jonson perhaps excepted, Renaissance tragic dramatists do not scruple to flatter their audiences as preternaturally wise, generous, and well-born arbiters of taste. Not many, however, ask them so pointedly to compare a play's representations against their own experience.

A play resembling the works considered so far, not only in its documentary appearance but in its preoccupation with rank, is *A Yorkshire Tragedy,* which likewise deals with domestic murder. Despite similarities, however, *A Yorkshire Tragedy* must in certain respects be distinguished: unlike Arden, for example, the Husband of this play is not fundamentally insecure about his status—outwardly he is unambiguously gentle. Nor does the play explicitly reflect upon the social meaning of tragedy. That said, it recalls the plays already discussed in deviating from tragic practice, notably in an absence of idealization or in treating contemporary events and emphasizing the familiarity rather than remoteness of their contexts.[31] This "realistic" approach—an emphasis upon the domestic, ordinary, and country (a *Yorkshire* tragedy)—means abandoning "the high and excellent Tragedy," which we may conservatively define as violent, terrible happenings in grand milieux, "still maintained," as Sidney said, "in a well-raised admiration" and generating in the spectators, by "stately speeches and well-sounding phrases," a feeling of awe.[32] Rather than giving us this sort of story, the play is preoccupied with a contrast in the Husband between gentility and brutality: if he is "a gentleman by many bloods" (2.61), his forefathers' lustrous name has been besmirched by his gambling and cruel treatment of his wife. The play is deeply absorbed in this contradiction between gentility as a birthright and as an ideal of conduct (hence the repeated references to "The ancient honour of his house and name" [2.9]).[33] The preoccupation with rank, and with the problematization of gentility (is this man gentle, given his irrational, bestial behavior?), climaxes in the torment overtaking him on the too-late realization that his profligacy has beggared his children, a despair that precipitates the murders. It is worth quoting from the speech in which he comprehends the enormity of his situation:

> What is there in three dice to make a man draw thrice three thousand acres into the compass of a round little table, and with the gentleman's palsy in the hand shake out his posterity thieves or beggars? 'Tis done; I ha' done't, i'faith; terrible, horrible misery! How well was I left? Very well, very well. My lands showed like a full moon about me. But now the moon's i'th' last quarter, waning, waning, and I am mad to think that moon was mine. Mine and my father's and my forefathers', generations, generations. Down goes the house of us; down, down it sinks. Now is the name a beggar, begs in me. That name, which hundreds of years has made this shire famous, in me and my posterity runs out. (4.64–77)

He will kill his boys rather than let them endure the ignominy of poverty: "My eldest beggar, thou shalt not live to ask an usurer bread, to cry at a great man's gate, or follow 'good your honour' by a coach; no, nor your brother. . . . Bleed, bleed rather than beg, beg. / Be not thy name's disgrace" (4.100–102, 105–6). *A Yorkshire Tragedy* is overwhelmingly concerned with rank (its tragedies occur because of the Husband's uncontrollable dismay at his fall in degree), and to explore these complexities of social standing it abandons the idealizing "grave Cothurnate Muse,"[34] which tries to awe its audience with a "swelling scene" (*Henry V,* prologue), in favor of a more realistic and analytic approach, in which the ethical and social ideal of gentility may be interrogated by reality. The play contrasts what ought to be with what is, social distinction with natural frailty. *A Yorkshire Tragedy* rings some changes on the mode of tragedy, but the variations it effects are intimately bound up with its primary interest in degree.

If *A Yorkshire Tragedy* significantly departs from conventional tragedies because of a preoccupation with the pressures and ambiguities

of distinction, Thomas Heywood's *A Woman Killed with Kindness*
prepares its audience for a tragic outcome only, in crucial respects, to
reverse that expectation. We suppose Anne Frankford merely speaks
probability when she says, after her adultery is discovered, "He cannot be
so base as to forgive me" (13.139), yet Frankford does, and it is
presented as the superior course. But the play does more than arouse and
overturn generic expectations. Important for our purposes is its tendency
to situate those expectations (especially the tragic desire for revenge) in
the context of a specific social group's code of conduct. Unlike the plays
examined so far, Heywood's adopts a critical attitude toward this
tradition. In the end, one set of socially identifiable values is substituted
for another.

Sir Francis Acton is positive about how he would have acted had he
been Frankford: "had it been my case, / Their souls at once had from
their breasts been freed; / Death to such deeds of shame is the due meed"
(17.20–22). The play contrasts aristocratic lawlessness, expressed in a
code of honor sanctioning violence and revenge in certain situations, with
a civic or bourgeois ethic of "kindness." The bloody storm that breaks in
the hunting scene (scene 3), when a brawl over a sporting wager leaves
two servants dead, is the crucial scene for the aristocratic party;[35]
significantly the next scene shows a reflective Frankford indoors. His
placid, intelligent satisfaction in his home life ("How happy am I amongst
other men / That in my mean estate embrace content" [4.1–2]) throws
into relief the ferocity and wildness of the previous scene. There the
noble virtues (competitive love of honor, readiness to take up arms to
maintain it) are viewed coldly by the corpses of Acton's huntsmen, as the
aristocrat Mountford comes to his senses:

> My God! what have I done? what have I done?
> My rage hath plung'd into a sea of blood,
> In which my soul lies drown'd. Poor innocents,
> For whom we are to answer . . .
>
> (3.42–45)

Of course the ethical contrast of the play isn't quite that simple. Acton,
in a surprise change of heart, extends a kindness to Mountford by
marrying his sister, thus freeing him from the obligation he feels himself
under to his enemy for having had him released from debtors' prison; this
act of charity parallels Frankford's kindness to Anne.[36] And Frankford's

content may be compared to Mountford's when living humbly with his sister Susan ("All things on earth thus change, some up, some down; / Content's a kingdom, and I wear that crown" [7.7–8]). Nevertheless, the natural bearer of such values in the play is Frankford: Acton is wonderfully converted to kindness, after almost destroying Susan Mountford; Mountford discovers content in poverty. (His hands, too, are stained with the blood that flowed in scene 3.) To the extent that these characters change positively, then, they become more like Frankford, who thanks the maid who providentially restrains him from striking Wendoll, Anne's lover: "thou like the angel's hand / Hast stay'd me from a bloody sacrifice" (13.68–69). The contrast between nonaristocratic, middling-gentry civic values and a sanguinary aristocratic honor code remains.

Anne Frankford dies, but the tone of the play's close is Christian, sentimental, and pathetic rather than turbulently passionate (or "tragic," by the criterion of stormy and gloomy emotionalism that the clownish Comedy and stridently confident Tragedy of *A Warning* defer to, not to mention Prince Hamlet). Anne's salvation is assured ("Pardon'd on earth, soul, thou in Heaven art free" [17.121]), and she and Frankford are reunited: "And with this kiss I wed thee once again" (17.117). Some commonsense skepticism is injected into this high-minded, nearly mawkish scene by Frankford's loyal servants (Nicholas will "sigh and sob" but "not die" [17.100] for Anne, as his betters say they would) but this does not off-balance it.[37] This resigned, decorous atmosphere is not, at any rate, the somber, full-throated end to tragedy Heywood assumes in *The Apology for Actors:* "Comedies begin in trouble, and end in peace; Tragedies begin in calmes, and end in tempest."[38] The relative serenity of the play's end can, I think, be read as an unostentatious rejection of tragedy, or a rejection of the sort of outcome that, throughout, has been associated with a noble-aristocratic code of conduct, and which is here supplanted by a consciously nonelite ethic. In both plots a potential tragedy is overtaken by an antithetical outlook embodied most explicitly in a character from the middling strata of society.

More than the other plays discussed here, *A Woman Killed with Kindness* invokes tragedy to critical effect, so that it becomes a problem in the play rather than a mode that is subtly distanced but not essentially challenged. And indeed tragedy is such an authoritative, prestigious form in the period that we would not expect many plays to undo it. But each of these plays, by bringing the form into relation with a conventionally nontragic world, invites attention to its social specificity, and raises the question of its "truth," such truth being conceived either fairly narrowly, in terms of fact (does it harmonize with "real," or socially undistinguished, life?) or, more broadly, in terms of its ethical claim on its audience (is it true? should we order our lives by it?). But however these plays differ from each other, each testifies to an interest in reflecting upon tragedy as a socially symbolic mode.

3

Shakespeare and the
Social Symbolism of Art

A Midsummer Night's Dream, The Taming of the Shrew

"To begin, then, with Shakespeare. He was the man who of all modern, and perhaps ancient, poets, had the largest and most comprehensive soul."[1] Dryden's tribute resonates in many ways, but for this study we may single out one implication—the social. We can credit Dryden with the identification of a characteristic quality of the Shakespearean text: its capacity to comprehend vast social differences, its sheer sociological inclusiveness and richness, and it is in this sense that one may, still, be allowed to speak of the "universality" of Shakespeare. Again, Dryden's praise reminds us of that other quality traditionally attributed to Shakespeare and variously signified: his "myriad-mindedness" (Coleridge)[2] or "multidimensionality" (Robert Weimann),[3] his complementary, open, or profoundly dramatic technique (essentially an art of contrast), his dialectical approach, where, as Germaine Greer has put it, every play is in the nature of an "experiment" and every idea receives "full imaginative development."[4] Thus much seems implicit in Dryden's "comprehensive." Of course the two senses of the word drawn out here—the sociological and "philosophical"—may not be unrelated: if particular social strata can have exclusive values, ideologies, or "structures of feeling"[5] attributed to them, then the dialectical energy of Shakespeare's art and thought may be grounded in the seeming rich mimesis of Shakespearean drama, its tendency to convey the effect of a total representation of social life.[6] Obviously, this would not be the whole story—not every conflict in a Shakespeare play is ideological or the expression of a social contradiction (in particular, distinctions *within* a social group may be dramatically, let alone historically, as or more important than those marking it off from other strata). Nonetheless, there seems nothing inherently implausible in attempting to relate the dialectical method of Shakespeare's art to the plays' social dialectics—seeing a many-sidedness of viewpoint as produced by the poetic evocation of a complex, various, differentiated social scene. Clearly, this approach would be related to the far more ambitious project of a Marxist criticism of Shakespeare, whereby the richness of his drama would be grounded in an interpretation of the age as one of fundamental—indeed, epochal—historical transition. But while such a total synthesis of economic, social, political, and cultural factors in the period has obvious, immense appeal, the problems involved in conducting an argument of such generality are also immense, possibly insuperable.[7]

I propose to take a narrower approach than this Marxist one, considering social complexity in a few Shakespeare plays selected because, like Nashe's texts or the plays considered in chapter 2, they seem especially interested in social differences, turning "degree" into poetic subject matter, and because their interest in playing with radical social contrasts tends to involve the complication or problematization of literary mode. I shall anticipate the argument a little by suggesting that where these plays seem preoccupied with social differences, they are correspondingly self-aware about the social meaning of literary modes and "art" generally (and, vice versa, that literary self-consciousness is accompanied by attention to social distinctions). Thus the extremely complicated social character of these plays (they are all "mixed" in some sense) induces, I suggest, a certain self-consciousness about form, literary forms being conspicuously implicated within (indeed, unthinkable outside of) broadly social or "nonliterary" distinctions. To put this in more concretely dramatic terms: interplay between high and low characters or milieux throws the work into an attitude of critical self-awareness about the social character of its modes. (We have seen how Nashe's work—like Shakespeare's in its tantalizingly various and complex social affiliations—is also highly self-conscious about literary form as social form, deliberately adopting and playing off against each other putative popular and elite modes, or exploiting their social ambiguity. Certainly, in respect of such "comprehensiveness," Nashe is as dialectical as Shakespeare: a key element in many texts by both authors is a rich interplay—among, of course, every other kind of contrast—between supposed aristocratic and nonelite manners, attitudes, modes of expression, and so on.) I should add that, as with claims for the individuality of Shakespeare's characters (such as Pope's),[8] claims for the social diversity of Shakespeare's texts are apt to be exaggerated: not every Shakespeare play is equally interested in manipulating or playing with social hierarchy, or in exploring the social symbolism of modes. Of course, social differences exist in all the plays, because all have some commitment to a rhetoric of mimesis or representation. But not all such differences are as vividly or profoundly evoked as they are in, say, *A Midsummer Night's Dream* or the *Henry IV* plays—works that would be unrecognizable were the social contrasts in them diminished or erased, their structure and meaning hinging upon a to-and-fro between noble and common spheres of life. But in a play such as *Much Ado About Nothing,* while the resolution of the Hero-Claudio imbroglio turns upon the discoveries of the lower-class watchmen, we need not suppose the play to be developing a really significant contrast between the nobility and the Dogberry group. Other distinctions are just as important, one of the most obvious being that between one kind of heroine and another. Again, Ralph Berry has pointed out that there are important scenes involving, or passages alluding to, the common people in *Richard II* (the "poor groom" and his description of "roan Barbary" [5.5.72, 78], for instance, who now bears Bullingbrook rather than Richard), but, except for these brief glimpses of the common people, the play concerns itself almost exclusively with nobles and is not concerned to elaborate detailed social contrasts.[9] Instead, the real focus of interest is the aristocratic power game, and popular characters, the allegorizing gardeners of 3.4, for example, are subordinated to it.[10] So the play does not aim at the impression of a complete, dialectical anatomy of society. It is where this interest in comprehensiveness occurs, I think, that there may arise a critical self-awareness about the social functions, meanings, and limitations of literary modes. But before turning to the plays, it will be useful briefly to consider why some of the period's drama should register a sensitivity to social hierarchy and to the social symbolism of modes of writing. It will be necessary, then, briefly to touch again upon the question of how to formulate the social meaning of the English Renaissance stage.

Marxist critics, working on the sociology of the Elizabethan stage and its complex relation to populace and elite in the period (a line of inquiry originally opened up by such scholars as Alfred Harbage, Muriel Bradbrook, and C. L. Barber) have tended to stress the contradictory social character of Shakespeare's theater.[11] Although there are substantial problems with this formulation, especially in the area of who precisely attended the theaters, and although the term "contradiction," implying some notion of class struggle, is most likely misleading about the character of early modern social relations, the basic emphasis on the social complexity and heterogeneity of the institution is probably correct. A part of this complexity involved the relatively humble origins of the writers. One needs to stress "relatively": in Stratford terms Shakespeare's family was, as Samuel Schoenbaum has reminded us, an important one, with aspirations to gentility.[12] Nashe, as we saw—like Peele, Greene, and Marlowe—was able to tread a more conventional path to respectability than Shakespeare's: the university degree. Still, each of these writers improved his situation while contending with the uncertain status of the professional writer. (Greene's anxiety about this ambiguity is especially clear: witness the defensiveness of "Utriusque Academiae in Artibus magister" on the 1591 title page of *Greenes Farewell to Folly,* as well as his snobbish attacks on the "upstart crow" and on players in general.)[13] Professional men of letters, then, were, like the players, another gray area in the traditional or ideal hierarchy of Tudor-Stuart England.[14] The important point here, however, is that, given the ambiguous position of these writers, it would not be strange if they displayed in their works a special interest in rank (we may note emblematically that the play that might be taken as beginning the modern movement in Elizabethan tragedy, *Tamburlaine,* is the story of a shepherd turned conqueror-king),[15] and the wager of this book has been that in certain texts this interest informs the manipulation of literary modes, which are themselves understood in terms of social hierarchy. Indeed, the marginal, anomalous social position of the commercial stages suggests the possibility of their writers enjoying a certain freedom in their handling of hierarchical relations, as C. L. Barber has argued: "The stage . . . was a middle-class property and point of vantage. In the commercial theater, Shakespeare could use the power of dramatic form to develop aggressive, ironic understanding of the court world."[16] I proceed, then, from the assumption that Shakespeare (like Nashe and, in all probability, those professional playwrights considered above) did not, like a Sidney, inherit art as his birthright—that is, the high modes of literature that were in his world the symbolic property of the aristocratic elite.[17] Thus these "bourgeois" professional writers do not live a simple relation to the institutions or modes of literature,[18] but manipulate the forms of elite culture more as outsiders than insiders; and this ambivalent, complicated relation to literature may itself be articulated in particular works—we may find, that is, that certain works register an awareness of the socio-cultural meaning and force of literary modes or that they register the author's own sense of outsiderness with respect to the institutions of art. None of which implies that, because these writers do not naturally inhabit the aristocratic

modes they manipulate, they are therefore on the side of the angels and
to be identified with an oppositional "popular culture"—literature after all
being precisely the means by which they advance, or seek to advance,
themselves. We should not suppose that their ambiguous position with
regard to elite culture requires that they have (as Barber in the quotation
above too readily assumes) an interest in attacking, ironizing, or generally
subverting it. (Perhaps the opposite, in fact—their real interests lying in
manipulating elite modes as effectively as possible, so hitching their
wagon to the court's.) Yet we can expect that the relation of such outsiders to the modes of elite culture is bound to be complicated.

   A Midsummer Night's Dream (1595–96; pub. 1600) is one of Shakespeare's plays that works with a radical social contrast and that is also
deeply self-conscious in its use of dramatic form and art in general. I
shall suggest that the play's sensitivity about differences of rank is the
basis for its consciousness of genre and the potential social uses of art.
This is a play notably ambivalent about social hierarchy, soliciting from
its audience both pleasure and alarm at the confusion of social boundaries.[19]

   "Bless thee, Bottom, bless thee! Thou art translated" (3.1.118–19). So
Quince on Bottom's metamorphosis. *A Midsummer Night's Dream* is a
play about "translation," or change, and this has from the first a conspicuous social dimension. Bottom moves from the human to the fairy world,
but he is also transformed, apparently, into a gentleman: "gentle mortal,"
"gentleman" are Titania's titles for him (3.1.137, 164). And of course
Bottom's fancy language upon his elevation ("I beseech your worship's
name. . . . I pray you commend me to Mistress Squash. . . . I shall desire
you of more acquaintance" (3.1.179–80, 186, 188–89) is preposterously
refined and gentle—or at least attempts refinement and gentility. The
comedy of these scenes depends on the incongruity between what Bottom
is (a weaver) and what he becomes (a courtier, and an especially favored
one at that). The play can, then, be characterized as delighting in the
promiscuous mingling of rank in the Bottom/Titania complication. Puck's
voice, at any rate, is gleeful: "My mistress with a monster is in love. /
Near to her close and consecrated bower, / While she was in her dull and
sleeping hour, / A crew of patches, rude mechanicals, / That work for
bread upon Athenian stalls . . . " (3.2.6–10). The tantalizing force of this
is all in the idea of the proximity of the mechanicals to the "close and
consecrated bower." Clearly the play has some fun (we might call it its
utopian aspect) with the upsetting of hierarchy and decorum: there is
excitement and pleasure in this suggestion of the bottom becoming (for

a time only, of course, and with every qualification) the top. But Shakespeare's presentation of this reversal is nonetheless ambiguous. First, it is only by virtue of Oberon's manipulation of events (admittedly bungled in one important respect) that the play can have its fun with hierarchy: we know, in other words, that order will be restored, that "Jack shall have Jill; / Nought shall go ill: / The man shall have his mare again, and all shall be well" (3.2.461–63), that social prerogative and "degree" will once again be in place. Seen thus, comedy takes on a conservative appearance, effectively guaranteeing the social structure: it is because Bottom's ascent is so temporary that it can be allowed to be enjoyable—indeed, that it can happen at all. Second, the nature of this elevation is itself ambiguous. It is, after all, an as(s)cent: in proportion as Bottom is exalted he is humbled. We might think of this particular humiliation, the "ass's nole" (3.2.17), as the price of promotion: a control on the potentially destabilizing implications of Bottom's career. By making Bottom even more ridiculous than he already is, any threat in this suspension of normal hierarchical relations is defused. (Against the notion of this suspension being reduced to absurdity must be balanced Bottom's supreme, victorious confidence in his role, his ability to take us along with him, or that general buoyancy of his which disarms a belittling, condescending laughter. I shall return to this point later in a comparison with Shakespeare's Christopher Sly; for now we may note that, to the extent that Bottom is a figure of fun, we find the idea of his elevation correspondingly ludicrous.) Further, this revolution in the social system takes place in an enchanted, exotic wood, in a play striving for a lyrical and fantastic atmosphere, and consequently, it might be argued, there can be no danger in imagining such an upset, since there is no pretence of addressing reality. (By comparison, we might note the revulsion social rising generates in the tragic and politically realistic context of *King Lear,* where the "finical" Oswald is sinister proof that the time is out of joint [2.2.19].) Even so, from the first our delight in Bottom's change is mingled with less pleasant feelings. For Oberon it is part of a grotesque disorder, a "hateful fantas[y]" (2.1.258) properly evoking pity rather than pleasure ("Her dotage now I do begin to pity" [4.1.47]). But Bottom's and Titania's liaison looks different from Bottom's humble position, and the play is careful to include this perspective. For him it has been ineffably lovely, "past the wit of man to say what dream it was" (4.1.205–6). But Titania, restored to reason, can only exclaim, "O, how mine eyes do loathe his visage now!" (4.1.79), and Oberon observes that when Titania adorned Bottom's head with flowers

> . . . that same dew which sometime on the buds
> Was wont to swell like round and orient pearls,
> Stood now within the pretty flouriets' eyes,
> Like tears that did their own disgrace bewail.
>
> (4.1.53–56)[20]

From a ruling-class perspective (here identified with Nature), Bottom's "translation" can only ever have a "tragic" significance—or rather tragicomic, since things are put right in the end. Merely by including this conservative attitude, however, the play can once again be said to attempt the "containment" of the radical possibilities of translation.[21]

If *A Midsummer Night's Dream* takes an ambivalent pleasure in complicating hierarchical relations, we are more or less always aware that these are to be reinstated by the end. But the text's playful attitude to hierarchy is also obvious with the lovers' time in the wood, likewise a "translation" though, in contrast to Bottom's, one that moves downward. For there is a general suspension of gentle behavior: Demetrius is rude to Helena, Lysander can abandon Hermia, Helena thinks the others cruelly mock her: "I thought you lord of more true gentleness" (2.2.132, to Lysander), and later:

> If you were civil and knew courtesy,
> You would not do me thus much injury.
> . . . .
> If you were men, as men you are in show,
> You would not use a gentle lady so;
> . . . .
>   None of noble sort
> Would so offend a virgin . . .
>
> (3.2.147–60)

It is easy to see in the lovers' bewilderment and unhappiness how far they have come from the polite, sophisticated court of Theseus. There is a sense in which the move from Athens to the wood is a move from a relatively idealized and (in the terms of this play and of other texts we have considered) thus an elite or aristocratic milieu, to a less cultivated one. For the wood, while it is sociologically a various place, is in part, and in the aspect in which the lovers encounter it, seen as a place of naïve, folkloric wonder and surprise. Of course it is impossible to fix the character of this wood in sociological or in any other terms: it is at once Ovidian and literary and the setting of old wives' tales, beautiful and ugly, incomparably charming and terrifying as well.[22] The noble Oberon and Titania are at home in it, the craftsmen frightened out of it. Nonetheless, for the aristocratic lovers it is an obscure locale utterly different from the urbane, enlightened Athenian scene, presided over by a self-styled connoisseur of the arts. We can read the lovers' discomfiture partly in terms of a "translation" to a folk realm of fancy and superstition. The important point is that this translation is unpleasant, that in contrast to Bottom's dream it is more akin to nightmare, and that in this play whether something is tragic or comic seems to depend quite a lot on which social level you belong to: Bottom's sojourn with the Faerie Queene is exquisitely pleasurable, but the lovers experience the wood's uncertainties as tragical, and comedy may be said to mean their restoration to themselves, or, perhaps, to truer versions of those selves, a crucial aspect of this restoration being reinstatement in a courtly, aristocratic milieu. The comic end of the play thus involves a return of the lovers not only to themselves and their true desires, but also to a leading place in the social hierarchy after a disturbing period of estrangement from it. "Playing" with social hierarchy, "playing" with social position—this adequately describes some of the play's interests, so long as we keep in mind the different emotional contents such "play" can have, contents that tend to divide along social lines, as we have seen.

If the various loosenings of social order are open to different generic constructions—tragic or tragicomic from the point of view of elite characters, intoxicatingly comic and splendid from the point of view of the major plebeian character—then the figure who embodies the text's fascination with social interplay is Puck. His social character, as we have noted, is extraordinarily difficult to pin down: he is a "shrewd and knavish sprite" (2.1.33) who, like Nashe's personae, combines in himself the perspective from above and from below.[23] On the one hand, Puck is linked with common village life, is given a homely speech, and is less ethereal ("thou lob of spirits" [2.1.16]) than the other fairies. His role as servant and jester also separates him from the elite of the play. Yet equally plain is his feeling of difference from the "hempen home-spuns" (3.1.77), as well as from the unseen but vividly evoked cottagers and "villagery" (2.1.35) inhabiting the nonelite social space of the play.[24] But if he is a richly complementary figure, neither strictly high nor low, and thus an instance of the play's social dialectics, his radical indefinability in terms of hierarchy, his anomalous and mixed social character, is presented not as threatening but as overwhelmingly delightful. Of course, we may feel that it is precisely because he is presented as a figure of fancy that he is unthreatening. The unreality of *A Midsummer Night's Dream* thus begins to appear as the means by which a liberated social interplay is both licensed and contained.

The temptation, then, to concur unreservedly with Elliot Krieger's assessment of the play—that its movement overall is conservative, leading toward the reaffirmation or regrounding of hierarchy (a hierarchy all the stronger and more inevitable and necessary for its temporary upsetting)—is compelling. (In line with this assessment, we may suppose that what Krieger calls the "second world" of the play, the green wood, performs a crucial function in naturalizing this hierarchy, a legitimation achieving its richest expression in Puck's valedictory blessing of the house and couples at the end.) Krieger is surely right to see the playlet of *Pyramus and Thisby* performing an important role in this conservative reordering ("putting the mechanicals in their place" by virtue of their awkwardness in the aristocratic setting).[25] Yet there are certain problems involved with assuming that the play's overall cast is therefore conservative. I shall argue with this interpretation in subsequent pages; for the moment, following Krieger, I should like to consider the function of genre and tragedy in the reimposition of hierarchy in the play.

Perhaps the first thing to notice about the playlet is that it is another form of "translation," this time plebeians translated into the conditions of noble life and story. At least, such is the intention—in fact, the effort of the mechanicals to assimilate themselves to elite society is so inept as to reemphasize their proletarianness, as Krieger shows. Secondly, we should notice the social role of the performance itself, for it is through its clumsiness that the court group reaffirms its own solidarity (originally threatened in the opening, quasi-tragic, scene). Thus the play presents a true knowledge of art, of genre and of decorum, as a not insignificant factor in ruling-class unity. (The mechanicals' ignorance underscores their exclusion from this class, but it does more than that: their amateur miscomprehensions in art reaffirm their incapacity in politics, a knowledge of one implying competence in the other. The implication is that the principle of decorum and fitness, involving notions of subordination and degree, is as fundamental to politics as to poetics.)[26] Thirdly, *A Midsummer Night's Dream* is clear about the social meaning of tragedy, because though the poetry and performance of *Pyramus and Thisby* are incredibly poor, it is not only the badness of the piece that is in question. What is also felt as ridiculous is the connection of the idea of tragedy with plebeians. Tragedy is consciously taken to exclude lower-class experience, and the juxtaposition of the two is clearly an incongruity to be savored:

plebeian tragedy is comical tragedy. In short, social and poetic categories are not separated out. Finally, for the courtiers one of the silliest aspects of the entertainment is simply its generic incoherence:

> "A tedious brief scene of young Pyramus
> And his love Thisby; very tragical mirth."
> Merry and tragical? Tedious and brief?
> That is hot ice and wondrous strange snow.
> How shall we find the concord of this discord?
>
> (5.1.56–60)

This orthodox, neoclassical assertion of the purity of genres is, I think, the assertion of a social, as well as aesthetic, conservatism: it reasserts ideals of order, stability, and decorum, after the "discord" of those scenes of radical social mixing and translation (confusion, from one point of view) in the wood. (We may note that Theseus's aesthetic language just before the lovers' return to the city and the official recognition of their loves "in the temple" [4.1.180] also expresses this apparent restoration of the status quo, with its talk of a "musical confusion / Of hounds and echo in conjunction" [4.1.110–11]—that is, of an order robust enough to include and contain "confusion.") The social symbolism of *A Midsummer Night's Dream* may thus be thought of as describing dramatically a contradiction between disorder and order akin to the stylistic opposition between Nasheian variety and Lylean order: the contrast is similarly imagined as between what is essentially a court aesthetic and ideology and something potentially undermining it. In any case, we may see a tension in the play between the "impure," discordant, dialectical impulse toward translation, involving a promiscuous interplay between social groups, and the opposed ideal of a hierarchy of genres and ranks inhibiting this impulse. Although, as we have seen, the conservative ideal is perhaps dominant by the end of the play, its middle scenes exhibit a heady interest in social translation.

We can appreciate the daring of the social dialectics in the wood of *A Midsummer Night's Dream* by comparing the more conservative version of metamorphosis offered in the induction to *The Taming of the Shrew* (1593–94; pub. 1623). Like Bottom the Weaver, Christopher Sly the tinker is temporarily translated into a gentleman. A nobleman finds him dead drunk outside a tavern, and decides to play a joke on him. "What think you," he asks his huntsmen,

> . . . if he were convey'd to bed,
> Wrapp'd in sweet clothes, rings put on his fingers,
> A most delicious banquet by his bed,
> And brave attendants near him when he wakes,
> Would not the beggar then forget himself?

1 Hun: Believe me, lord, I think he cannot choose.

2 Hun: It would seem strange unto him when he wak'd.

Lord: Even as a flatt'ring dream or worthless fancy.

(induction, 1.37–44)

This reference to dream, as well as the lush, richly decorative rhetoric singing the delights of the new life Sly has entered upon ("Wilt thou have music? Hark, Apollo plays, / And twenty caged nightingales do sing" [induction, 2.35–36]) in some ways anticipates Bottom's idyll with Titania. While Sly is thus translated, so is the lord, taking on the role of a servant. Clearly the nobleman's fascination with this social experiment is the play's too: the reversal of social status is itself felt as dramatically interesting (an interest in such social translation perhaps helping to explain, as suggested in the Introduction, the pervasiveness of humble disguises in both comedy and tragedy in the period).[27] As in *A Midsummer Night's Dream,* this scene of elaborate social interplay is at the same time occasion for a certain artistic consciousness, especially an awareness of genre. A messenger tells Sly,

> Your honor's players, hearing your amendment,
> Are come to play a pleasant comedy,
> For so your doctors hold it very meet,
> Seeing too much sadness hath congeal'd your blood,
> And melancholy is the nurse of frenzy.
> Therefore they thought it good to hear a play,
> And frame your mind to mirth and merriment,
> Which bars a thousand harms and lengthens life.

Sly: Marry, I will, let them play it. Is not a comonty a Christmas gambold, or a tumbling-trick?

Page: No, my good lord, it is more pleasing stuff.

Sly: What, household stuff?

Page: It is a kind of history.

(induction, 2.129–41)

Here the allusion to comedy is at once a formal definition ("a kind of history") and a crucial separating out of high and low milieux, seeming almost to safeguard hierarchical difference against the mixing that has, albeit in a highly restricted sense, taken place.[28] If the crossover of Sly and the lord momentarily (and playfully) upends distinctions of degree, making them appear manipulatable and open to change, it is in this moment of aesthetic self-awareness that they are reinstalled: Sly's immovable plebeian-ness is emphasized in his ignorance of the nature of comedy, just as the mechanicals' low status is affirmed through their ignorance of the nature of tragedy. Thus "art" is, it seems, in either play deployed to consolidate social hierarchy. What is remarkable about this scene from the *Shrew* and *Pyramus and Thisby* is that formal self-consciousness is so closely implicated in an awareness of rank, and emerges out of a scene of explicit interaction between ranks. Thus the meeting with the drunken Sly is followed by the entrance of the players and the lord's Hamlet-like compliment to them, displaying his own discrimination in such affairs: "that part [Soto's] / Was aptly fitted and naturally perform'd" (induction, 1.86–87; compare Philostrate's disparagement of the plebeian players in the *Dream:* "not one word apt, one player fitted" [5.1.65]). The important thing to note in both plays is just how the discourses of art and hierarchy merge.[29] Yet the social dialectics of the *Shrew*'s induction are in no way as intense as those of the *Dream,* for where in the former the reversal is safely stage-managed by the nobleman, in the latter the young aristocrats' bewilderment and Titania's sense of disgrace toward the end of the play are genuinely felt and powerfully disorienting emotions. Moreover, despite the fact that the mechanicals are to some extent "put in their place" by *Pyramus and Thisby,* we feel no compulsion to second the smugness of the aristocrats, whom we have watched behave in ways scarcely less absurd than Bottom and his friends.[30] The elite characters of this play, then, are more challenged by translation than in the *Shrew* induction. Bottom, in addition, does not cut the purely buffoonish figure Sly does: apart from his possessing a realistic, commonsensical wisdom (his philosophic remarks on reason and love, for instance [3.1.142–47]), as well as an imaginative impressionability of which the tinker shows scant evidence, Titania's election of Bottom is an intense, ecstatic experience of a different order altogether from the mirthless, deliberate practical joke played on Sly. And where with Sly we are conscious only of his unsuitability for the greatness thrust on him, the harsher, more disciplinarian comedy of that play inviting us to laugh with the lord and servants at him, with Bottom as courtier we register the incongruity, but are amazed at the capacity almost to bring it off: there is a sense in which he manages to convince despite everything. In any case, both plays are remarkable for their showing social hierarchies and art to imply each other: both imagine intriguing scenarios of social mixing and interplay, but art counts as a deeply conservative check to this imagining.

In *A Midsummer Night's Dream*, I have suggested, art appears as a means by which basic social distinctions are rediscovered after a potentially disturbing (or liberating—the play allows for both evaluations) interval in which they have been suspended, an interval of topsy-turvydom or translation, and I have also suggested that a similar thematization of the conservative social role of art occurs in *The Taming of the Shrew*.[31] In this play, it seems, the theater and poetry are represented not in terms of any liberatory or subversive potential, but as means for enforcing social norms and hierarchies. Thus the disorderly Sly, who "will not pay for the glasses [he has] burst" in the tavern, defies the town constabulary, and is "fourteen pence on the score for sheer ale" (induction, 1.7–8, 11–15, 2.23) is made to watch a "pleasant comedy" (induction, 2.130) whose moral is intensely conservative, and which enforces the familiar analogy of patriarchal and political authority, or "aweful rule, and right supremacy" (5.2.109).[32] The lord enlists, we should remember, professional players in this "pastime passing excellent" (induction, 1.67); what is notable about this scene is its self-consciousness, with the theater presented as enforcing social order.[33] It is true that the experimental, open element of play—of social translation, whereby a tinker becomes a nobleman and a nobleman a servant—is also present, and this is what makes the *Shrew* a companion to *A Midsummer Night's Dream*. But the central difference between the two works lies in the overriding emphasis on "art" in the *Shrew,* on the lord's virtuoso, illusion-making art (indeed, the art of the theater-poet), and the consequent closing down of social possibilities such an art seems to imply. It is this social power of art that is emphasized, its ability to control and manipulate appearances and thus social relations, even to create subjects whose self-understanding is fantasized by the powers-that-be. We have seen that, by comparison, the translations in the *Dream* are more vertiginous and apparently unpredictable (not even Oberon gets everything right first go round), and this lack of control suggests a corresponding measure of possibility. This is the case even though, as suggested above, the very daringness of the play's manipulation of hierarchy is predicated upon the comic guarantee that "all shall be well"

(3.2.463). (For about even this supposed restoration of decorum at the close of the play there is, as we have also seen, a striking irony, as the courtiers condescend to a play almost as unreasoning as their own love adventures.) But in the induction to the *Shrew,* the emphasis is all on the nobleman's control and skill, on a virtuosity, including a powerful eloquence, capable of overcoming Sly's resistance to manipulation. The induction, then, figures the theater as a social force, in a fantasy of total authority: the nobleman possesses a Prospero-like power for manipulating others, which is founded upon theater and capable of fashioning the very identity of his auditors:

> *Sly:*   Am I a lord, and have I such a lady?
> Or do I dream? Or have I dream'd till now?
> I do not sleep: I see, I hear, I speak;
> I smell sweet savors, and I feel soft things.
> Upon my life, I am a lord indeed,
> And not a tinker, nor Christopher Sly.
>
> (induction, 2.68–73)

What this passage and the scene as a whole suggest is a role for the theater in the ideological formation of subjects: the outsider Sly is through theater led to identify with aristocratic culture.[34] And it is specifically the theater, with its duplicitous techniques of impersonation, which effects this "false consciousness," or mystified experience of social reality: thus the directions to "Barthol'mew my page," who must be "dress'd in all suits like a lady" to impersonate Sly's noble wife, and who will be able to "rain a shower of commanded tears" by "An onion . . . / Which in a napkin (being close convey'd) / Shall in despite enforce a watery eye" (induction, 1.105–6, 125–28). Art is represented as a mode of elite social authority, employing fancy or the imagination for orthodox ends.[35] (By contrast, the *Dream* sets fancy in powerful opposition to social orthodoxy, as a mode for its—temporary, perhaps, but in no way easily forgotten—undoing.) What is crucial is the emphasis in the *Shrew* on *technique* or manipulation. Where in *A Midsummer Night's Dream* the disruptions of the social system have a magical or uncanny authority, so that they cannot be dismissed as merely illusory—at least not by the audience, Bottom, or the lovers—in the *Shrew* there is no such suggestion of an alternative, more fluid social reality; instead we see art serving authority, and we realize, even if he doesn't, that Christopher Sly is only a tinker and will remain one. The translations in the *Dream,* however, are not nearly so obviously unreal, so simply the result of technique—it is not clear that Bottom is now a mere weaver, for in an important sense he remains the consort of the Faerie Queene, able "to discourse wonders" (4.2.29); nor are the social translations of the play engendered, and so contained, by an aristocratic "art," but are on the contrary imagined as profound alternatives to the rigidity and conservatism of art: art is brought in to recontain and close down the dizzying possibilities for social relations, felt as fearful and delightful all at once, which are released by the play.[36] The disturbingly frank (for modern taste) identification of the art of the poetic theater with aristocratic authority in the *Shrew* turns upon genre: it is because what Sly watches is not "a Christmas gambold, or a tumbling-trick"—not a naïve popular entertainment but an example of deliberate and socially sophisticated art, a "kind of history"—that ensures that the lesson of the drama is essentially conservative. It will be useful to turn now to this "kind of history" itself, for it too, in the context of play with social distinctions and hierarchy, seems to recognize the power of art, its functioning as a mode of elite social symbolism and control.

It was suggested some pages back that the unreality of the *Dream* was necessary for its pleasurable loosening of the social structure, and thus that its fantastic aspects must be regarded as functioning conservatively, rendering the notion of social translation an "antic fable" or harmless "fairy toy" (5.1.3). Yet a comparison with the undoubtedly conservative *Taming of the Shrew* has shown that such a reading too easily accepts Theseus's complacent and facile dismissal of what has occurred in the night, and it is by now a critical truism that "the story of the night . . . / . . . grows to something of great constancy" (5.1.23, 26), and that the play throws into disarray ruling dualisms like reality and dream.[37] Thus, "strange and admirable" (5.1.27) as the play's envisioning of social translation might be, it is not canceled out by the end of the play; and its exoticism, fancy, and magic is to be compared with the contemporary and, in the body of the play, harshly materialistic and urban setting of the *Shrew,* which imposes, it seems, its own limitations on the idea of social translation—or at least gives this notion a conservative meaning. What I am suggesting is that upsets of social relations in the *Shrew* are more anxiety-producing affairs than in the *Dream:* to the extent that the play experiments at all with such reversals they are invariably the occasion for cuffs and blows, for verbal sparring and comic anger, and in general for the aggressive high spirits of slapstick. Vincentio's stupefaction, rage, and bewilderment at Tranio and Biondello's non-acknowledgment of him are typical (see 5.1.45–111). We are, of course, still in a comedy, even if, by comparison with the *Dream,* a highly realistic, unromantic one, so these instances of complication and reversal of traditional relations are not equatable with the anguish, disbelief, and shock that social translation gives rise to in, for example, *Lear,* where even the impudence of an Oswald is implicated in a narrative of cosmic ruin—yet the connection with comic versions of the same process is there, and *Lear* exploits it. An undercurrent of violence and tension pervades the social relations of the *Shrew:* "Was ever man so beaten? Was ever man so ray'd? Was ever man so weary?" complains Grumio on arriving at Petruchio's country house (4.1.2–3). Yet in their turn the servants are incorrigibly saucy: Grumio and Biondello are maddening quibblers and logic choppers (see, for example, the exchanges with Petruchio and Baptista at 1.2.5–44 and 3.2.30–41). These playful yet aggressive "sets of wit"[38] underscore one's impression of social relations characterized by a tendency toward force and violence (Kate's shrewishness has to be seen within the context of this generalized aggressivity), and this competitive, tense atmosphere clearly sets limits to the kinds of social translation imaginable. Nonetheless, the play does experiment with certain reversals of degree: "Tranio is chang'd into Lucentio" (1.1.237) so that the latter might have access to Bianca (the stage direction at 1.2.217 giving us "Tranio brave" and, at 2.1.38, "Lucentio in the habit of a mean man"). Still, such translations of social role do not suggest the profound renovation of social hierarchy hinted at in *A Midsummer Night's Dream;* and the reason for this reluctance of the play to press the idea of translation seems connected, once again, with the role of the foregrounded dramaturgical principle of "art" as a conservative check on this process. Thus the play's emphasis on "counterfeit supposes" (5.1.117), or on the "mystaking or imagination of one thing for an other" (prologue to Gascoigne's *Supposes*)[39] as a result of deliberate counterfeiting (such as Lucentio, Tranio, Biondello, Hortensio, Gremio, and Petruchio all engage in), is an emphasis on deft technique entirely absent from the *Dream.* This stress on the artful, theatrical manipulation of social reality lacks the implication of a thoroughgoing (and lasting) revision of the social structure that we encounter in the *Dream;* for the *Shrew,* with its emphasis on clever deceit, or the strategic trickery of art, preserves the notion of an unchanging social reality only temporarily distorted by these fictions and subterfuges. The reversal of role Tranio and Lucentio engineer ultimately only confirms the "truth" of the established order: finally, Tranio is Tranio and Lucentio is Lucentio; and when this is not so, it is because of the feigning of art—but what Bottom experiences in the woods, whatever it is the lovers undergo, is not a mere "suppose." Rather it is something that transcends or is more mysterious than "art," in something of the same way that the enigmatic, remote Hippolyta is a stranger, more alluring figure than the day-lit Theseus. In the *Shrew,* therefore, social translation operates in accordance with a technical rhetoric, or in terms of clever impersonation and the crafty manipulation of appearances; in the *Dream* it involves a far-reaching enchantment and wonder and poses, briefly but memorably, an alternative social reality. The notion of art is central: for in the *Shrew* the emphasis is on strategy, intrigue, and the manipulation of other people and social situations or, at a higher level of abstraction, of the plot by an author. (A manipulation Petruchio figures: obviously, he uses, along with physical force, a histrionic-poetic power to subdue Kate, even as Sly is subdued by this faculty in the nobleman's hands: just as Sly is made to identify with aristocratic life, so is Kate with patriarchy). This calculating, unillusioned rhetoric of art, characterizing the *Shrew*'s version of social interplay, seems appropriate to the "realistic" atmosphere of a town and its life of unapologetic getting and gaining: Athens and its wood is finally an ampler, less crowded place, its social structure less defined and constricting, than Padua. We may think of the change in Kate as like the translation Bottom undergoes—but unlike Bottom's, its logic is conservative, toward the reassertion of a hierarchical social relation rather than its unorthodox overturning or problematization. What we seem to see in the *Shrew* is Shakespeare's recognition of art's role in backing up "aweful rule, and right supremacy"; in the *Dream* art is similarly represented as a conservative force, but the play is more dialectical than the self-satisfied courtiers at its end, and they and their art do not have the last word. The point, then, is that none of the rearrangements of social role in the worldly, metropolitan comedy of the *Shrew* (the lord's, Lucentio's, Petruchio's—who is "mean apparell'd" at his wedding, so that it is "shame to [his] estate" [3.2.73, 100]) suggest that quality of wondrous, revisionary enchantment experienced in the apparently artless mix-up of social relations in the *Dream.*

I have suggested that the social dialectics of particular Shakespeare plays underlie or provoke a formal awareness—that their complex social makeup fosters an attitude of self-consciousness about form and that this involves an awareness of the social provenance, meaning, and potential uses of modes and of art generally. This suggestion can be further explored in a play with some striking similarities to *A Midsummer*

Night's Dream: George Peele's *The Old Wives Tale* (ca. 1588–94; pub. 1595). Describing this work's social character is difficult, since it unites the most diverse material. On the one hand it is, in Muriel Bradbrook's words, a fantastic popular "medley," derived from folktale and naïve tradition; on the other hand, its use of this material is sophisticated, knowing, and literary.[40] This sophisticated viewpoint is located in the three pages of the play who, lost in a wood, are welcomed into his cottage by Clunch the Smith, and who persuade his wife Madge to pass the night by telling them an old winter's tale:

> *Antic:* . . . methinks, gammer, a merry winter's tale would drive away the time trimly. Come, I am sure you are not without a score.
>
> *Fantastic:* I'faith, gammer, a tale of an hour long were as good as an hour's sleep.
>
> *Frolic:* Look you, gammer, of the giant and the king's daughter, and I know not what. I have seen the day, when I was a little one, you might have drawn me a mile after you with such a discourse.
>
> (lines 85–90)

The tone is witty and aware, yet sympathetic rather than merely condescending. Like the Nashe texts examined, or like the Shakespeare of *A Midsummer Night's Dream* or some of the late plays, Peele's play is consciously double in its social affiliations, both of and not of a "popular tradition." The meeting between Antic, Fantastic, and Frolic, and Madge and Clunch, is a socially inclusive scene, but the important thing about it is that this meeting between a nobleman's clever pages and simple country people is also a scene of aesthetic self-consciousness, as is evident from the device of the frame itself (once Madge has actually begun her tale this frame does not play much of a role, though it is in the theater a potentially continuous visual presence). As Patricia Binnie observes,[41] the beginning of Madge's tale is a veritable catalogue of folk motifs—clearly Peele wants to make these particular (popular) conventions as visible as possible:

> *Madge:* Once upon a time there was a king or a lord or a duke that had a fair daughter, the fairest that ever was; as white as

snow and as red as blood; and once upon a time his daughter was stolen away, and he sent all his men to seek out his daughter, and he sent so long that he sent all his men out of his land.

Frolic: Who dressed his dinner, then?

Madge: Nay, either hear my tale, or kiss my tail.

Fantastic: Well said! On with your tale, gammer.

Madge: O Lord, I quite forgot! There was a conjurer, and this conjurer could do anything, and he turned himself into a great dragon, and carried the king's daughter away in his mouth to a castle that he made of stone, and there he kept her I know not how long, till at last all the king's men went out so long that her two brothers went to seek her. O, I forget! She (he, I would say) turned a proper young man to a bear in the night and a man in the day, and keeps by a cross that parts three several ways, and he made his lady run mad. Gods me bones! who comes here?

Enter the Two Brothers

Frolic: Soft, gammer, here some come to tell your tale for you.

(lines 113–34)

The first thing to say about this passage is that it is under conditions of social mingling that these conventions are recognized as such. (This attitude of self-consciousness is maintained in the rest of the play, where, as in Madge's introduction, fairy-tale motifs are foregrounded by their very abundance.) Moreover, these conventions are not treated as if they were poetic only—we are not dealing with a merely formal self-con-sciousness—but instead are presented in terms of their putative social character, that is, as conventions of popular narrative. The pages can enjoy such tales as Madge's, but the play is concerned to represent their distance from them as well (Frolic's "Who dressed his dinner, then?" is a reminder of this distance).[42] Again, artistic self-consciousness is predicated upon social- or rank-consciousness. We may call this particular attitude of the text a "realism," because conventions are viewed realisti-cally, from outside, in a detached, critical way, and because artistic conventions are referred to social, economic, and political reality (instead of simply responding to the story, it is itself contextualized, and we apprehend it as popular). The techniques of "epic theater" are relevant as a modern parallel to this sixteenth-century dramatic "realism," but Maynard Mack has also set out the terms for its discussion in his analysis of that "fine poise" in the Elizabethan theater "between elements making for engagement and those making for detachment."[43] Thus *The Old Wives Tale* can be analyzed in terms similar to those we have brought to bear on other Renaissance works, where the text's complicated social situation is seen as precipitating a formal self-consciousness or a distancing of particular discursive modes as social-cultural forces: so-called bourgeois tragedy, in attempting a serious treatment of nonaristocratic life, develops a critical distance on tragic conventions, and Nashe, in a move interpretable as articulating his own ambiguous social position, plays off against each other elite and "popular" discourses to produce a socially undecidable, ironic, and elusive body of writing. *Realism* is an appropriate term for describing the characteristic stance of these texts, for each sees modes and conventions as aspects of social reality or as articulations of degree, and art as expressing elite social authority. In this respect *The Old Wives Tale* forms something of an exception to the texts examined so far, its self-consciousness regarding the social character of literary modes being directed not at art but at the naïve notion of the tale.

The Two Noble Kinsmen

Let me turn now to some other Shakespeare plays that seem, by a significant manipulation of social interplay, to explore the social meaning of literary modes or art. I am not concerned here with plays that explicitly reflect upon the social-symbolic function of cultural modes. Nevertheless, I shall attempt to show that notions of art in *The Two Noble Kinsmen* (1613; pub. 1634), assumed to be a collaboration by Shakespeare and Fletcher, have an implicitly conservative social value, and contrast with the social and generic mixing experimented with in the lower-class plot of the Jailer's Daughter and her love for the noble Palamon. This is a play acutely conscious of the connections between literary and social distinctions, but it explores them without the overt interest of *A Midsummer Night's Dream* or *The Taming of the Shrew*. In *Coriolanus* (1607–8; pub. 1623) and *King Lear* (1606; pub. 1608, 1623) there is also no explicit reflection on the social symbolism of art and its modes, but I shall argue that in these plays, too, a commitment to a radical and demanding form of social interplay is central to a strategy for critically distancing elite life, and tends to problematize, on social grounds, the mode of tragedy itself. No doubt it is paradoxical to say of perhaps the greatest tragedy ever written that it problematizes its mode, but I shall suggest that much of the humanity of *King Lear* is predicated on this problematization. Again, my interest is in how these plays generate a detached perspective on the cultural modes of an aristocratic elite, a perspective we may suppose the privilege of a "bourgeois," or at least unaristocratic, author. In all three plays elite culture constitutes some kind of problem—and in *Coriolanus* and *King Lear* this means that a preeminent aristocratic mode, tragedy, is also a problem: both plays depart from some of the fundamental social assumptions of their modes. Once again, we return to the basic fact of Shakespearean drama, its dialectical energy or "comprehensiveness," for it is these plays' interest in the exploitation of (among other contrarieties) social distinctions that produces a detached attitude toward a traditionally exclusive or restrictive cultural mode.

The Two Noble Kinsmen has a strong interest in social rank. It gives an ideal, rather nostalgic picture of an aristocratic ruling class and its chivalric ideology. By contrast, the court of Theseus in *A Midsummer Night's Dream,* with its sophisticated, clever, and hedonistic courtiers, is more contemporary in feel, modeled less upon an idealized notion of ancient virtue. But the later play tries to suggest an exotic and ideal aristocratic culture. Ann Jennalie Cook has written illuminatingly on some Shakespearean explorations of the notion of "the gentlemen," plays, that is, which take up a problem (how to define a gentleman) extensively treated in nonfiction of the period.[44] *The Two Noble Kinsmen* is likewise preoccupied with gentility: thus the "noble" of the title should be given its full weight, for the play really is about the aristocratic ideal, and everything in it evokes that ideal as sensuously and magnificently as possible (so a good part of its diction—words like "clear," "virtuous," and "pure"—comprises synonyms for "noble"). The emphasis on nobility is plain: the First Queen's opening lines appeal to Theseus to right wrongs (Creon's refusal to allow the queens "to urn [the] ashes" of their "sovereigns" [1.1.44, 39]) for "true gentility's" and "pity's sake" (1.1.25). Characterization is extremely slight, even by the standards of late Shakespeare: the emphasis is really collective, on the nobility as a class rather than on individuals. Indeed, we may feel that the play takes a virtually anthropological approach to its subject—as if its real interest were in the culture of chivalry and nobility rather than in the characters themselves. At least, they are seen as the subjects of a specific, radically strange and exotic culture. Thus the paradoxical nature of Palamon's and Arcite's relations: nobility demands that, even as rivals in love, they honor each other (so the extraordinary scenes [3.3, 3.6] in which Arcite feeds and arms Palamon in order to self-respectingly kill him in combat: we can sense the interest here in probing the rigorous artificiality of a social code). So it is nobility that makes Theseus "prorogue" (1.1.196) his marriage to avenge "rotten kings" and "blubber'd queens" (1.1.180), and nobility again that sustains the great friendships of the play: Theseus and Pirithous, Palamon and Arcite, Emilia and "Flavina" (see 1.3.54–97). Of Palamon and Arcite it can be said that their every word and deed must be referred to this supreme cultural ideal. This isn't to imply that the treatment of chivalry is one-sided: though presented at its most golden, aristocratic culture is occasionally viewed ironically and realistically. Thus vows of undying friendship metamorphose into hate minutes after Emily's appearance in the courtyard visible from the prison window (a "romantic realism"—love subverting high-flown ideals—familiar from Shakespeare's comedies: Lucentio's prompt abandonment of Aristotle and the Stoics on sight of Bianca [Shrew, 1.1], for example, or the fate of the love scoffers in Love's Labor's Lost or Much Ado). Still, it seems these contradictions have to do with the play's interest in a cultural elite (and the stresses and strains of its way of life) and that, overall, the play offers a magnificently idealized vision of this aristocratic milieu.

The concern with rank is evident in the prologue, and here it takes, for my purposes, a particularly interesting form. The play, we are assured, has "a noble breeder and a pure, / A learned, and a poet never went / More famous yet 'twixt Po and silver Trent." The actors must do justice to its "nobleness" (15), otherwise

> How will it shake the bones of that good man,
> And make him cry from under ground, "O, fan
> From me the witless chaff of such a writer
> That blasts my bays and my fam'd works makes lighter
> Than Robin Hood!

By invoking the learned Chaucer,[45] the play defines itself against naïve popular narrative (the "witless" or "artless" storytelling The Old Wives Tale, for instance, purports to supply), and this self-characterization is evident in the masterly first act (extravagantly praised by De Quincey),[46] with its conspicuously highborn and stately, or artificial, mood. This is, indeed, from the first a play of "art," of extreme formality and dignity, possessing a composure that contrasts strikingly with the experiment in the rhetoric of popular simplicity Shakespeare undertook a few years earlier in *Pericles,* where Gower's "song that old was sung" must sue for a kind reception "in those latter times, / When wit's more ripe" (Chorus, 1, 11–12).[47] "Ancient Gower" is unpretentiously an entertainer, singing "a song" (a "mouldy tale," Jonson would call it), "To glad your ear and please your eyes," which "hath been sung at festivals, / On ember-eves and holy-ales; / And lords and ladies in their lives / Have read it for restoratives" (2, 1, 5–8). These unsophisticated, old-fashioned "rhymes," dedicated to "pleasure" (12, 14) and frankly associated with festivity and traditional pastime, show up the loftier tone of the prologue to *The Two Noble Kinsmen,* where what is at stake are "fam'd works" and finished "art" (20, 28), and a "story . . . / constant to eternity" (13–14). This "art," the laureate art of a "good man" (Chaucer is crowned with "bays" [17, 20]) is, by contrast with the more homely Gower, conceived exclusively in terms of the authority and prestige of a social elite: "art" here has a clear aristocratic connotation (even the notion of a "good man" implying, along with an ethical distinction, a social one). I suggest that the prologue's emphasis on "art" is sustained throughout the play in its idealization of aristocratic culture, and that this art has a fundamentally conservative social meaning. As in *A Midsummer Night's Dream,* it expresses a commitment to principles of degree and social order.

I have suggested that the play explores the artificiality of an elite way of life, and the extravagancies and paradoxes this life involves. It would be more accurate to say that the play generalizes "art" to include society: this golden Athens—more lustrous than the recognizably Elizabethan, "brazen" Athens of the *Dream*—is so stylized as to suggest the kind of transfiguring of the real advocated in Sidney's idealizing aristocratic poetics. The view that elite society in the play has an "aesthetic" perfection can be taken literally: I mean that that beautiful mood of gravity and solemnity which pervades almost all the high-life scenes (it is relatively unrelieved by the flippancy and irony flourishing in the more casual court of *A Midsummer Night's Dream* or the witty, sharp, satiric court of *Love's Labor's Lost*) is a mood of decorum. Society in the play has a kind of formal rigor, expressed in the heavy codification as well as the studied ceremoniousness of manners. It is as if social relations were a kind of art governed by decorum. In Theseus's world style is all. The first scene sets the tone: we open with "Hymen with a torch burning; a

Boy, in a white robe, before, singing and strewing flow'rs; after Hymen, a Nymph, encompass'd in her tresses, bearing a wheaten garland; then Theseus, between two other Nymphs with wheaten chaplets on their heads; then Hippolyta, the bride, led by Pirithous." Another Shakespeare-Fletcher collaboration, *Henry VIII*, attempted such a ritual ceremonialization of politics, but that play's idealism was more than a little constrained by its intractably historical monarch; here it is untrammeled.[48] The suggestion, then, is that the degree of idealization, of heightening, in *The Two Noble Kinsmen* is unique in Shakespeare—no other play is as consistently grave, decorous, and "artificial" in its representation of society. (The Roman plays exploit the prestige of antique aristocratic culture, but are also studies in political realism.) Of course, this is a matter of language: the idiom of the play is generally higher than, say, the more varied *lexis* of a comparably romantic play like *The Tempest*, in which the speech of the court party encompasses a broader repertory of social registers than that of a Theseus, Palamon, or Arcite, which always betokens nobility.[49] No less is it a matter of the elegantly artificial visual language of the stage. Verbal and spectacular aspects of this heightening are obvious in the opening tableau:

> *Enter three Queens, in black, with veils stain'd, with imperial crowns. The first Queen falls down at the foot of Theseus; the second falls down at the foot of Hippolyta; the third before Emilia.*
>
> *1 Queen:* For pity's sake and true gentility's,
> Hear and respect me.
>
> *2 Queen:*   For your mother's sake,
> And as you wish your womb may thrive with fair ones,
> Hear and respect me.
>
> *3 Queen:* Now for the love of him whom Jove hath mark'd
> The honor of your bed, and for the sake
> Of clear virginity, be advocate
> For us and our distresses! This good deed
> Shall raze you out o' th' book of trespasses
> All you are set down there.
>
> *Theseus:* Sad lady, rise.
>
> *Hippolyta:*   Stand up.
>
> *Emilia:*   No knees to me.
>
>   (1.1.25–35)

This stylization of aristocratic life is typical and more complete than anywhere else in Shakespeare. The propriety of Athenian society contrasts vividly with the gross moral, political, and religious disorder of Creon's tyrannized Thebes, where "mortal loathsomeness," the unburied bodies of the dead kings, offends "the blest eye / Of holy Phoebus" (1.1.45–46). That society itself is a work of art is palpable in the elaborate ceremonial of 5.1, when Arcite, Palamon, and Emilia pray to their respective deities; but throughout one is impressed by the finish, artifice, and exquisiteness of social life. Yet this aestheticization of the social is profoundly conservative. To see how this is so, we must turn to the plebeian subplot, the story of the Jailer's Daughter.

Her story is easily summarized: falling in love with the prisoner Palamon, she frees him, goes mad when her love is not returned and, finally restored (more or less) to sanity, marries her betrothed (whom, however, she is still sufficiently deluded to think Palamon). In all this the Daughter strikes us as freer, less constrained by a self-consciously artificial code of conduct, than the upper-class characters: "Let all the dukes and all the devils roar, / He is at liberty!" she declares splendidly, flouting patriarchal and ducal authority. "Farewell, father; / Get many more such prisoners and such daughters, / And shortly you may keep yourself" (2.6.1–2; 37–39).[50] In the course of her madness, she joins a group of rustics, and dances a morris with them before Theseus. Her fresh, natural spontaneity contrasts with the rigid artifice, deliberate virtue, and codified manners of the elite circle. As pastoral, this part of the play throws into relief the refinement and civilization of the elite story. Yet more is at stake here than lower-class rustic contrast. Let us recall the intrinsic seriousness of the Daughter's predicament:

> Why should I love this gentleman? 'Tis odds
> He never will affect me. I am base,
> My father the mean keeper of his prison,
> And he a prince. To marry him is hopeless;
> To be his whore is witless . . .
>
> (2.4.1–5)

Empson suggested pastoral posits a "beautiful relation between rich and poor," that it "breaks through" the class system, making "the classes feel part of a larger unity or simply at home with each other."[51] Rather as with Bottom's unorthodox sojourn with the Faerie Queene, this pastoral story entertains the utopian idea of a "base" commoner marrying a noble.

Pastoral here appears as an imaginative mode of disorder revising the principle of hierarchy in the elite world (expressed aesthetically as decorum and beauty). The Daughter is associated with an artlessly lovely Nature not easily assimilated to this hierarchical ideal of social decorum. The Wooer's Ophelia-like image of her near "the great lake that lies behind the palace" (4.1.53) contains a profound mingling of the folk and low, and the lyrical:

> The place
> Was knee-deep where she sat; her careless tresses
> A [wreath] of bulrush rounded; about her stuck
> Thousand fresh water-flowers of several colors,
> That methought she appear'd like the fair nymph
> That feeds the lake with waters, or as Iris
> Newly dropp'd down from heaven. Rings she made
> Of rushes that grew by, and to 'em spoke
> The prettiest posies—"Thus our true love's tied,"
> "This you may loose, not me," and many a one;
> And then she wept, and sung again, and sigh'd,
> And with the same breath smil'd, and kiss'd her hand.
>
> (4.1.82–93)

The emphasis is on an uncontrived quaintness: instead of an aristocratic art, a naïve nature; instead of learned "poetry," "posies."[52] Yet we might not feel that nature was alternative to an elite aesthetic of social decorum were it not that it is in this low milieu that a transgression of social boundaries is entertained. As in *A Midsummer Night's Dream,* the mode of the imaginative and naïve raises social possibilities uncontemplatable in elite "art," which can only attempt their demystification, as dream, fancy, or madness. So this enchanted image of the Daughter by the lake (probably by Fletcher)[53] has a magical aspect, contrasting strongly with the disciplined, cultivated world of Theseus, Palamon, and Arcite, and reminiscent of that similarly artless, socially fluid, wood in the *Dream.* The lake "behind the palace" (the Daughter is on its "far shore" [4.1.54]) and the wood, where the country people dance (3.5), are removed from the artificial world of the elite and from the social rigidity that art connotes. As in *A Midsummer Night's Dream,* an opposition between Nature and Art has a social significance, elite life in this play, in its high elaboration and formality, being contrasted with a Nature that appears to undo some of the assumptions of this milieu. Art as a social value, the sophistication of life into highly developed forms (the rigorous code of chivalry), is contrasted with a realm of common life that is freer and more natural, and in which the rules of social life, its art, have less sway, so that a "beautiful relation" (romantic love) between the classes may be imagined. Indeed the Daughter's madness, an "extravagant vagary" (4.3.73) in its fantastic coining (4.3.40) and in the energy and imagination of its nonsense, is the clearest contravention of the dominant group's ideal of decorum, and has an explicit utopian character: "She is continually in a harmless distemper, sleeps little, altogether without appetite, save often drinking, dreaming of another world and a better" (4.3.3–5).

If the Art/Nature opposition of this play is socially symbolic, and if this is ultimately a play of art, or decorum, in which the disruptive desire of the Jailer's Daughter is finally channeled into its proper social level,[54] the play's complication of hierarchy is nonetheless adventurous. Here the generic question is paramount and difficult. For it quickly becomes obvious that the opposition set up here between high and low story is not wholly adequate: for the distinction of this subplot over the conventional clown material of Elizabethan and Jacobean drama[55] is precisely that it does not form a simple contrast with the aristocratic narrative. Of course, in some ways it does provide this contrast: the rustics the Daughter accompanies constitute just this kind of trivial nondramatic lower-class stage business. Yet this episode merely underscores the relatively more complex mood of the Jailer's Daughter plot as a whole. After his inspired account of the Daughter singing among "the rushes and the reeds" of the lake, one of the Wooer's audience responds with an "Alas, what pity it is!" (4.1.61, 94): it is a remarkable feature of this play that while it is not concerned with effecting some thorough transmutation of social relations such as Bottom enjoys, it does not "put the Daughter in her place" through ridicule. In the Wooer's solemn speech, and in the Daughter's madness generally, the play eschews comedy. Indeed, it seems interested in taking the action as close to tragedy as possible, entertaining the idea of her death (she is rescued from drowning herself by the Wooer). Her romantic predicament is not obviously ludicrous. She is not a conventionally humorous plebeian: her speech is less elevated than the elite's (though often in verse), and it is sometimes bawdy, but her simplicity makes her situation even more affecting. (There is a sense in which this simplicity even associates her with the noble characters—for it seems analogous to those qualities of purity and clearness I have suggested are the ethical signs of nobility in the play.) Palamon's solicitude for her at his near-execution undoubtedly stresses the hero's generosity, yet it also dignifies her by suggesting that she is worthy of concern. It seems possible, then, that part of the play's intention is to present a humble character as an object of serious interest: so her mad talk is in general riddling, evocative, and sentimental rather than demeaning.[56] Thus the story presents a generic problem, for in its relatively serious presentation of the Daughter's desire for Palamon it raises the self-contradictory notion of a lower-class tragedy. But there is a profounder problem than this "formal" one. Such a tragedy would be a consequence of the rigid social structure of the play, its normative aesthetic conception of society. But in bringing her story to the brink of tragedy, and in exploiting the pathos of her predicament, the play raises as a problem this principle of social decorum, which naturally cannot countenance Empson's "beautiful relation between the classes" (or has an unliberal conception of what that would be). Of course, in resolving the girl's lovesickness happily, the generic problem of the tragedy of a lower-class woman is averted. But at a deeper level the rigid, exclusive, aesthetic social ideal has also been problematized.

The elite culture of this play is, then, bracketed off, or critically distanced, and the significance of the Jailer's Daughter story is twofold. First, it shows a readiness to experiment with the traditional social character of a generic mode: the tale transcends the comic register typical for stories of common life, indeed approaches a tragic seriousness. Second, although it does not form a conventional generic contrast with the Palamon/Arcite story, the social contrast renders even more conspicuous the elite character of the aristocratic narrative. It underscores the chivalric story's artificiality: the texture of that narrative—the loftiness of its knightly ethic, its exalted religion of love, its all-wise prince and noble friendships, its tourneys and combats, gods and goddesses, above all the great inscrutable machinery of cosmic justice—("Never fortune / Did play a subtler game. The conquer'd triumphs, / The victor has the loss; yet in the passage / The gods have been most equal" [5.4.112–15])—is seen "realistically," as elite artifice, or from a social vantage point outside aristocratic culture. In other words, the pronounced social contrast of the play foregrounds its main plot as an elite cultural mode. Here we recall that most of the play's character-interest is displaced into its sentimental lower-class half. Thus, to recast in sociological terms a point made some pages ago, if we are drawn to care for the Jailer's Daughter in a way uncharacteristic of most treatments of plebeians in English Renaissance drama, we are not likewise involved with the fortunes of the elite figures: the emphasis is not so much on those characters as on a radically other culture (chivalry), or on the character of a particular rank. An account of this play, then, might reformulate in social terms Maynard Mack's description of Elizabethan and Jacobean dramaturgy as fostering both audience "engagement" and "detachment"; we are distanced from the elite of the play (apprehended as the subjects of a specific culture), and we are engaged with the principal plebeian character (whose naturalness contrasts with the artifice of ruling-class life). If the play does critically distance this story of two noble kinsmen as aristocratic cultural symbolism, it gains this realistic perspective on the interimplications of degree, literary mode, and aesthetic discourse without recourse to the overt self-reflection of other plays considered here.

King Lear, Coriolanus

My purpose has been to argue that the social dialectics of some of Shakespeare's plays, their interest in the interplay of heterogeneous spheres of social life, often involves (by contrast with Nashe and with most of the plays discussed in chapter 2) a negative attitude toward the modes of elite culture—and now I suggest that it may be the basis for a similarly critical attitude toward a genre that has usually been socially restrictive. As I have argued, simply the presence of lower-class characters in a tragedy may initiate a certain internal distance in the mode. Thus one of the effects of Hamlet's exchange with the grave diggers is to distance slightly from us, or frame, his predicament: what is conveyed is that "the general" (2.2.437), the populace, are not directly involved in Hamlet's story. This is unremarkable until we consider what it enables Shakespeare to do with tragedy, which is to render visible the social contours of the mode, or remind us of what tragedy, as traditionally conceived, leaves out of account. Thus the grave diggers' detached, irreverent, ironic demeanor distances this tragedy as concerning only the rulers. Popular misfortune is not rendered as tragedy; yet even the brief allusion to the "twenty thousand men" Fortinbras is marching off to their death "even for an egg-shell" (4.4.60, 53) recalls from oblivion a world of popular experience complementing the lonely trials of the tragic hero. This doesn't mean that the marginal, plebeian point of view summoned up "subverts" tragedy: Hamlet is mourned no less for it at the end of the play, and those soldiers are not. But by introducing the relatively disengaged point of view of the grave diggers, or in this oblique but telling reference to popular life, Shakespeare allows the supreme and isolated hero of tragedy to be seen realistically or from below, contextual-

izing his story in the larger reality of the whole society rather than
working unproblematically within tragedy's aristocratic assumptions. The
grave diggers supply the play, then, with a certain critical distance on the
aristocracy.[57] (Thus Ophelia is treated simply as one of the "great folk,"
and her death occasions not the hysterical grief of a Laertes or a Hamlet
but a piece of social observation, if not criticism: "If this had not been a
gentlewoman, she should have been buried out a' Christian burial"
[5.1.27, 23–25].) A critical light is also thrown upon tragic assumptions
in *King Lear*, where the suffering of the king and other elite characters
(Gloucester, Kent, and Edgar) is understood in the context of the daily,
anonymous, untragic suffering of the mass of society, "[loop'd] and
window'd raggedness" (3.4.31). A measure of Lear's ethical rehabilitation
is a newfound concern for this mass[58]—and implicit within this is the
recognition, remarkable indeed for a tragedy, that the misery of poor
people weighs as much as a king's. This recognition amounts, it may
seem, almost to an ethical dismantling of the social basis of tragedy. Thus
the Gentleman's comment on Lear: "A sight most pitiful in the meanest
wretch, / Past speaking of in a king!" (4.6.204–5) invokes elitist
assumptions natural to tragedy but which the hero, we may well feel, has
largely relinquished. It seems that, by vividly evoking lower-class
privation, the play forces a critical distance on the tragic privileging of
the hero's pain: a relative sense of his suffering is gained by situating it
within a differentiated social reality. We may even suspect that this social
contextualization is the basis for the play's famous grotesque comedy,[59]
as elite characters are made to submit to the indignities and humiliations
of common life: the irony of the play would then be at bottom a leveling
one. So the aristocratic genre of tragedy, which would prioritize noble
suffering, is not accepted on its own terms: runs against the grain, in fact,
of the play, which stresses the moral desirability (though not, we must
perhaps admit, the capability) of identifying with the poor and oppressed.
Like *A Midsummmer Night's Dream*, then, *Lear* has a radical and
demanding version of social "translation": just as Bottom's stay in the
wood constitutes a dizzying suspension of rigid social relations, so Lear
on the heath symbolizes a move away from an elite to a popular social
space, or, if the heath is to be seen as a locus of general human suffering,
to one which does not exclude the popular. So the play seems to describe
not simply a (ironically conceived) transition from "civilization" to
"wilderness," but a move that takes the king deep into the world of the
play's dispossessed, who are, though seldom directly seen, among its
principal characters.[60] For the heath can be regarded as the play's

"political unconscious," the repressed underside of the play world in which are confronted the miseries of the weakest members of society. Thus the ejection of the basically good characters of the play—Lear, Gloucester, Edgar, Kent, and the Fool—from the seats of aristocratic power comes to seem as much a repudiation of the arrogant heartlessness of such places as it does banishment: it literalizes the play's departure from the elitist assumptions of tragedy. It is necessary to stress that this transition from the castles to a netherworld of popular suffering is eventually coherent as a gesture of rejection. The profound lessons Lear learns on the heath lead him to turn against an unjust society, and it is here also that he appears to win a deep and explicitly anti-elitist humility: "Take physic, pomp, / Expose thyself to feel what wretches feel" (3.4.33–34). It is here, in this "translation" into the life of "houseless poverty" (3.4.26), that the play effects its critical distancing of the aristocratic mode of tragedy, or the exclusive and unexamined preoccupation with the noble hero's suffering: it is a movement not merely from courts but from the courtly assumptions of tragic ideology. Thus Lear himself acquires a crucial vantage point within the play, as, to different degrees, do Gloucester, Edgar, and Kent, from which the life of the elite can be perceived ironically—can seem indeed profoundly alien or ridiculous. Lear, it is true, remains "every inch a king" (4.6.107), yet it is implied that moral progress is bound up with becoming an outsider[61] —and it is this complicated double state of insiderness/outsiderness with regard to aristocratic, or tragic, life and assumptions that seems to interest Shakespeare, who as professional author and client of the court also lives a complicated insider/outsider relation to aristocratic culture, to its modes and values. The attitude of an outsider underlies the caustic satire of Lear's speeches; the attitude of an insider, their self-lacerating passion. The radical distantiation of elite life is clear in the speech unmasking elite justice or "authority" (4.6.154–73), and is most explicit in the detached amusement that Lear imagines himself and Cordelia enjoying as "God's spies," regarding indifferently the absurdities, as they now appear, of "court news" and "gilded butterflies" and "pacts and sects of great ones" (5.3.13–18). There is, of course, in this notion of "God's spies" the idea of a radical religious overcoming of the world. Yet its wry detachment also suggests the quizzical, ironic attitude toward elite life given to humble characters like *Hamlet*'s grave diggers. The "old tales" (12) Lear and Cordelia are to tell each other at least suggest a spirit of simplicity and unpretentiousness, one contrasting with the feverish insiders' chatter about "Who loses and who wins; who's in, who's out," which Lear sees himself and Cordelia engaging in only ironically. We should remember, too, that the social translation that characters such as Lear, Edgar, and Kent undergo is not a matter of "counterfeit supposes," not, that is, a case of theatrical technique, such as we saw in the *Shrew.* Like Hamlet's madness, Edgar's "Poor Tom," even Kent's "Caius," are, despite the superficial resemblance to play-acting, not mere roles, lightly put on and off. They constitute a stranger, more terrible and uncontrollable experience than technique or role can suggest, akin in this respect to the ecstatic translations of Bottom or the lovers, and seem to promise, for Edgar and his kingdom, permanent and beneficial effects.[62]

It is important to stress the social, and radical, character of this translation in *Lear.* Lear's suffering involves not only "the winds and persecutions of the sky" (2.3.12) or the torment of ingratitude, but the deepest social humiliation. Thus the repeated references to the "hovel" that Kent leads him to (3.2.61, 78; 3.4.174; and compare Cordelia: "to hovel thee with swine and rogues forlorn" [4.7.38]), which is implicitly contrasted with Gloucester's "hard house" (3.2.63), now controlled by Cornwall, Goneril, and Regan. It is outside these hard houses that the reevaluation of tragic values begins. This humiliation, and Kent's, stocked "as basest and [contemned'st] wretches" (2.2.143), occurs amid the harshest awareness of hierarchy. So the violence of Lear's and Kent's response to Oswald's "weary negligence" (1.3.12): "whoreson dog," "slave," "cur," "rascal," "base football player," "I'll teach you differences" (1.4.81–90)— a rhetorical violence expressing a tension in social relations that the Fool expresses satirically or proverbially: "Truth's a dog must to kennel, he must be whipt out, when the Lady Brach may stand by th' fire and stink" (1.4.111–13); "Fortune, that arrant whore, / Ne'er turns the key to th' poor" (2.4.52–53). The preoccupation with hierarchy continually recurs, in characters good and bad: Lear's contempt for "this detested groom" (Oswald, 2.4.217), or Kent's (2.2.14–24), is matched by Regan's and Cornwall's for the "dog," "villain," "peasant," "slave" (3.7.75, 78, 80, 96) who tries to rescue Gloucester. This sensitivity to rank renders all the more striking the humiliations various characters undergo. Lear simply cannot accept that anyone would knowingly set Kent in the stocks: "What's he that hath so much thy place mistook / To set thee here?" (2.4.12–13). The irony of Kent's taunt to Oswald is, however, that the "differences" he is to "teach" the servant are those Lear unlearns in his discovery of "the thing itself," "unaccommodated man" (3.4.106–7).

And yet this is, it must be faced, conceivably to sentimentalize a play the social ironies of which are fiercer than the account so far suggests.

For is it really the case, as has perhaps been too sanguinely proposed, that Lear does unlearn "differences" in an access of common feeling? Or is it rather—terrible irony this—that the play represents, in language of immense persuasive power, the feeling of unity with the poor instead of its reality, a longing for a kinship with oppressed humanity rather than its achievement? For in the end we must, I think, agree with Lear that he remains "every inch a king"—that his overwhelming self-obsession is a royal rather than a simply "personal" characteristic (and it is senseless to speak in his case of a personality not bound up with kingship), and that this tremendous noble egoism, excepting perhaps in the strange lull of the scene with the Doctor ("I am a very foolish fond old man. . . . If you have poison for me, I will drink it" [4.7.59, 71]), never really dissipates or changes into something new. Thus emerges the truly harsh irony that Lear never does abandon the "lendings" (3.4.108) of social place to rediscover the natural or unaccommodated man beneath: that he is condemned to himself, and that moments of sincerest humility and sense of fellow-feeling are equally moments of kingly assertiveness. Lear's voice is always loudest, and even the penitent meekness of the speech beginning, "Come, let's away to prison" (5.3.8) has about it a domineering, controlling and, of course, patriarchal egoism; in any case, this tone is passing, replaced by the punching aggressiveness of "A plague upon you, murderers, traitors all! . . . I have seen the day, with my good biting falchion, / I would have made [them] skip" (5.3.270, 277–78). It may be said that an extraordinary sense of self is proper to tragic heroes, and that there can therefore be attached to it no special significance here. True—that the hero be large-souled, magnificent, is merely conventional, and we must therefore suppose Shakespeare to be playing against the traditionally elitist egocentrism of the tragic protagonist Lear's desire for, or fantasized sense of, a common humanity. If this view is correct, the play does not so much "dismantle" tragedy as ironically and depressingly reaffirm its social limitation.

Like *The Two Noble Kinsmen* and *King Lear, Coriolanus* is among Shakespeare's most hierarchy-conscious plays. Like them too it lacks any specific reflection on genre. Nevertheless, here as well, in an approach somewhat different to *Lear*'s, the presence of humble characters, along with the play's interest in the conflict between patricians and plebeians, occasions a critical, politically realistic perspective on tragedy. Both plays accord a central importance to common people. I suggest then that, as in *King Lear,* the preoccupation of *Coriolanus* with rank entails a distancing of tragic values. Certainly the presence of a proletarian viewpoint in the play complicates our sense of the tragedy of Coriolanus, from the first "a very dog to the commonalty" (1.1.28–29). Rather than presenting his fall solely from his own point of view, or even from that of the patricians, the play provides a different perspective, the plebeians', opposed to both of these and impossible to ignore.[63] (Thus *Coriolanus,* like *King Lear,* is a play about which the critic cannot avoid the language of social contradiction, a language I have suggested is often inappropriate for describing the social relations of Renaissance texts.) We may say, then, that the purity of the genre, which would mourn Coriolanus's downfall, is compromised by an interest in social conflict (the intrusion of a nonaristocratic viewpoint). It is true that *Coriolanus* does not explicitly criticize tragedy. But in complicating our response to the hero, by grounding his career in the broader social, economic, and political reality of Rome, and making it impossible to understand that career in purely aristocratic terms, the play opens up the genre to social complexity. The tragic hero and his death are seen "realistically," or from the viewpoint of the *polis* as a whole (thus the citizens' debate over Coriolanus's worth to the commonwealth [1.1.25–46]).[64] Even at his most authoritative and charismatic—for example, at the taking of Corioles, where he ought to command as a god—Coriolanus's *ethos* is not allowed to go unquestioned, and Shakespeare supplies in the common soldiers a skeptical, unheroic, and commonsensical perspective opposed to that of the warrior-aristocrat.[65] Our sense of Coriolanus as a tragic hero deserving our admiration is thus complicated by awareness of a justifiable popular suspicion. We remain strangely detached: we do not make the emotional investment in Coriolanus that we do in, say, Macbeth, whose characterization by Malcolm as a "dead butcher" (5.9.35) does not match our experience of him.[66] Shakespeare seems determined to bleach the play of tragic emotion. (Bradley noted the peculiar dispatch of Coriolanus's end[67]—a feature Brecht fastened upon in his adaptation, with its outrageously brusque, unelegiac, and bureaucratic conclusion: the people's tribunes forbidding Volumnia and Virgilia the customary prerogatives of mourning.) If an audience cannot overlook the antipatrician perspective in the play, neither can the patricians, for whom the people remain a permanent factor in any political calculation. Thus Coriolanus's rise to power in Aufidius's army is based on his popularity with the troops, and he cannot be assassinated until the people have been prepared (5.6.14–15). The citizens, then, are throughout an independent if unpredictable political force. Frank Kermode has rightly called *Coriolanus* an "inhospitable play,"[68] and the difficulty we have in sympathizing with Coriolanus is clearly grounded in the play's uncompromising dialectical method, as Coriolanus's "tragedy" is compared with popular complaint. Thus the objective quality of the play: this tragedy obliges us to take into account a perspective hostile to the tragic hero. While *King Lear* encourages identification with its protagonist even as it alienates his suffering through a socially critical irony (we cannot forget the general suffering over which Lear has reigned), Coriolanus, in this respect not unlike Palamon and Arcite, appears as the bearer of an impossibly exotic and exclusive, indeed alienating, ideology. (However, if the antique aristocratic spirit Palamon and Arcite embody is intended to seem "other" to a modern Jacobean audience, it is also not harsh and repellent, as it is with Coriolanus, but is advanced as cause for wonder.) Shakespeare, then, does not allow us to remain unproblematically within the values of tragedy, but requires the recognition that tragic esteem and sorrow for Coriolanus is a point of view—one, moreover, only fully available to the aristocrats of the play. *Coriolanus,* then, also exhibits a socially critical attitude toward tragedy, seeing the form from outside and problematizing it on the grounds of its elite character.

Let us consider further how Shakespeare alienates tragic emotion from this play. Coriolanus is like no other Shakespearean tragic hero. One way in which he differs from Romeo, Richard II, Hamlet, Brutus, Lear, Othello, Macbeth, or Antony is in the relatively narrow social range of his personality. The social character of Shakespeare's tragic heroes is usually more complex. We are used to thinking of Shakespeare as endowing his tragic protagonists with a certain social breadth, or comprehensiveness, so that even if we cannot endorse the sentimental idea that *King Lear* shows in its hero an ever wider and more inclusive identification with society, we can agree that Lear's social character is not as severely restricted as Coriolanus's. To take the most obvious way in which this is so, Lear is not incapable of compassion or simple kindness toward the poor, and it is his voice that articulates the powerful if unrealized ethical ideal of becoming like them. Indeed, a peculiarly Shakespearean achievement is the depiction of noble protagonists who have a more rounded and textured social identity than, for example, the heroes of ancient tragedy. Nothing could be less like Coriolanus than Hamlet's rapport with the grave diggers, suggesting some affinity despite the drastic social divide; and Antony, Othello, and Romeo all suggest a capacity to behave in ways that are not merely or only elite. In other words, Shakespeare's noble heroes (or heroines: Cleopatra is a wrangling strumpet as well as a monarch [1.1.13, 48]) tend to incorporate aspects of life not essentially or distinctively noble—they seem larger, socially richer, figures than Coriolanus, suggesting contact with less elevated modes of life. And if the rhetoric of *King Lear,* at least, is expansive and collective, moving toward the people, *Coriolanus* traces instead a withdrawal into an ever more wintry and aggressive self-sufficiency, an elitism of one. He is, of course, a far more inflexible character than Lear: in Bradley's words, "if Lear's thunderstorm had beat upon his head, he would merely have set his teeth,"[69] and the rigidity is social as well as psychological: unlike any other Shakespearean tragic hero, Coriolanus, as Ralph Berry has said, "is defined by his class. . . . there is nothing left over."[70] As with Palamon and Arcite, it is impossible to think of Coriolanus without continuous reference to an ideal of aristocracy. What I suggest is that Shakespeare has made Coriolanus as absolutely aristocratic as possible, in a way unprecedented in the other tragedies. In terms of this emphasis on rank, then, *Coriolanus* bears the comparison with *The Two Noble Kinsmen.* Like Palamon and Arcite, Coriolanus embodies elite culture. Like them he is self-consciously aristocratic, and the play is about the destruction wreaked by this self-consciousness. In both plays aristocratic culture is imagined in the most exotic terms: in both there is that almost anthropological interest in exploring it. But whereas Palamon and Arcite move in a dramatic structure that confirms this way of life, Coriolanus's world is less sympathetic. The essential point, in any case, is that Coriolanus is exclusively aristocratic, and that therefore the legitimate complaint that he lacks "humanity" is to be explained in part by the "objective" appearance he has of simply embodying an aristocratic "line": he is patrician "ultra" ideology.[71] Where other Shakespearean tragic heroes have that larger set of potentialities or concerns with which they might be associated, Shakespeare confines Coriolanus to the sheerest expression of patrician arrogance; and Volumnia is chillingly clear on his having been raised to embody an ideal of aristocratic, especially military, virtue. By presenting such a radically stripped-down tragic figure, Shakespeare sets up an internal distance on tragedy and its traditional social assumptions. So this drastic reduction of social character in this, possibly last, tragic hero of Shakespeare tends to undermine tragic identification: the dreadful, all-but-total consistency of Coriolanus's character renders him uniquely and terribly other. And we may note that tragic affect in *Coriolanus* is complicated by a method directly counter to that of *Lear:* for while both heroes are crucially defined by their relations with the common people, on a rhetorical level *King Lear* throws into question the authority of the distinctions—certainly the crueller inequalities—of hierarchy, and proposes the desirability of rediscovering "unaccommodated man" beneath the artificial "lendings" making for differences between people; in *Coriolanus,* it is the opposite, extremist emphasis on aristocratic privilege and exceptionalism that inhibits tragic emotion.

What I am suggesting is that like the other texts treated in this book, *Coriolanus* attains, through social interplay, a detached view of a literary mode as a culturally or socially symbolic mode. The play takes the long view, not the hero's. So Brecht, planning his own adaptation of *Coriolanus,* found in Shakespeare's play warrant for his desire that his version concern not only Coriolanus: "We must . . . be able to 'experience' the tragedy not only of Coriolanus himself but also of Rome, and specifically of the plebs."[72] Brecht's Shakespeare shows "the field of forces within which [the hero] operates."[73] Thus Coriolanus can be understood "objectively," as the expression of one pole of a general contradiction between patricians and plebeians, a contradiction to which he is subordinated and that is independent of him. The essential crisis of the play—the struggle between haves and have-nots—does not originate in Coriolanus and is elaborated before he appears. Thus of this "tragedy" Thomas Sorge observes that "the play is not organized solely around a central character," and that "its concern with the clash of political forces, rather than the exploration of characters" means that "its structure is incapable of ensuring the highest tragic effect at the moment of the fall of the hero."[74] The play has, then, a communal, rather than individualistic focus—and such a focus is set in obvious, catastrophic tension with the extreme individualism that Coriolanus expresses, in which one may "stand / As if a man were author of himself, / And knew no other kin" (5.3.35–37). Coriolanus is a hero, and the play is concerned with his fortunes, but these are incomprehensible without reference to a social process that he does not control. (With respect to Shakespeare's development, this de-emphasis on character is interesting in terms of the plays that will follow, where, too, individual character is less important than the pattern into which it is integrated.)[75] If *Coriolanus* is Shakespeare's last tragedy, as entertained by Philip Brockbank,[76] it suggests a new, more ironic relation toward the genre on the part of its author: a new assessment, perhaps, of the claims to a heroic individualism made in other tragedies, and a new interest in articulating the social character of experience, a dimension of life that tragedy, with its tendency to bring about a powerful identification with the individual hero, is less concerned to articulate. (*Lear,* as we have seen, pulls in both directions, allowing identification with the king, yet troubling this on communal grounds.) Coriolanus himself, however, is an especially unbending proponent of this tragic ideology of supreme individualism—yet the play as a whole shows self-authoring to be suicidal. Moreover, his assertiveness and egoistic absolutism are felt as alien even by the patricians themselves, for, as Anne Barton has suggested, he seems to embody a peculiarly archaic or primitive stage of aristocratic ideology, one less accommodationist than that now required, more suited to "the plains of Troy" than to "an evolving republic" developing complex political institutions.[77] This suggests a play in which the ideology of tragedy is criticized from the viewpoint of the public good: Coriolanus's heroic self-regard is dangerously outmoded from the point of view of the commonwealth. No other Shakespearean tragic hero is from the outset so completely antisocial, a point emphasized in the incivility of Coriolanus's first lines, a discourtesy Macbeth, for example, has descended to only by the end of that play. The First Citizen's comment that all Coriolanus's deeds have been done not for Rome but "to please his mother, and to be partly proud" (1.1.38–39) is perceptive: Coriolanus disdains all custom and communal symbolism, such as the "gown of humility" (stage direction, 2.3.39). No other Shakespearean tragedy articulates so explicitly this conflict between a collective viewpoint and tragic egoism. The suggestion here, then, is that Coriolanus embodies a social-cultural mode that in literary terms would be called tragic, but which this "tragedy" criticizes as ideology. Coriolanus is a tragic hero in a post-tragic world, in which exceptional personalities are measured against the claims of increasingly institutionalized collectivities —he is out of place in a world in which tragic values are being superseded by a political conception of life.[78] If this is so, *Coriolanus* can yet be spoken of :n terms similar to those we might bring to the analysis of other Shakespearean tragedies, for it articulates a sense of historical change found in *Richard II, Lear, Hamlet,* and *Macbeth:* a sense of the passing of an old order and the wrenching birth of modernity. But at the same time *Coriolanus* resembles *Lear* in another respect: the appearance of going beyond the tragic evocation of historical crisis and change to a perspective at odds with the social assumptions of tragedy itself.

Epilogue

This book has considered the social significance of some discursive modes and traditional literary forms in the English Renaissance. I have focused on works preoccupied with social difference (and articulating this, as I have emphasized, in a variety of ways) and that indicate an awareness of the possible public significance of modes—that see them as socially symbolic. Thus the essay has tried to combine the formal and social-historical study of Renaissance literature. Despite, by now, many cultural accounts of writing in this period, many of these neglect the modes of sixteenth- and seventeenth-century literature: it seems we still need a *history* of *forms* for this era, one accounting for the public meanings and roles of the age's literary and discursive conventions. There should be no barrier between historicist and formal approaches. Indeed, social descriptions of English Renaissance literary culture that lack an account of modes and forms, including the First Folio genres as well as others, are probably incomplete social descriptions.

A social account of types of writing involves a conception of society. But contemporary historicist studies of English Renaissance culture sometimes have a rather reductive, oversimplified view of this period's social relations, which derives ultimately from what Heather Dubrow and Richard Strier have called the "covert and at times overt Marxism" of the new historicism.[1] How should we conceive of social relations, and thus to some degree of social-literary relations, in sixteenth- and seventeenth-century England? Probably the most important task now with regard to this question is to revise that anachronistic perspective that sees Elizabethan and Jacobean society as always and fundamentally characterized by class animosity and conflict. We need to think again about approaches that appear to assume that all social life is basically a "more or less veiled civil war" between classes, periodically exploding into "open revolution."[2] Indeed, reexamining this "metaphysical philosophy of

history"[3] and its influence on approaches to English Renaissance culture
may be what is needed to grasp the nuanced quality of social-literary
relations in the period.

Abandoning, in our accounts of English Renaissance culture, the
monochromatic interpretation of Early Modern English society as a scene
of fundamental, drastic, and continuous tension, and even violent conflict,
between rich and poor, rulers and ruled, is not simply to reject the work
of Marxist literary scholars. It is, however, to recognize that such work
tends to focus on a corner of a whole picture. Radical approaches to
Early Modern England are good on certain social tensions (for example,
those between landlords and tenants). They are not so good at attending
to, or analyzing, other types of social conflict—for instance, the fact that
the typical targets of popular wrath were not ruling elites but prostitutes,
"foreigners, Catholics, Dissenters, profiteering middlemen"[4] (in other
words, those living on the margins of society). Nor do such approaches
much clarify aspects of the stability of Early Modern English society: the
desire and capacity, for example, of different social groups to live
harmoniously together, or the stabilizing effect of social norms such as
deference and neighborliness, of institutions such as patronage, or of
patriarchal ideals such as "godly magistracy."[5] Many historicist approaches to English Renaissance culture are uninterested in the ways in which
society formed a unity, and stimulated by certain social tensions and their
relation to discourse. But to downplay what might be called the successes
of the society, to overlook the resolution or even absence of tensions, is
to give at best a one-sided interpretation of social, and thus perhaps of
social-literary, relations in Renaissance England.

Although Marxism is indeed describable as a universal, antihistorical
"historiosophy,"[6] a feature of some academic cultural Marxism has been
a respect for the local situatedness of literary works. Doubtless the now
frequently disowned, "scientific" pretensions of classical Marxism lie
behind this commitment, but Walter Cohen's recent criticism of
neohistoricism for being insufficiently empirical, preferring a casual,
synechdochic approach to past culture rather than a "systematic survey of
. . . available evidence," is in the spirit of this detailed, contextualizing,
topical cultural criticism.[7] Such a survey, however, will produce a more
textured, variegated picture of Tudor-Stuart social relations than that
which informs much historicist work. For some critics nothing succeeds
like failure: it is precisely those moments when English Renaissance

society breaks down into conflict that are taken to define it. But while it may be difficult to make interesting stories out of social concord, it is a simplification to see Early Modern England as characterized chiefly by class conflict and hatred.

The tendency in some historical studies to see English Renaissance social and cultural relations in terms of highly dramatic conflicts is discernible in Annabel Patterson's *Shakespeare and the Popular Voice.*[8] In many ways this book departs from familiar emphases in contemporary historical approaches, most obviously in its attempt to reconstruct a nonelite culture. Nevertheless, aspects of its approach are shared by other historicizing treatments of English Renaissance literature, and are usefully considered here.

Shakespeare and the Popular Voice is a contentious title, for even if we accept (what is controversial) that there was in Shakespeare's day a "people," a distinct entity with its own perspective or "voice," a problem arises as to number: why not "voices"? Why should "the people" view their world in one rather than many, even incompatible, ways? The book accepts the existence of "class divisions" (2) in sixteenth-century England, arguing for "a cultural tradition of popular protest" (38), which Shakespeare, whom "common sense suggests . . . would have placed himself . . . in the category of the 'commons'" (3), articulates. Again "the popular voice" seems overly restrictive. Was this voice, traced back to the 1381 Peasant Revolt, always, even mainly, one of protest? Or is only the note of protest authentic? But the popular voice (if it existed) was very likely less monotonous than this (otherwise, it is hard to understand why England was not regularly disturbed by radical conflict). (By "commons" is meant "the people" or "those below the rank of the landed aristocracy or gentry" [2]; it is difficult to understand why Shakespeare, whose father acquired arms in 1596, who bought a comfortable Stratford house—built by a Lord Mayor, no less—and who is "gent" in his will, would count himself among "the people.")[9] On the cultural tradition of popular protest it is acknowledged that "the most important evidence" for its existence is in "texts of the dominant culture," such as Shakespeare's plays, and this preservation of symbolic protest in elite literary and nonliterary works is called "ventriloquism," after Macherey (41). This term, however, itself raises the complex problem of the status of these texts, how far they record "the popular voice" and how far, instead, they endow what is mute or inarticulate with a voice expressing elite perceptions of popular beliefs, attitudes, motives, and so on. This source problem is particularly delicate in Tudor England, where there seems to have existed a tendency among the elite to exaggerate the likelihood of popular disorders or, when they did occur, their extent and severity. These "ventriloquizing" texts suggest that sixteenth-century England was riven by class conflict. How likely is this?

Patterson discusses *A Midsummer Night's Dream* in the context of "the abortive Oxfordshire rising of November 1596, when Bartholomew Stere, a carpenter, and Richard Bradshawe, a miller, had planned an anti-enclosure riot of distinctly violent proportions" (55). The play's relation to "festivity" needs to be carefully interpreted, "not least because . . . [it was] easy . . . for festival or carnival events to get out of control and become riots, or . . . serve as the pretext of organized class warfare" (56). The "surfac[ing]" of a popular "class consciousness" (57) in the *Dream* is analyzed, the approach being based on a social context of violent class confrontation, especially in London, where there were "at least thirteen disturbances in 1595 alone . . . of which twelve took place between 6 and 29 June, that is to say, in . . . Midsummer season" (56). Midsummer in 1591 and 1592 had been marred by other disturbances: "the small but highly dramatic rebellion [or 'popular uprising' (37)] of the crazed prophet William Hacket in July 1591" (35), and a "riot" (37) the next year by "Southwark feltmakers" (35) outside the Marshalsea Prison, which is seen as a class protest against social injustice. Around the time he came to write *A Midsummer Night's Dream,* it is argued, Shakespeare's "environment was, if anything, even more disturbed than it had been in 1591–2" (56): the tumult of 29 June, for instance, "involved 1,000 rioters, a mixture of artisans and apprentices . . . , took several days to suppress, and concluded . . . with the execution of five persons" (56).

This situating of the play in an environment of fierce class contradiction has methodological and interpretive problems that, as I have suggested, are not unique to *Shakespeare and the Popular Voice.* For what is missing in the invocation of these events is precisely that density of historical context which, to be fully understood, they need. They require themselves to be historicized. To take the first event first, William Hacket's antics. As Christopher Haigh describes it, Hacket, having "decided he was the new Messiah . . . announced that Elizabeth had been deposed. He sent his two apostles out into the streets of London 'and tell them in the city that Christ Jesus is come with his fan in his hand to judge the earth. And if any man ask you where he is, tell them he is at Walker's house, by Broken Wharf.' "[10] As Patterson acknowledges, only a small number of people heeded Hacket's call. The question then arises whether such an incident, involving very few people (and led by a madman), merits being considered a "popular uprising"? Surely the significance of this event for understanding the social "environment" of London in the early 1590s is at least unclear. Similarly with the events (or rather nonevents) in Oxfordshire. What is the social significance of a "rising" that never happened, that "came to nothing" because its "leaders could find no followers" (55)?[11] This incident may tell us many things about Oxfordshire in 1596, but turbulent class conflict is not among them.

With the 1592 disturbance outside the Marshalsea, or the riots of June 1595, we are on firmer ground: in each case something substantial occurred. But the significance of these events becomes less certain when we examine them closely and in context. At the least, we have to admit their meaning is not obvious.

Roger B. Manning, whom Patterson cites, says of the circumstances surrounding the 1592 disturbance:

> The trouble began when the deputies of the knight marshall [a royal official] arrested and imprisoned a felt-maker in a particularly violent manner. [Some time after] . . . a large group of felt-makers made plans to break into the Marshalsea Prison and rescue him. As they approached the Marshalsea, the knight marshal's men sallied forth and attacked the felt-makers with cudgels and daggers.[12]

Patterson considers the felt-makers' protests evidence of "political consciousness" and their "focus on the prison . . . a way of appealing, symbolically, against injustice conceived on a broader scale" (36). Here the empirical thickness of these events begins to fade before the abstract notion of class struggle. Clearly the felt-makers were retaliating on behalf of one of their number, who had been roughly and high-handedly treated by the marshalmen (an original offense compounded by their later thuggery outside the prison). But what requires the view that the felt-makers' actions were *political,* that they were acting as "the people" against specifically *elite* oppression ("injustice conceived on a broader scale")? The felt-makers were certainly protesting an abuse (and were, we should note, afterward backed up by one member of the city elite: the Lord Mayor, who, Steve Rappaport notes, "wrote to the queen's lord treasurer suggesting that the marshalmen be admonished for their behaviour and warned to use more discretion in the future when serving warrants").[13] The Privy Council rebuked the felt-makers' "bad and mischeivous intencion," but we cannot regard this as necessarily the same thing as a "seditious intention" (35), for what the Council regarded as seditious was often not that, at least not in any meaningful sense of the word—unless we suppose that virtually any disorderly conduct in Elizabethan England "symbolically" challenged the regime. As presented, however, the events do not compel the interpretation that the felt-makers were acting as a class against the injustice of a ruling group or social system. Nor do they require this symbolic interpretation to be explained.

The June 1595 "food riots"[14] were grave enough. But there is danger in treating this episode in isolation, as if it was symptomatic of a chronically diseased body politic—when the crucial point is that it was atypical. Even if the riots *could* be shown to be lower-class insurrections against the social structure, their significance would be lost unless it was recognized that they were exceptional in size, duration, and severity. Generally speaking, disturbances in sixteenth-century London were small-scale, brief affairs.[15] And even the 1595 riots, occurring in a period that saw, with four bad harvests, the worst distress of the century, were hardly apocalyptic: "It appears," writes Rappaport of the riot on the 29 June (the most serious in many years), "that no one died in [it], that there was little damage to property, and that it faded from memory soon after its end."[16] Indeed, notwithstanding these riots or the many other difficulties London faced in this period, its "fundamental stability . . . is not," for Ian Archer, "in question."[17] This stability, like the kingdom's as a whole, had many causes, and it is worthwhile recalling some of them. I rely here especially on Archer's *The Pursuit of Stability*. Archer, it should be noted, is no Merrie Englander: he acknowledges tensions between social groups but stresses as well the factors integrating City life. Above all, he is concerned to explain why it was that, though "the social fabric was highly flammable, . . . it failed to ignite" (257).[18]

A main cause of stability was England's success in feeding itself, so that, despite "sustained population pressure" after 1520, there was, as John Guy notes, no "major national subsistence calamity."[19] In London, though poverty existed, most people "were not merely subsisting" and "the middling sort" were the majority.[20] The London rulers were not indifferent to the life of the populace, and in hard times "energetically organised the provisioning of the capital": "that London escaped serious disorder in the 1590s is tribute to the elite's responsiveness to popular grievances" (259).[21] Moreover, while "ameliorative social policies" (149) did not always meet demand, they did defuse tensions;[22] generally, Poor Relief reinforced "habits of deference and subordination,"[23] casting the needy "in the role of petitioners . . . [dependent] on their wealthier neighbours" (99; see also 203). Another factor enhancing stability in London was the small number of City dynasties: as a result, "the elite may . . . have been popularly perceived as open to men of talent" (51).[24] The rulers, often of relatively humble backgrounds, seem not to have regarded themselves as a race apart: "the corporate ideal" was strong in the City (259).[25]

Perhaps ideology was the most important cause of stability. The prevailing familial or paternal theory of government[26] restrained rulers, encouraging them to govern for the commonweal. The responsibilities of the powerful to the weak were continually stressed: "Magistrates repeatedly had held before them the patriarchal ideal, combining as it did love with justice."[27] As Archer puts it:

> The character of sixteenth-century government cannot be understood without reference to the ideals which shaped magisterial performance. . . . The primary obligation of the magistrate was to ensure that the word of God be set forth in preaching. . . . But rulers also had wider obligations to their subjects. The rich in general were constantly reminded that they held their wealth as stewards and therefore that they had an active duty to care for the poor, in giving alms, in not rack-renting their tenants, and in showing forbearance to poor debtors. . . . It would be wrong to present the elite as an oligarchy of rapacious extortioners ruling entirely in their own interests. 'Commonwealth' ideals clearly played a part in their approach to the government of the City. Their rule was shaped by the prevailing religious rhetoric.[28]

Social cohesion in Early Modern times was also enhanced by "the universal phenomenon of patronage," which, as Perez Zagorin has emphasized, encouraged "vertical integration and the formation of solidarities between higher and lower status groups"—a main reason for the vertically bonded character of revolts (or their tendency to unite people from widely different social levels).[29] The centrality of patronage in every sphere of life in Early Modern England is stressed by Derek Hirst: "All must look upwards for advancement and aid; and in doing so they acknowledged the demands of hierarchy."[30] Apprenticeship, of course, was fundamentally a patronage relation (216–17), and, in general, "vertical solidarities" were probably more significant, in town and country, than horizontal, or class, ones.[31] The ethic of neighborhood, embodied in parish and local government, was important in generating "loyalties which [could] transcend social divisions" (82; see also 80–92). On the other hand, solidarity among the less well-off seems to have been rare: in London, for instance, there is little evidence of livery companies cooperating to attain popular goals, and commonly they were in conflict. Indeed, while London's rulers

> were united, . . . the populace they ruled was weak and divided. A model of social relations based on the straightforward dichotomy between elite and populace has serious limitations because of the divisions among the poorer inhabitants of the City. The craft-bounded horizons of many Londoners acted as a barrier to common action, and craftsmen in different companies with common grievances, for example against aliens and foreigners, were competitors on other issues. (258; see also 98, 145–48)

In an essay, "The Social Order of Early Modern England: Three Approaches," Keith Wrightson has attempted a solution to a problem that has clearly been at the center of this book: the relative strengths in this period of "vertical" and "horizontal" social ties.[32] There is evidence for the importance of both these commitments, yet often they are seen as incompatible. Wrightson thinks this either/or approach inadequate, proposing instead that "'vertical' and 'horizontal' social alignments are not mutually exclusive":[33] people can and do conceive of themselves, at different times and in different circumstances, as related primarily to people on their own social level, or to people above or below them. Instead of thinking of Renaissance England as either "a vertically aligned hierarchy or a class society," Wrightson argues, we need "to recognize the variety, flexibility and ambivalence of social relations in this period rather than to explain them away."[34] Wrightson's approach is not, it seems to me, merely a case of splitting the difference; what it commends is a dynamic, realistic, empirical interpretation of Tudor-Stuart social life. Currently, historicist accounts of English Renaissance literary culture often rely upon a rigid, overdrawn conception of Early Modern society that focuses on social contradiction to the exclusion of much else that is important. This book has tried to convey something of the "variety, flexibility and ambivalence of social relations" in Early Modern England as they are articulated in, and articulate, modes of writing. It has argued that certain English Renaissance texts are engaged with social difference pervasively, profoundly, and variously, and that they understand literary and discursive modes as socially symbolic, or as inextricably related to social hierarchies. It has, however, rejected the assumption that the only significant social relations in this period are ones of contradiction, or that only these social relations count in the period's literary art. There is work to be done in developing styles of analysis flexible enough to comprehend the ways in which this complex society inscribes itself in literature.

Notes

Introduction

1. Date of composition and of the royal performance are taken from the edition by Arvin H. Jupin (New York, 1987), 3, 15. There were at least seventeen editions between 1598 and 1668 (9), and there is other "ample evidence" (30) of the play's popularity (see 28–32). All references, by scene and line numbers, are to the text edited by Russell A. Fraser and Norman Rabkin in vol. 1 of their *Drama of the English Renaissance* (New York, 1976).

2. Muriel Bradbrook, "Shakespeare and the Use of Disguise in Elizabethan Drama," notes that Elizabethan "disguises generally mean a drop in social status" (she cites *Mucedorus, Edward IV, George a' Greene,* and *When You See Me, You Know Me*), and that Robin Hood seems to lie somewhere behind the convention: see her *Aspects of Dramatic Form in the English and the Irish Renaissance* (Brighton, England, 1983), 35.

3. I borrow the term from Durkheim, who intends by it the "exterior" (or objective), as well as "coercive," character of social phenomena: see *The Rules of Sociological Method,* 8th ed., trans. Sarah A. Solovay and John H. Mueller; ed. George E. G. Catlin (New York, 1966), 1–14.

4. This leveling sentiment, along with others like it, is recorded in R. W. Dent's *Proverbial Language in English Drama Exclusive of Shakespeare, 1495–1616: An Index* (Berkeley, 1984), 450.

5. G. K. Hunter's account of *Mucedorus*'s generic self-consciousness (in his *English Drama: 1585–1642,* forthcoming in the *Oxford History of English Literature*) may be compared to Jupin's in his edition, who likens the play to Peele's *Old Wives Tale* as a "self-conscious" ironization of romance conventions (71). Hunter's "Flatcaps and Bluecoats: Visual Signals on the Elizabethan Stage," *Essays and Studies* 33 (1980), analyzing dramatists' manipulation of the significance of Tudor dress codes, and stressing the extent to which character in sixteenth- and seventeenth-century drama is an effect of social station (visually indicated by such codes), has been useful to me in formulating the concerns of the plays discussed here.

6. A play reminiscent of *Mucedorus* in this respect is the anonymous *The Rare Triumphs of Love and Fortune* (written 1582 and published 1589; ed. John Isaac Owen [New York, 1979]), in which Venus (or Comedy) and Fortune (or Tragedy) debate the outcome of a romance between Hermione and Fidelia. The self-consciousness about genre here seems, again, tied to an interest in the complications of status, the play veering

Notes

Notes 153

Notes

toward tragedy (and the hero being banished from court) because Fidelia's father King Phizantius has been "Unwitting of his [i.e., Hermione's] linage" (line 1771): "for had I knowne it so, / [Hermione] had never tasted of this woe" (lines 1769–70). Likewise, the reconciliation of comedy and tragedy, in which "every thing united is by love" (line 1833), turns upon a discovery of proper social identities and relations: "For tis not so; he is not borne so base / . . . but of a noble race" (lines 1757–58). The quotation from the *Monk's Tale* is taken from *Chaucer's Major Poetry*, ed. Albert C. Baugh (Englewood Cliffs, N.J., 1963), line B3182.

7. See vol. 8 of *A Select Collection of Old English Plays* . . . by Robert Dodsley . . . , 4th ed., revised and enlarged by W. Carew Hazlitt (London, 1874), 205. The texts in Dodsley are based on the editions of 1601. Further references, also by volume and page, are included in the text.

8. Cf. 8.153: "No man must presume to call our master / By name of Earl, Lord, Baron, Knight, or Squire; / But simply by the name of Robin Hood."

9. Cf. Janet Spens, *An Essay on Shakespeare's Relation to Tradition* (Oxford, 1916), on *As You Like It* and *The Two Gentlemen of Verona*: "What Shakespeare gets [from Munday's plays and the Robin Hood legends] is the suggestion of the free life in the forest" (33).

10. On the ideal of a "divinely appointed hierarchy" underpinning the Tudor social structure, see D. M. Palliser, *The Age of Elizabeth: England under the Later Tudors: 1547–1603* (London, 1983), 80, and 79–83. A book still useful for its articulation of the official self-image of Tudor society—though misleading if taken as a simple gloss on the period's literature, and requiring to be supplemented by an awareness of the actual "fluidity" of Elizabethan society (Palliser, *Age of Elizabeth*, 84)—is E. M. W. Tillyard's *The Elizabethan World Picture* (London, 1943).

11. Disguise features prominently: Robin is a "citizen" (8.126), the Bishop of Ely a poor countryman (8.180ff.), John a "woodman" (8.199; 195–99).

12. Andrew Gurr, *Playgoing in Shakespeare's London* (Cambridge, England, 1987), 49. On "the Tudors' obsession with status," and its daily expression in conventions of speech and behavior, dress, diet, tombs, architecture, and so forth, see Palliser, *Age of Elizabeth*, 77, 81–83. Lawrence Stone, *The Crisis of the Aristocracy: 1558–1641* (Oxford, 1965) likewise regards Tudor-Stuart people as "obsessed" with status (223). Harold Perkin's discussion of "the formal sense of hierarchy" in "the old [i.e., pre-nineteenth century] society" in England emphasizes that "differential status was part of the given, unquestioned environment into which men were born, and they proclaimed it by every outward sign: manner, speech, deportment, dress, liveried equipage, size of house and household, the kind and quantity of the food they ate": *The Origins of Modern English Society: 1780–1880* (London, 1969; repr. 1976), 24–25. The phrase "social symbolism" is borrowed from Fredric Jameson, *The Political Unconscious: Narrative as a Socially Symbolic Act* (Ithaca, N.Y., 1981).

13. In "The King Disguised: Shakespeare's *Henry V* and the Comical History," in *The Triple Bond: Plays, mainly Shakespearean, in Performance*, ed. Joseph G. Price (University Park, Pa., 1975), Anne Barton shows how disguise in Heywood's *Edward IV* and Peele's *Edward I* and *George a' Greene* realizes a romantic fantasy of relaxed popular-ruler interaction (96–99). J. Churton Collins, ed., *The Plays and Poems of Robert Greene*, 2 vols. (Oxford, 1905) gives *George a' Greene* "tentatively" to Greene (2.163).

I use his text (in vol. 2); references to it are by line number. Laura Caroline Stevenson, *Praise and Paradox: Merchants and Craftsmen in Elizabethan Popular Literature* (Cambridge, England, 1984) gives dates of first performance as ca. 1587–93 (230). "Popular" is used at this point in Stevenson's restrictive sense: that is, works supposed to have enjoyed a wide audience (see *Praise and Paradox,* 11–15). A *Pinner* (or *Pinder*) is defined by *OED* 2 as "an officer whose duty it is to impound stray beasts."

   14. See the title page of the 1599 edition reproduced in *Plays and Poems of Robert Greene,* 2.181.

   15. Hunter, *English Drama,* notes this contrast in the play between courtly vice and country virtue. That "horizontal" social divisons ("class") were not the only or even chief divisions of Tudor and later society is emphasized by many historians and is obviously relevant to descriptions of the main contrasts of plays like *George a' Greene.* For Perkin, *Origins of Modern English Society,* "permanent vertical links" rather than "the horizontal solidarities of class" characterized even late eighteenth-century England: "most workers were too scattered, too isolated, too dependent upon a face-to-face relationship with a paternal employer" to have very strongly developed class feelings (49, 32). Joyce Youings, *Sixteenth Century England* (London, 1984), sees Tudor society as "remarkably . . . free from class tension" and characterized by "deep vertical, as well as horizontal divisions" and "bonds" (129, 358), rebel armies, for instance, tending to be "a microcosm of contemporary society" (209). Palliser, *Age of Elizabeth,* agrees: conflicts more often than not united "lords and their tenants . . . against other lords and tenants, villagers against men of another village" (79). All of which underscores the contemporary pertinence of M. St. Clare Byrne's warning about the need to be wary of anachronism in references to a "social order" different from our own (see "The Social Background," in *A Companion to Shakespeare Studies,* ed. Harley Granville Barker and G. B. Harrison [New York, 1934], 196 and passim). On the traditional Marxist thesis that "class divisions" have been the "chief factor determining social change" in virtually all civilizations, see Leszek Kolakowski, *The Founders,* vol. 1 of *Main Currents of Marxism: Its Origins, Growth, and Dissolution,* trans. P. S. Falla (Oxford, 1978), 357 (also his "Commentary on historical materialism," 363–75, esp. 369). Possibly French and English conditions differed greatly: in Fernand Braudel's *The Wheels of Commerce,* vol. 2 of *Civilization and Capitalism: 15th–18th Century,* trans. Siân Reynolds (London, 1982), France's peasantry is seen as "in perpetual conflict with its oppressors" and quite typical and "frankly modern" class struggles are identified in the Lyons printing industry as early as 1539 and 1572 (495, 499).

   16. "Yeoman status was accorded to men who farmed a substantial acreage, usually in excess of fifty acres. . . . Farmers of smaller acreages . . . were generally accorded the name 'husbandman'": Keith Wrightson, *English Society: 1580–1680* (New Brunswick, N.J., 1982), 31–32. Yet while they were among the "more substantial farmers," yeomen, unlike the gentry, actually worked with their servants and laborers: Youings, *Sixteenth Century England,* 121–22.

   17. See Heywood's "To the Reader," preface to *The English Traveller,* in vol. 4 of *The Dramatic Works of Thomas Heywood* (London, 1874; repr., New York, 1964), 5.

   18. For a discussion of *Edward IV, If You Know Not Me, You Know Nobody,* and *The Downfall* and *The Death of Robert Earl of Huntingdon,* plays whose "relation to history is often tenuous," see F. P. Wilson, "The English History Play," in *Shakespearian and*

Other Studies, ed. Helen Gardner (Oxford, 1969), 46, 45–53. Certainly none of these qualify as a history by Wilson's definition (that its "chief interest" be "political" [4]). For the title page to *Edward IV,* see *The Dramatic Works of Thomas Heywood,* 1.1; except for the *Four Prentices* I quote from this edition; further references, also by volume and page number, are included in the text. For the latter play I have relied upon Mary Ann Weber Gasior, ed., *The Four Prentices of London: A Critical, Old-Spelling Edition* (New York, 1980); references are by line number. Probable dates of composition for Heywood's plays are provided by Otelia Cromwell, *Thomas Heywood: A Study in the Elizabethan Drama of Everyday Life* (New Haven, Conn., 1928), 162, 44–46, and 49–50; I have followed, however, the more conservative dates in Blakemore Evans's *Annals* (but see Gasior, xiv–xv, who is fairly confident on a date of 1594 for the *Four Prentices*).

19. A similar case could be made for the anonymous "history" *The Famous Victories of Henry the Fifth* (ca. 1583–88; pub. 1598) which, less politically shrewd than Shakespeare's *Henry IV,* features an easygoing Prince whose participation in the disreputable world of Sir John ("Jockey") Oldcastle, Ned and Tom is wholehearted rather than strategic ("We are all fellowes, I tell you sirs, and the King / My father were dead, we would be all Kings" [lines 93–94]). Although the dissolute companions are actually knights, the casualness of Henry's demeanor betokens a certain rapport with less sophisticated types (even if the strictly low-life world of the play, embodied in Dericke the clown, is not one with which Henry is associated). Hal, of course, is a more complex, remote figure, more obviously regal, than the Harry of *Famous Victories*—and Shakespeare, of course, does not show him committed to the Fleet (line 370): see the 1598 text in vol. 4 of *Narrative and Dramatic Sources of Shakespeare,* ed. Geoffrey Bullough (London, 1962). Samuel Rowley's *When You See Me, You Know Me, or The Famous Chronicle Historie of King Henrie the Eight, With the Birth and Vertuous Life of Edward Prince of Wales* (1604; pub. 1605), ed. Karl Elze (Dessau, 1874), also enjoys situations of unorthodox social interplay: so Henry is mistakenly thrown in the Counter, which is transformed for "one night" into "king Henry's court" (37); a certain rough comradeliness arises there between him and the notorious "masterless man" Black Will (36); and note the sometimes amazing extent to which Will Summers's "tongue is privileged" (42): "Out of my way, old Harry . . . " (7).

20. Most historians agree that the "crucial" social distinction was between gentleman and commoner, gentility being defined as "the virtue, education, and capacity necessary to govern"; Palliser, *Age of Elizabeth,* 70. Cf. Wrightson, *English Society,* 22–26: "A gentleman stood apart, and the possession of gentility constituted one of the most fundamental dividing lines in society" (23); see also L. A. Clarkson, *The Pre-Industrial Economy in England: 1500–1750* (London, 1971), 36. A slightly different point of view is represented by Youings, *Sixteenth Century England:* "the great distinction" was between those who, although not noble or even gentle, were "of a 'sufficiency'" and so capable of "public responsibility," and those others who "were fit, in Sir Thomas Smith's phrase, 'only to be ruled' " (45–46).

21. D. M. Lucas, ed., *Poetics* (Oxford, 1968), comments that *spoudaios* and *phaulos* "indicate the two ends of the ordinary, aristocratically based, Greek scale of values. . . . It is the mark of the *spoudaios* to concern himself with the pursuit of *aretē* [excellence], which . . . is centred on honour. The *phaulos* is an inferior being . . . because his capabilities and ambitions are mean" (63); he cites Thucydides 7.77.2 for *phaulos*

meaning "common soldier." S. H. Butcher, *Aristotle's Theory of Poetry and Fine Art,* 4th ed. (1911; repr. New York, 1951), translates *spoudaious/phaulous* as "men . . . of a higher or a lower type" (11), commenting that "Aristotle does undoubtedly hold that the chief actors in tragedy ought to be illustrious by birth and position" (237); French neoclassicism, however, erroneously made him say that "outward rank [was] the distinguishing feature of tragic as opposed to comic representation" (238). Cf. Raymond Williams, *Modern Tragedy* (Stanford, Calif., 1966), who argues that among the Greeks, "rank and heroic stature" indicated "the general importance of the action," but medieval to neoclassic notions of tragedy tended to stress "exalted rank" for its own sake (22, 25).

22. See vol. 2 of *Elizabethan Critical Essays,* ed. G. Gregory Smith (Oxford, 1904), 35. On the distinction between tragedy and comedy as based mainly on rank, see J. E. Spingarn, *A History of Literary Criticism in the Renaissance,* 2d ed. (1908; repr. New York, 1954), 60–74.

23. Note, for example, the following headings: "In what Forme of Poesie the Great Princes and Dominators of the World were Honored" (Book One, Chapter xvi); "Of Historicall Poesie, by which the Famous Acts of Princes and the Vertuous and Worthy Lives of Our Forefathers were Reported" (Book One, Chapter xix); "In what Forme of Poesie Vertue in the Inferiour Sort was Commended" (Book One, Chapter xx). Comedy, "never medling with any Princes matters nor such high personages," deals "commonly of marchants, souldiers, artificers, good honest housholders, and also of unthrifty youthes, yong damsels, old nurses, bawds, brokers, ruffians, and parasites" (2.33).

24. This self-consciousness about modes resembles the "baring of the device," or *ostranenie* (making strange) of form, which Viktor Shklovsky found typical of modern art; and Brecht's *Verfremdungseffekt* is another parallel. Yet such concepts must be invoked cautiously for, as Fredric Jameson notes, they are implicitly "polemic," dedicated to "the negation of the existing habits of thought or perception"; and such a "critical" or "revolutionary" stance (familiar in modernist aesthetic culture, with its manifestoes, movements, avant-gardes, and bellicose rhetoric) is often absent in the sixteenth-century works under consideration (which often have a complicated, ambiguous relation to the modes they defamiliarize). See *The Prison-House of Language: A Critical Account of Structuralism and Russian Formalism* (Princeton, 1972), 90, 43–101.

25. I draw here on Stephen Greenblatt's *Shakespearean Negotiations: The Circulation of Social Energy in Renaissance England* (Berkeley, 1988): "Mimesis is always accompanied by—indeed is always produced by—negotiation and exchange" (12).

26. See Priscilla Parkhurst Ferguson, Philippe Desan, and Wendy Griswold, "Mirrors, Frames, and Demons: Reflections on the Sociology of Literature," *Critical Inquiry* 14 (1988): "In one way or another the reflection model supports practically all work in the sociology of literature" (427). The authors complicate this "discredited" (428) model by arguing that literature produces "structured misreflections" of the real (429)—a formulation, of course, still involving referentiality.

27. Claims to gentility became more frequent throughout the period (Youings, *Sixteenth Century England,* 320), but according to Wrightson, *English Society,* contemporary descriptions of the social hierarchy reveal some degree of confusion about "criteria of social rank" (19); Palliser, *Age of Elizabeth,* notes that "the lines of social demarcation were often blurred" (60). Cf. *The Rare Triumphs of Love and Fortune,* where the following exchange takes place between a Parasite and a Servant:

Penulo: Horeson pesant, seest thou not what I am?

Lentulo: Troth, sir, I see you have a good dublet and a pair of hose;
          But now a dayes there is so many goes
          So like Gentlemen, that such a poore fellow as I
          Know not how a Gentleman from a knave to spye.

                                                    (lines 683–87)

28. Date of composition and first performance is taken from Sheldon P. Zitner, ed., *The Knight of the Burning Pestle* (Manchester, 1984), 10–12; the play was published in 1613 (1). All references, by act and line number, are to this edition, and included in the text.

29. See, for example, their remarks to the Merrythoughts at 3.190–97, 3.287–89, and 3.539–49.

30. Nell softens at one point to remark that Merrythought is "a fine old man" (2.474–75)—but the general attitude is disapproval.

31. Thus, according to Edwin Haviland Miller, medieval romances (and ballads, jest-books and bawdy tales) were probably enjoyed by the Tudor elite, and became definitely low-brow only after about 1625: *The Professional Writer in Elizabethan England: A Study of Non-Dramatic Literature* (Cambridge, Mass., 1959), 75–85. (But see also Louis B. Wright, *Middle Class Culture in Elizabethan England* [Chapel Hill, N.C., 1935], who suggests that from about the midsixteenth century onward knightly romances appealed mainly to the "middle" or "lower classes" [376].) Frances Yates has discussed the romantic "refeudalization" of the Elizabethan court: see her "Elizabethan Chivalry: The Romance of the Accession Day Tilts," in *Astraea: The Imperial Theme in the Sixteenth Century* (1975; repr. London, 1985), 108. Even by the eighteenth century Johnson apparently had a life-long "fondness" for "romances of chivalry"; see Boswell, *Life of Johnson,* in the revised edition by R. W. Chapman (Oxford, 1970; repr., World's Classics, 1980), 36.

32. Robert Weimann, "Shakespeare (De)Canonized: Conflicting Uses of 'Authority' and 'Representation'," *New Literary History* 20 (1988), sees the gap I have noticed between Rafe and his Hotspur role as a *contradiction* operative on the Elizabethan stage generally, where "plebeian actors" impersonate royal or aristocratic personages. For Weimann, this is a relation of tension and conflict: "The represented role will clash with the representing actor" (79).

33. Nell's claim is not as outrightly laughable as the Clown's boast to Autolycus in *The Winter's Tale* after he is rewarded by Leontes: "You are well met, sir. You denied to fight with me this other day, because I was no gentleman born. See you these clothes? Say you see them not and think me still no gentleman born. You were best say these robes are not gentlemen born. . . . Give me the lie, do; and try whether I am not now a gentleman born" (5.2.128–34). The phrase "gentleman born" had proverbial status and is used seriously in Deloney (the motto to *The Gentle Craft,* Part One [pub. 1598] is "A Shoomakers sonne is a Prince borne"; see the reproduction of the 1627 title page in *The Novels of Thomas Deloney,* ed. Merritt E. Lawlis [Bloomington, Ind., 1961]). In Dekker's *The Shoemaker's Holiday,* ed. R. L. Smallwood and Stanley Wells (Manchester, England, 1979), Simon Eyre the shoemaker is not ridiculous, though made to exclaim "Peace, am I not Simon Eyre? Are not these my brave men, brave shoemakers, all gentlemen of the

Gentle Craft? Prince am I none, yet am I nobly born, as being the sole son of a shoemaker" (sc. 7, lines 47–50). *The Oxford Dictionary of Proverbs,* 3d ed., revised by F. P. Wilson (Oxford, 1970), has 1592 for the first usage of "gentle craft" (in Greene's *Quip for an Upstart Courtier*).

34. The amateurism of privileged milieux is conspicuous in the dedication to the *Old Arcadia:* "This idle work of mine. . . . which I am loath to father"; "a trifle, and that triflingly handled"; see *The Countess of Pembroke's Arcadia: (The Old Arcadia)*, ed. Jean Robertson (Oxford, 1973), 3. Richard Helgerson, *Self-Crowned Laureates: Spenser, Jonson, Milton and the Literary System* (Berkeley, 1983), discusses Renaissance literary amateurism, including Sidney's (21–39).

35. On Jonson as (at least temporarily) "the King's poet," moving "with confidence in the exclusive circle of the rich, the well-born, the powerful, and the learned," see Helgerson, *Self-Crowned Laureates,* 162. Nashe was at one time friendly with the family of Sir George Carey, but seems early on to have given up hope of noble patronage: Donald J. McGinn, *Thomas Nashe* (Boston, 1981), 22–23, 18.

36. This term is used by Palliser, *Age of Elizabeth* (77), in an attempt to avoid the implications "middle *class*" carries (in particular, "rise of"). While rejecting any such rise in sixteenth-century England—as well as the concomitant assumption of a distinct bourgeois "class consciousness," or, in Tawney's words, "an outlook on religion and politics" peculiar to the "business classes" and opposed to a "godless" court and "spendthrift" aristocracy: *Religion and the Rise of Capitalism* (1926; repr. West Drayton, Middlesex, 1948), 207–8—Palliser does point to "a growing self-awareness" among "'the middling sorts of men'"—this sense of common "identity" (77; see also 75–77) being distinguishable from the agonistic concept of class-consciousness. According to Kolakowski's reading of Marx, "class" necessarily involves the idea of "class-struggle": "An essential condition of the existence of a class is . . . that there should be at least the germ of class-consciousness, an elementary sense of common interest and shared opposition to other classes"; he quotes from *The Eighteenth Brumaire of Louis Bonaparte,* in which Marx writes of the French peasants of his day that "in so far as . . . the identity of their interests begets no unity, no national union and no political organization, they do not form a class" (*Main Currents,* 356).

37. See Thomas Heywood, *An Apology for Actors* (pub. 1612) in the Shakespeare Society edition (London, 1841), 49.

Chapter 1. "Playing the Knave": Social Symbolism and Interplay in Thomas Nashe

1. Ann Rosalind Jones uses these terms, with implications rather different from the approach to Nashe's writing I shall propose, in "Inside the Outsider: Nashe's *Unfortunate Traveller* and Bakhtin's Polyphonic Novel," *ELH* 50 (1983): 61–81.

2. The distinction between popular and elite cultural life is for this period somewhat arbitrary: C. L. Barber, for instance, notes how Elizabethan "Courtly entertainments . . . reflected the popular tradition of seasonal holidays" and that "courtiers themselves" took part in "traditional popular pastimes" on Elizabeth's progresses (*Shakespeare's Festive*

Comedy: A Study of Dramatic Form and Its Relation to Social Custom [Princeton, 1959], 30, 31), and Palliser, *Age of Elizabeth,* rejects "any division of Tudor culture into 'literary' and 'popular'" as simplistic (353). Courtiers read "popular" literature (see introduction, n. 31), H. H. Furness remarking of the jest-book Beatrice refers to in *Much Ado About Nothing*—namely, *The Hundred Merry Tales*—that "there is a tradition that this book and others like it, were the solace of Queen Elizabeth's dying hours"; and he quotes from "an intercepted letter" among Venetian diplomatic correspondence, where, after describing her ailments, it is noted that she "delighteth to heare some of the 100 merry tales": see his *New Variorum* edition of *Much Adoe About Nothing* (Philadelphia, 1899), 72. (I owe this reference to G. K. Hunter.) Participation in "popular" entertainment by the elites of pre–eighteenth-century Europe makes Peter Burke stress the difficulty of drawing a clear division between learned and popular culture, between which there was a "two-way traffic"; see *Popular Culture in Early Modern Europe* (London, 1978), 24, 58. Cf. L. C. Knights, *Drama and Society in the Age of Jonson* (London, 1937), invoking the idea of "organic community" (313) and citing Yeats: "the art of the people was as closely mingled with the art of the coteries as was the speech of the people . . . with the unchanging speech of the poets" (11; and see 141). A similar perspective is found in Marxist scholarship on the Elizabethan theater, though here the stress is on a "unity-in-contradiction"; cf. Robert Weimann, *Shakespeare and the Popular Tradition in the Theatre: Studies in the Social Dimension of Dramatic Form and Function,* ed. Robert Schwartz (Baltimore, 1978; repr., 1987): the public theater was "a national institution . . . 'a theatre of the people and of the court'"; Shakespeare's "multidimensionality would have been impossible without the deeply rooted contradictions of the Elizabethan social order" (172; 246). See also Walter Cohen, *"The Merchant of Venice* and the Possibilities of Historical Criticism," *ELH* 49 (1982): "Shakespeare's plays" were "an achievement that depended on a comparative social and cultural unity, long since lost, in the nation as well as the theater" (766). See, finally, the important review article by David Harris Sacks, "Searching for 'Culture' in the English Renaissance," *Shakespeare Quarterly* 39 (1988), which criticizes notions such as "popular" or "elite" culture for the impression they give of some absolute separation between the two: "Once we assume the existence of dominant and subordinate classes, no class can be said to have a truly independent culture. For culture will be shaped in the relationship between the contesting groups. . . . each group may have an independent viewpoint regarding key issues and ideas, but all must participate, if only in conflict and disagreement, in the common culture formed by their relationships to one another" (480).

    3. The title page is reproduced in *The Complete Works of John Lyly,* ed. R. Warwick Bond, 3 vols. (Oxford, 1902), 2.1. Further references, also by volume and page number, are included in the text. G. K. Hunter analyzes what title pages of Elizabethan plays reveal about contemporary aesthetic expectations in "Shakespeare's Tragic Sense as It Strikes Us Today," in *Shakespeare: Pattern of Excelling Nature,* ed. David Bevington and Jay L. Halio (Cranbury, N.J., 1978), 81–88. The epigraph from Lyly is in Bond (1.272). Cf. Apelles in *Campaspe* (ca. 1580–84; pub. 1584): "For as in garden knottes diversitie of odours make a more sweet savor, or as in musicke divers strings cause a more delicate consent, so in painting, the more colours, the better counterfeit" (Bond, 2.340).

    4. Of the "fower partes belonging to Elocution," explains Wilson, "exornation" is that overseeing the "gorgious beautifying of the tongue with borrowed wordes, and change of

sentence or speech with much varietie"; figural language too "helpeth much for varietie": see the extracts in *English Literary Criticism: The Renaissance,* ed. O. B. Hardison (Englewood Cliffs, N.J., 1963), 38, 40, 45.

5. *Essays of John Dryden,* ed. W. P. Ker (Oxford, 1900), 1.70–71.

6. *Timber, or Discoveries,* in *Ben Jonson,* ed. Ian Donaldson (Oxford, 1985), 568. Cf. Dryden in "To the Memory of Mr. Oldham": "A noble Error, and but seldom made, / When Poets are by too much force betray'd": vol. 1 of *The Poems of John Dryden,* ed. James Kinsley (Oxford, 1958), 389.

7. *Endeavors of Art: A Study of Form in Elizabethan Drama* (Madison, Wis., 1954), 6, 20.

8. Theory "lagged behind" the drama in Renaissance England and Spain: ibid., 10—a circumstance probably facilitating Shakespeare's drama: see Wolfgang Clemen, "Characteristic Features of Shakespearian Drama," in *Shakespeare's Dramatic Art: Collected Essays* (London, 1972).

9. *Themes and Conventions of Elizabethan Tragedy,* 2d ed. (Cambridge, England, 1980), 35. Peter Alexander, *Shakespeare's Life and Art* (London, 1939) finds "Gothic" variety in Shakespeare (6), and Susan Snyder sees the "Elizabethan passion for variety" in multiple plotting and the use of multiple perspective: *The Comic Matrix of Shakespeare's Tragedies: "Romeo and Juliet," "Hamlet," "Othello," and "King Lear"* (Princeton, 1979), 29. G. K. Hunter notes that Elizabethan playwrights "seem to have sought to include as many modes of entertainment as possible and to have regarded the narrative chiefly as a means of stringing together as many and as diverse episodes of traditional entertainment as possible": *John Lyly: The Humanist as Courtier* (London, 1962), 111. A systematic account of narrative variousness and abundance in Elizabethan drama is Richard Levin's *The Multiple Plot in English Renaissance Drama* (Chicago, 1971). Levin also defends the variousness of Elizabethan plays against the homogenizing tendencies of thematic interpretations in *New Readings vs. Old Plays: Recent Trends in the Reinterpretation of English Renaissance Drama* (Chicago, 1979). Stanley Wells, "Shakespeare and Romance," in *Later Shakespeare,* ed. J. R. Brown and Bernard Harris (New York, 1967), stresses variety as a central feature of Elizabethan romances (55).

10. *English Literature in the Sixteenth Century, Excluding Drama* (Oxford, 1954), 19.

11. Cf. Rosalie Colie: "literary invention . . . in the Renaissance was largely generic" (*The Resources of Kind: Genre-Theory in the Renaissance,* ed. Barbara K. Lewalski [Berkeley, 1973], 17). Meres's mapping of contemporary literature in the most traditional generic terms seems not to have been unusual, however bizarre it seems today: see the extracts from *Palladis Tamia* (pub. 1598) in vol. 2 of *Elizabethan Critical Essays,* ed. Smith, 319–21. That "the heavens" were "hung with black" (*1 Henry VI, 1.1.1*) for tragedies would indicate that poetry was automatically thought of by genre even among the players, as G. K. Hunter has pointed out to me.

12. See, however, a critique of progressive interpretations of Renaissance culture in Hunter, *John Lyly,* 1–5. Nashe's antimedievalism is typical of humanism: see Lewis, *Sixteenth Century* (1–66), and cf. Ann Thompson, *Shakespeare's Chaucer: A Study in Literary Origins* (New York, 1978), on the Elizabethans' belief "that theirs was a new era, cut off from the darkness and ignorance of the past" (8). An archly ironic expression of the view that this "glistering" age (*Winter's Tale,* 4.1.14) was one of ever-greater literary, cultural and social sophistication occurs in Middleton's preface to Dekker's *The*

Roaring Girl, or Moll Cutpurse (ca. 1604–10; pub. 1611); see vol. 3 of *The Dramatic Works of Thomas Dekker,* ed. Fredson Bowers (Cambridge, England, 1958), 11:

> The fashion of play-making, I can properly compare to nothing, so naturally, as the alteration in apparell: For in the time of the Great-crop-doublet, your huge bombasted plaies, quilted with mighty words to leane purpose was onely then in fashion. And as the doublet fell, neater inventions beganne to set up. Now in the time of spruceness, our plaies followe the nicenes of our Garments, single plots, quaint conceits, letcherous jests, drest up in hanging sleeves, and those are fit for the Times, and the Tearmers: Such a kind of light-colour Summer stuffe, mingled with diverse colours, you shall find this published Comedy.

13. Cf. T. S. Eliot, *Elizabethan Essays* (London, 1934): "The art of the Elizabethans is an impure art," desiring "every sort of effect together" (15, 18). Perhaps *The Faerie Queene* is the period's greatest example of this general tension between a classical commitment to a closed, regular form (the projected Aristotelian scheme) and what has been called "the half-Gothic luxuriance of Elizabethan art" (see vol. 1 of *Ben Jonson,* ed. C. H. Herford and Percy Simpson [Oxford, 1925–52], 60)—that is, the romantic urge against closure, and towards multiplicity and variety (the "endlesse worke" [*F.Q.,* 4.12.1] of story).

14. Cf. Thomas Heywood, *Apology for Actors,* 53: "playes are writ with this ayme . . . to teach the subjects obedience to their king, to shew the people the untimely ends of such as have moved tumults, commotions, and insurrections." Franco Moretti, "'A Huge Eclipse': Tragic Form and the Deconsecration of Sovereignty," cites passages from Elyot, Sidney, and Puttenham assigning tragedy the role of showing the evil ends of tyrants: see *The Power of Forms in the English Renaissance,* ed. Stephen Greenblatt (Norman, Okla., 1982), 17–18. J. W. H. Atkins, in *English Literary Criticism: The Renascence,* 2d ed. (London, 1951), argues that it is at this time that properly literary values begin to supersede a medieval "utilitarian outlook" on poetry (15); nonetheless, "ethical considerations" (101) remained central, and one required of poetry "factual truth and moral teaching" (358). On the age's assumption that poetry had an ethical, didactic purpose, see Spingarn, *A History of Literary Criticism in the Renaissance,* 47, 58; E. K. Chambers, *The Elizabethan Stage* (Oxford, 1923), 1.259–60; F. P. Wilson, *The English Drama, 1485–1585,* ed. G. K. Hunter (Oxford, 1969), 85; Doran, *Endeavors of Art,* 88–97; Kenneth Muir, *Shakespeare's Comic Sequence* (New York, 1979), 3–6; and Miller, *Professional Writer,* 25.

15. Christopher Haigh, *Elizabeth I* (London, 1988), 34.

16. For the concept of order in Tudor thought, see Tillyard, *Elizabethan World Picture,* 7–15, and as the central doctrine of European Christian humanism, Douglas Bush, *English Literature in the Earlier Seventeenth Century: 1600–1660,* 2d ed. (Oxford, 1962), 35–38. Anthony Fletcher, *Tudor Rebellions* (London, 1983), quotes from the 1547 *Homily:* "Where there is no right order there reigneth all abuse, carnal liberty, enormity, sin and babylonical confusion" and refers to "the dread of anarchy," which "obsessed" official discourse (4). Paul Slack, "Poverty and Social Regulation in Elizabethan England," *The Reign of Elizabeth I,* ed. Christopher Haigh (Athens, Ga., 1985), cites Patrick Collinson on the "collective paranoia" among the better-off about growing numbers of poor people as a source of disorder, and notes that "in the latter half of

Elizabeth's reign people in authority felt threatened by rising populations, large numbers of vagrants and paupers, and the disorders they provoked" (238, 225–26); Palliser, *Age of Elizabeth*, agrees: "all Tudor governments were obsessed with the fear of revolts" (309), even though these were rare (311). Cf. Stephen Greenblatt on "the great ruling class nightmare in the Renaissance: the marauding horde, the many-headed multitude, the insatiate, giddy, and murderous crowd": "Murdering Peasants: Status, Genre, and the Representation of Rebellion," in *Representing the English Renaissance* (Berkeley, 1988), 5; and *Gorboduc* (1562; pub. 1565, 1570): "So giddy are the common peoples mindes, / So glad of chaunge, more wavering than the sea" (5.1.72–73), in *Chief Pre-Shakespearean Dramas*, ed. Joseph Quincy Adams (Boston, 1924).

17. True probably of neoclassicism generally: note how Dryden's Neander insinuates a political absolutism into the idea of aesthetic order: "coordination [that is, lack of unity] in a play is as dangerous and unnatural as in a state": *Essays*, ed. Ker, 1.71.

18. Bradbrook thinks "grave disturbances" at the playhouses "negligible": *The Rise of the Common Player: A Study of Actor and Society in Shakespeare's England* (Cambridge, Mass., 1962), 51; but for the view that the theaters were sources of crime and disorderliness, see Chambers, *Elizabethan Stage*, 1.264. Whether the stage contributed to a more important disorder, preparing the way for the "English Revolution," has recently been much debated: see Walter Cohen, *Drama of a Nation: Public Theater in Renaissance England and Spain* (Ithaca, N.Y., 1985): "the Civil War provides the main basis for assigning a progressive political impact to the drama" (27; also 161–62), and Jonathan Dollimore, *Radical Tragedy: Religion, Ideology and Power in the Drama of Shakespeare and His Contemporaries* (Brighton, England, 1984), 3–4; see also Moretti, "'A Huge Eclipse,'" 7–8. Reading these later conflicts back forty odd years into sixteenth-century society is obviously hazardous, and unconvincing to Joyce Youings, who stresses the essential resilience of Tudor society: "few Elizabethans can have had the slightest premonition" of the problems to come: *Sixteenth Century England*, 383, 384. J. P. Kenyon, *Stuart England* (London, 1978), notes that fears for the government's stability were first expressed in 1628–29 and also rejects explanations setting the war's origins deep in the past (41–42). Christopher Hill's understanding of Charles's execution as the culmination of a profound social-economic revolutionary process is totalizing and teleological according to Peter Laslett, *The World We Have Lost Further Explored*, 3d ed. (London, 1983), 182–210: "it is natural, though it may not be justifiable, to suppose that great events have great causes" (199). The view that the war had mainly "accidental," "contingent" political causes, rather than social ones, is critically discussed in the introduction to *Conflict in Early Stuart England*, ed. Richard Cust and Ann Hughes (London, 1989), 1 and passim.

19. That the players were subjected to censorship indicates this. For a discussion of the office of Master of the Revels, see Gerald Eades Bentley, *The Profession of Dramatist in Shakespeare's Time: 1590—1642* (Princeton, 1971), 145–81; according to Andrew Gurr, the censorship duties of the Master of the Revels were "taken seriously": *The Shakespearean Stage: 1574–1642*, 2d ed. (Cambridge, England, 1980), 74.

20. For the criticism of *Pericles*, see "On *The New Inn. Ode. To Himself*," in *Jonson*, ed. Donaldson, 502. Jonson's strictures of "Tales" and "Tempests" are related to this conservative suspicion for, although referring mainly to the old-fashionedness of these plays, they also take to task the debased appetite for such primitive "drolleries," an

appetite which—in flight from "nature" and truth—bespeaks a moral-social corruption: see the induction to *Bartholomew Fair* (1614; pub. 1631) in *Ben Jonson: Three Comedies*, ed. Michael Jamieson (Harmondsworth, England, 1966), lines 116–17.

21. "Population growth and inflation" were important factors of change over most of the Tudor-Stuart period: Paul Slack, *Poverty and Policy in Tudor and Stuart England* (London, 1988), 43; vagrancy was a particular problem in Tudor times, as the unemployed looked for work (44–45). The long-term price rise in England from 1500 to 1650, especialy in food (caused largely by parallel population expansion) was a general European trend: see D. C. Coleman, *The Economy of England: 1450–1750* (Oxford, 1977), 21–28.

22. *A Defence of Poetry* (pub. 1595) in *Miscellaneous Prose of Sir Philip Sidney*, ed. Katherine Duncan-Jones and Jan Van Dorsten (Oxford, 1973), 114.

23. For the judgment that this was a progressive period, witnessing "considerable economic, social, and political integration," see Palliser, *Age of Elizabeth*, 5, 378.

24. Shakespeare's histories reflect this sense of the premodern, pre-Reformation period as one of national turmoil, when lack of central control "made . . . England bleed" (epilogue, *Henry V*). For an exposition of the Elizabethan "horror of civil war," by reference to the homily *Against Disobedience and Wilfull Rebellion* (1574), see E. M. W. Tillyard, *Shakespeare's History Plays* (1944; repr. Harmondsworth, England, 1969), 75, 73–76.

25. *Jonson*, ed. Donaldson, 547. Language has an ethical dimension for Jonson: "Language most shows a man: speak, that I may see thee" (574; both quotations from *Timber*).

26. Haigh remarks "the limited coercive power of early modern governments": *Elizabeth I*, 173; and see Palliser, *Age of Elizabeth*, 302.

27. Weimann, *Shakespeare*, 173. The passage is found in Bond's edition, 3.115.

28. Stone, *The Crisis of the Aristocracy*, quotes Stubbes's *Anatomy of Abuses* (pub. 1583) on the dissolution of traditional social distinctions in dress: "such a confuse mingle mangle of apparell . . . that it is verie hard to knowe who is noble, who is worshipfull, who is a gentleman, who is not. . . . This is a great confusion & a general disorder" (28). J. B. Black, *The Reign of Elizabeth: 1558–1603*, 2d ed. (1936; Oxford, 1959) discusses the "'babylonian confusion' of classes" (268), especially as manifested in apparel: cited by Robert Weimann, "History and the Issue of Authority in Representation: The Elizabethan Theater and the Reformation," *New Literary History* 17 (1986): 468.

29. Williams, *Modern Tragedy*, rejected the "Elizabethan World Picture" conception: "the description of an Elizabethan and Jacobean sense of order [disregards] the extraordinary tensions of a culture moving towards violent internal conflict and substantial transformation" (53); and cf. Dollimore, *Radical Tragedy*: "The main tradition in Anglo-American literary criticism has been preoccupied, aesthetically and ideologically, with . . . 'a problem of *order*' " (5).

30. Greenblatt, "Murdering Peasants," 16.

31. G. R. Hibbard, *Thomas Nashe: A Critical Introduction* (London, 1962), 61–62. Stephen S. Hilliard, *The Singularity of Thomas Nashe* (Lincoln, Nebr., 1986), comments similarly on the "chaotic" *Unfortunate Traveller* (134).

32. *The First Part of the Return from Parnassus*, lines 1032–33 in *The Three Parnassus Plays: 1598–1601*, ed. J. B. Leishman (London, 1949).

33. For Chettle, see S. Schoenbaum, *William Shakespeare: A Compact Documentary Life,* rev. ed. (New York, 1987), 154.
34. Lewis, *Sixteenth Century,* 410–11. Crewe accepts the idea of "themelessness" in Nashe's writing as "a convenient term under which to approach an author who foregrounds performance as the irreducible . . . characteristic of his own work": *Unredeemed Rhetoric: Thomas Nashe and the Scandal of Authorship* (Baltimore, 1982), 2. Cf. Richard Lanham, "Tom Nashe and Jack Wilton: Personality as Structure in *The Unfortunate Traveller,"* Studies in Short Fiction* 4 (1967): "An inexplicable themelessness has been the real problem in almost all of Nashe's prose" (202).
35. On "copy" in Renaissance literary culture, see Doran, *Endeavors of Art,* 46–51. Crewe, *Unredeemed Rhetoric* ("The Loss of Decorum," 21–45), sees Nashe as having an ultimately "subversive" relation to decorum, rendering it "suspect or problematical" (33, 26), and notes Nashe's "early identification of good style with . . . good order in society" in the preface to Robert Greene's *Menaphon* (pub. 1589): *Unredeemed Rhetoric,* 108, n. 30.
36. T. S. Eliot, *"Ulysses,* Order, and Myth," in *Selected Prose of T. S. Eliot,* ed. Frank Kermode (New York, 1975), 177; for Eliot the Elizabethan period is one of "dissolution and chaos," "filled with broken fragments of systems" (*Elizabethan Essays,* 41, 52). Cf. Hilliard, *Singularity:* "all coherence [in this transitional era] was in question, if not yet gone" (3). In *Pierce Penilesse* modernity is the age of "Carterly upstarts, that out-face Towne and Country in their Velvets, when Sir Rowland Russet-coat, their Dad, goes sagging every day in his round Gascoynes of whyte cotton, and hath much a doo (poore pennie-father) to keepe his unthrift elbowes in reparations" (1.160; see also the tirade against "obscure upstart gallants," 1.173).
37. Quoted in Hibbard, *Thomas Nashe,* 63. Cf. also Campion's epigram *Ad Nashum* (in *Thomae Campiani Poemata* [pub. 1595]), in which he refers to Nashe's "bloody words" and "wounding humor," as well as his "wit born not without teeth" (*"cruenta verba," "vulnificos sales," "natos non sine dentibus lepores";* in *Nashe,* 5.146–47).
38. Hunter, *John Lyly,* stresses this prominence of "art," commenting that where, for example, "Shakespeare interlaces his groups [of characters] . . . Lyly keeps his separate" (348).
39. Hibbard, *Thomas Nashe,* sees the extemporal style as Nashe's attempt to distinguish himself from the professionals: extemporaneity was his "version, as a writer, of . . . *sprezzatura"* (45). This is, finally, more helpful than the analogy with the popular entertainer Tarlton—which, as I hope to show, has very definite limitations.
40. Weimann, *Shakespeare,* 128.
41. Weimann takes Hamlet's quip as a reference to Elizabethan graduates (ibid., 131).
42. Hilliard, *Singularity,* 3–4, 12. If Lyly's art "reflects an ordered universe," Nashe's "barely copes with chaos" (241).
43. Ibid.; especially 3, 136.
44. On Nashe's influence, see Neil Rhodes, *The Elizabethan Grotesque* (London, 1980), 91–100. As is often pointed out, the 1590s see a turn toward realistic, anti-idealizing modes of writing, a development in which Nashe plays a part: see Walter R. Davis, *Idea and Act in Elizabethan Fiction* (Princeton, 1969), 192–216.
45. The early novel attracts such formulations: cf. J. Paul Hunter, "'News and New Things': Contemporaneity and the Early English Novel," *Critical Inquiry* 14 (1988), on

its "distinctively . . . antiaristocratic tendency to encompass the daily, the trivial, the common, and the immediate" (496).

46. Nashe's "share" in the Martinist controversy is "fairly certain" (McKerrow, in *Nashe*, 5.64). On his stylistic indebtedness to Martin, see Hibbard, *Thomas Nashe* (44), and John Dover Wilson, "The Marprelate Controversy," in *Renascence and Reformation*, vol. 3 of *The Cambridge History of English Literature*, ed. Sir A. W. Ward and A. R. Waller (1909; repr. Cambridge, 1949), 398. On the political implications of sophisticated artistic ideas in the period, see Philip J. Finkelpearl, *John Marston of the Middle Temple: An Elizabethan Dramatist in his Social Setting* (Cambridge, Mass., 1969): he characterizes one advanced milieu, the Inns of Court, as "intellectual . . . critical, independent, aesthetically innovative, and politically concerned," but one too in which "orthodox ideals and ambitions mingled easily with licentious conduct" (25, 61).

47. McKerrow in his article "Marprelate Controversy" in the *Encyclopædia Britannica*, 11th ed. (1910–11).

48. Lewis, *Sixteenth Century*, 175.

49. See *A Dialogue Concerning Heresies*, ed. Thomas M. C. Lawler, Germain Marc'Hadour, and Richard C. Marius, in vol. 6 of *The Complete Works of St. Thomas More* (New Haven, 1981), 69.

50. It seems as well to note that where Nashe uses such an idiom he is giving us another style, as the Stage-Keeper in the induction to *Bartholomew Fair* (ed. Jamieson) seems to recognize: "And then a substantial watch to ha' stol'n in upon 'em, and taken 'em away with mistaking words, as the fashion is in the stage-practice" (lines 38–40). Shakespeare has been an occasion for discussion of the conventions, or "fashion," of Elizabethan literary lower-class speech: see N. F. Blake, *Shakespeare's Language: An Introduction* (London, 1983), 28–38; G. L. Brook, *The Language of Shakespeare* (London, 1976), 177, 181; Ludwig Borinski, "Shakespeare's Comic Prose," *Shakespeare Survey* 8 (1955), 62–63; and Margaret Schlauch, "The Social Background of Shakespeare's Malapropisms" in *A Reader in the Language of Shakespearean Drama: Essays Collected by Vivian Salmon and Edwina Burness* (Amsterdam, 1987).

51. The quotations from Martin are from *The Marprelate Tracts: 1588, 1589*, ed. William Pierce (London, 1911), 239, 118.

52. See *The Confutation of Tyndale's Answer*, ed. Louis A. Schuster et al., in vol. 8 of *Complete Works* (New Haven, Conn., 1973), 883.

53. Ibid., 896.

54. Hilliard, *Singularity*, 241.

55. More, *Dialogue*, 68–69.

56. *The Magic Mountain*, trans. H. T. Lowe-Porter (London, 1928; repr. 1948), 220.

57. Cf. Jonson on scandalous "controversiales scriptores": "Some controverters in divinity are like swaggerers in a tavern, that catch that which stands next them, the candlestick or pots; turn everything into a weapon. . . . These fencers in religion I like not" (from *Timber*, in *Jonson*, ed. Donaldson, 549–50).

58. Hibbard, *Thomas Nashe*, 46; cf. Rhodes, *Elizabethan Grotesque*: Nashe engages in "a deliberate abuse of standard *copia* techniques" (31).

59. On *Euphues*'s success, see Hunter, *John Lyly*, 72; on *Pierce*'s, Hibbard, *Thomas Nashe*, 59–60.

60. "Lyly as Shakespearian Precursor," in *Shakespearian Dimensions* (Brighton,

England, 1984), 154.

61. Quoted in Laslett, *World We Have Lost,* 35.

62. He was one of many for whom gentle status depended on attending university—a fact explaining the significant increase in the numbers of graduates during the sixteenth century: see Hugh F. Kearney, *Scholars and Gentlemen: Universities and Society in Pre-Industrial Britain: 1500–1700* (London, 1970), 26–27. Thomas's father was "apparently . . . not a university graduate," according to McGinn, *Thomas Nashe,* 13.

63. For Cook, *The Privileged Playgoers of Shakespeare's London: 1576–1642* (Princeton, 1981), not doing manual labor was the gentleman's main characteristic (24). Nashe styles himself "Thomas Nash Gentleman" on the title page to the 1592 edition of *Pierce Penilesse* (1.149) but as McGinn, *Thomas Nashe,* points out, in *Strange Newes, Of the Intercepting Certaine Letters* (pub. 1592) he appears to retract this claim or not care much about it: see 1.311–12. This disowning of gentility is an instance of that rhetoric of overcoming social distinctions which, I shall argue, is central to Nashe's writing.

64. See Palliser, *Age of Elizabeth,* 73–74. David Cressy, "Describing the Social Order of Elizabethan and Stuart England," *Literature and History* 3 (1976), accepts that the clergy and professions were considered superior to merchants, tradesmen, and craftsmen, but thinks them still basically subordinate to the landed gentry (35): "their gentle status was a concession to their abilities" (29, 37). An even more negative estimation of their place has been advanced by Youings in *Sixteenth Century England,* who writes that the parish clergy "were in no real sense gentry"; she classes them with the better-off yeomen, noting that the Cambridge matriculation registers grouped clergymen's sons "with those of tradesmen and farmers as *mediocris fortunae*" (319).

65. "The dominant value system" of Elizabethan society was "that of the landed gentleman": Stone, *Crisis,* 39. On the powerful attraction in this period of "the ideal of rural gentility," see Wrightson, *English Society,* 30, as well as Lawrence Stone and Jeanne C. Fawtier Stone, *An Open Elite? England 1540–1880* (Oxford, 1984), 11–16, who comment that land was a more "secure," if generally less lucrative, investment than business. But it also "signified power and status" (13), and men spent on country seats "because at bottom they were prestige-maximizers rather than profit-maximizers" (15).

66. Finkelpearl, *John Marston,* vii, 27–29.

67. Miller, *Professional Writer,* 12, 22.

68. On the kind of income necessary for an aristocratic life-style, see Stone, *Crisis,* 44.

69. According to Palliser, many individuals rose in status in the period: *Age of Elizabeth,* 77, and Stone, *Crisis,* observes an "unprecedented rate" of upward and downward social mobility (38). Cf. too A. L. Rowse, *The England of Elizabeth: The Structure of Society* (New York, 1951), 222.

70. Quoted in Laslett, *World We Have Lost,* 31.

71. For Bakhtin, see *Rabelais and His World,* trans. Hélène Iswolsky (Bloomington, Ind., 1984), and also *The Dialogic Imagination: Four Essays,* ed. Michael Holquist, trans. Caryl Emerson and Michael Holquist (Austin, Tex., 1981).

72. Weimann, *Shakespeare,* 180, 181. Cf. his reference to "popular uses of language . . . associated with Tarlton or Nashe" (205).

73. Both Weimann and Bakhtin tend to divide up certain qualities or values between

an elite and a populace. The folk are practical, irreverent deidealizers; the rulers, high-minded and solemn—dubious generalizations at any time. It is true, as we shall see, that Nashe exploits an elite "idealism" and a broadly nonelite "realism" in his texts—but that this reflects some essential historical opposition seems unlikely. In the English tradition there appears no insuperable barrier between the attitudes Weimann and Bakhtin find popular and elite ones—as Chaucerian *fabliaux* or academic "folk" plays like *Gammer Gurtons Nedle* (ca. 1552; pub. 1575) would suggest. The danger lies in stereotypes of either "popular" or "elite" culture: see Finkelpearl's description of the Revels at Gray's Inn in 1594–95, which combined "disorderly conduct, mock solemnity" and ribaldry with impeccable moral orthodoxy (*John Marston,* 38, 61).

74. This may not surprise: see Kolakowski's excellent discussion of the "monism" of Marx's "historiosophy," in which class struggle is the totality of the past. Historical materialism shares this essentialism, Kolakowski shows, with "all universal theories of history": *Main Currents of Marxism,* 366, 351–52, 363–71.

75. For the argument that class-consciousness in traditional society was restricted to the elite, see Laslett, *World We Have Lost,* 22–53.

76. In "Shakespeare and the Diction of Common Life," in *Shakespearian and Other Studies,* F. P. Wilson quotes the speech of a Parliamentarian full of proverbs (114), commenting that "to an Elizabethan the proverb was not merely or mainly of use for clouting a hob-nailed discourse" (117). Weimann, *Shakespeare,* says proverbs express "a mode of perception that had its roots in practical life and in the common man's concrete world of objects and ideas" (206; and see 237). One may ask: Do proverbs express the wisdom of common, that is, shared, life, or the specific experience of the "common man"?

77. See Hilliard, *Singularity,* 10, 241: *The Unfortunate Traveller* "subverts the literary and social conventions of the Elizabethan 'golden' age" and "undercuts both the traditional conception of society and the humanistic poetic" (123, 124). And see also Mihoko Suzuki's "'Signiorie over the Pages': The Crisis of Authority in Nashe's *The Unfortunate Traveller,*" *Studies in Philology* 81 (1984): 348–71, which argues that Nashe's text subverts political and "literary authority" (349).

78. Hilliard argues that "singularity," partly "forced on [Nashe] by his estranged status," was "a quality . . . that . . . threatened to become disruptive to the traditional social order" (*Singularity,* 3). Too serious an approach may distort it, however. The type of anti-establishment undergraduate humor that, rather than profoundly criticizing institutions, is essentially loyal to them (because of the privilege education confers) may be closer to the nature of Nasheian irony than the "subversion" of some approaches. On undergraduate culture in the sixteenth century, see Finkelpearl's opening chapter on the Inns of Court in *John Marston.*

79. Weimann, "*Fabula* and *Historia:* The Crisis of the 'Universall Consideration' in *The Unfortunate Traveller,*" in *Representing the English Renaissance,* ed. Greenblatt: Nashe's "authorship came to constitute and rely upon an authority distinctly his own. In this respect, Nashe (for all his political conservatism) was indeed a modernist" (191). Crewe, *Unredeemed Rhetoric* (68) uses the term "modernism" to indicate the self-consciousness of the writing rather than a literary-political radicalism. David Kaula, "The Low Style in Nashe's *The Unfortunate Traveller,*" *Studies in English Literature: 1500–1900* 6 (1966), stresses Nashe's pride in his originality and the impression he likes to give

of having refused the "discipline of imitation" (43–44).

80. Cf. Fredric Jameson on the "negative, critical, or revolutionary vocation" of modernism as interpreted by the Frankfurt School in his foreword to Jean-François Lyotard, *The Postmodern Condition: A Report on Knowledge,* trans. Geoff Bennington and Brian Massumi (Manchester, England, 1984), xvi.

81. Michael D. Bristol, *Carnival and Theater: Plebeian Culture and the Structure of Authority in Renaissance England* (New York, 1985), 95, 100, 96, 102.

82. Hilliard, *Singularity,* 68, drawing on Mark H. Curtis, "The Alienated Intellectuals of Early Stuart England," *Past and Present* 23 (1962): 25–44.

83. As will be already obvious, Nashe's relation to the elite involves broad questions about the relations between intellectuals and authority generally. Some illumination here is found in Gramsci's distinction between "organic" and "traditional" intellectuals, the former accepting their status as "an organic category" within a "fundamental social group" (thus "bourgeois" intellectuals, "proletarian" intellectuals) and the latter asserting independence from society: "Since . . . traditional intellectuals experience through an 'esprit-de-corps' their uninterrupted historical continuity and their special qualification, they thus put themselves forward as autonomous and independent of the dominant social group." The Nasheian persona is, as we shall see, in its emphasis on a certain autonomous, alternative, self-validating prestige, strikingly similar to the way "traditional" intellectuals define themselves: see *Selections from the Prison Notebooks of Antonio Gramsci,* ed. and trans. Quintin Hoare and Geoffrey Nowell Smith (London, 1971), 15, 8, 7.

84. "Tom Nashe and Jack Wilton," 207, 216, 206, 209.

85. "Inside the Outsider," 75, 74–75, 73, 74.

86. Ibid., 75, 71 (see also 66–67).

87. Ibid., 75, 78, 73.

88. Ibid., 75.

89. *The Unfortunate Traveller* is a "jarring confrontation" of "irreconcilable voices and mind-sets of [the] time" (ibid., 78).

90. Ibid., 75.

91. The Hamlet analogy is again useful: just as the prince's power over important, oppressive figures like Claudius and Polonius stems from his histrionic ability to move in their world ("the glass of fashion and the mould of form" [3.1.153]) while not being restricted to it, so Nashe's desired image is the knowing insider, freely moving in and out of aristocratic modes. Hamlet's ability to bewilder the court heavyweights and keep them guessing, his appearance of being the mirror of courtesy and yet uncircumscribed by the court, his very resistance to sociological or other types of analysis (we do not know, as Harold Jenkins points out, what he makes of the fustian of "mobled queen," but we know what Polonius thinks; see the note to 2.2.499 in the Arden edition [London, 1982])—such chameleonic unfixability of character suggests ways of understanding the social symbolism of Nashe's styles.

92. Kearney, *Scholars and Gentlemen,* 25.

93. I have in mind Walter Cohen's reading of the play in terms of a "lower-class subversiveness" (348) in *Drama of a Nation,* 322–56.

94. On the usefulness of this paradigm for understanding social relations in this period, see introduction, nn. 15 and 36. In *The World We Have Lost,* Peter Laslett argues that the

concept of class-conflict is more appropriate to nineteenth- and twentieth-century societies than to Tudor or Stuart England, where the ruling elite was the "only . . . body of persons capable of concerted action over the whole area of society," the "only . . . class in fact" (23). Laslett's argument depends upon "a distinction . . . between a status-group, which is the number of people enjoying or enduring the same social status, and a class, which is a number of people banded together in the exercise of collective power, political and economic" (22–23). Laslett's criticism of the usefulness of the concept of class for describing the social structure of Early Modern England finds support in J. H. Hexter's attack on "The Myth of the Middle Class in Tudor England" in *Reappraisals in History* (London, 1961): the Tudor "middle class" ("merchants, financiers, industrialists, the town rich, the *bourgeoisie*") lacked class consciousness: it had "no ideology of class war or even of class rivalry"; its most successful members aspired to join the aristocracy (75, 113). Cf. also Stevenson, *Praise and Paradox,* on the aristocratic, courtly nature of the literary praise of plebeian and bourgeois groups, especially her chapters "The Merchant as Knight, Courtier, and Prince," and "The Gentle Craftsman in Arcadia." For Palliser, *The England of Elizabeth,* the notion of "permanent antagonism" between rich and poor is fundamentally inapplicable to "a paternalist or deference society" like Tudor England (78, 80; see also 77–83). As regards the relation of literary culture to this problem, the lack of fundamental hostility to the elite in the most consciously plebeian author of the period, Thomas Deloney, is pertinent. The word "class" in reference to nonelite life is sometimes unavoidable, despite its often misleading implications; where it is used here it is usually a synonym for Laslett's "status-group." And rather than invoking a theory of general class-struggle (the real problem with the *systematic* application of the concept of class to this period), I continue in what follows to concentrate on the ambivalence, tension or uncertainty complicating the ideal hierarchy of society.

95. Thus the fool in medieval and Renaissance drama "reflects a dramatic and social position that rejects the assumptions of the mythical or heroic theme in favor of the common sense attitude of a plebeian . . . audience"; and "the popular tradition" in Shakespeare is seen as "supplementing, enriching, modifying, inverting, criticizing, or generally distancing the main action" (Weimann, *Shakespeare,* 13–14, 238). Although thus allowing for a multiplicity of relationships to "the main action," the book's emphasis tends to fall on the critical function.

96. Jameson, *Political Unconscious,* 80.

97. For an early sociology of the Elizabethan literary landscape, see John F. Danby's excellent *Poets on Fortune's Hill: Studies in Sidney, Shakespeare, Beaumont and Fletcher* (London, 1952), which proposes that Sidney was to literature what Elizabeth was to politics (31): "The *Arcadia* is Great House literature" (71).

98. Nevill Coghill, *Shakespeare's Professional Skills* (Cambridge, England, 1965), 59.

99. Weimann, *Shakespeare:* Hamlet mocks Polonius from the position of "popular commentator and parodist" (133); his wordplay generally "revives a late ritual capacity for reckless sport and social criticism" (150); in the scene with the "egalitarian" (240) grave diggers (who "challenge or complement some of the basic values of the play" [239]) the viewpoints of plebeian and prince merge: "the wit of the clown comes so near the experience of the courtier that it affects his language" (240). In sum, though Hamlet's relation with the court is "ambiguous" (231), the emphasis is on Hamlet as a vehicle for *"platea*-derived popular conventions and attitudes" (235), or on his solidarity with an

audience with a significant lower-class component and with characters "of lesser degree" (234). Although Hamlet is friendly with Marcellus and Barnardo, it is worth noting that they are "gentlemen," or officers, like Horatio (1.2.196)—he is apparently not intimate with the soldier Francisco.

100. An instance of Hamlet sentimentalism is Miklós Szenczi's "The Nature of Shakespeare's Realism," *Shakespeare Jahrbuch* 102 (1966), which speaks of "the instinctive connection of Hamlet, Lear, Othello, and Timon with the people" (53). Annabel Patterson, in *Shakespeare and the Popular Voice* (Cambridge, Mass., 1989), sees Hamlet as at times "a . . . spokesman for popular protest" (95). On the decline of deference toward the English nobility, relevant to Hamlet's complaint, see Stone, *Crisis,* 746–53.

101. We may compare with Hamlet's mad speech *Lear* 4.6, where torrents of "wild and whirling words" are evasive in a slightly different sense, talking down killing thoughts (such as responsibility). But here too such language seems a bid at empowerment, or survival, proceeding out of and trying to overcome through fantasy a real vulnerability: "No, they cannot touch me for [coining], I am the King himself. . . . Come, come, I am a king, / Masters, know you that?" (4.6.83–84, 199–200). The horrendously aggressive linguistic egoism of Lear's disordered speech (a speech to annihilate the world) is far removed in intensity from Nashe's often equally bewildering language play—but the common element of a frenetic assertiveness is there.

102. See Henry Knight Miller, "The Paradoxical Encomium with Special Reference to Its Vogue in England, 1600–1800," *Modern Philology* 53 (1956): 145–78, and Walter Kaiser, *Praisers of Folly: Erasmus, Rabelais, Shakespeare* (Cambridge, Mass., 1963). Kaiser thinks Nashe read Agrippa "more carefully than most" (143).

103. Nashe's stress on novelty, evident in this quotation, usually seems an attempt to distinguish himself as a special case transcending conventional social distinctions. David Margolies, *Novel and Society in Elizabethan England* (London, 1985) has argued that "most Elizabethan fiction writers accepted the role of entertainer" to the public (2). Nashe, however, does not want Tarlton's status.

104. See *OED,* "knave," sb. 2.

105. Why was Greene, during 1591–92, so preoccupied with the London low-life scene? Obviously pamphlets about it sold. But a secondary reason suggests itself. Like Nashe in eking out a precarious, vaguely disreputable living on the margins of the elite, and no doubt, as a graduate, anxious about his relationship to the vulgar, Greene finds the socially ambivalent conny-catcher an intriguing, perhaps solacing, figure. The rogue living by his wits, also surviving outside the traditional social structure, is hardly identifiable with his victims. The conny-catcher is a kind of sadistic revenge fantasy of the talented but impoverished professional author: he contemptuously takes in the clowns, including those of substance, and is not subordinate to the elite but rather a confident, raffish figure of glamorous power. On rogue, low-life, and prison literature, see Wright, *Middle Class Culture,* 410–11, 437–46.

106. The distinction is like that between Greene's underworld rogues and Deloney's upright plebeians.

107. Weimann, *Shakespeare:* a popular "realism of sentiment" shows up the "limits of idealism" (112, 111).

108. Cf. Bakhtin, *Rabelais:* "festive folk laughter . . . means the defeat of power, of

earthly kings, of the earthly upper classes" (92; and see 4 and passim). The gap between ideals and experience is a fundamental theme of Elizabethan fiction for Davis, *Idea and Act:* the experience of Jack Wilton "constantly gives the lie to ennobling formulations of the real" (215).

109. Cf. Jones, "Inside the Outsider": through Jack Wilton a "range of social classes and practices is seen from below" (64).

110. Cf. Lodge (1596): "Th. Nash, true English Arentine" (cited by McKerrow in *Nashe*, 5.147).

111. For Nashe and Juvenal, see Hibbard, *Thomas Nashe*, 63–64. Aretino is celebrated as a scourge of princes; but the stress is on the Italian's brilliance rather than on any dissenting stance—it is a personal distinctiveness that is emphasized, and Aretino is a humanist power fantasy: "The French king, Frances the first, he kept in such awe, that to chaine his tongue he sent him a huge chaine of golde, in the form of tongues fashioned" (2.265; see 2.264–66). Nashe emphasizes Greene's knavish quick wit in a retort to Harvey's attack on the dead writer (1.287–88). What is stressed is, again, a personal quality that excepts one from the social system. The same admiration for a prodigious, unconventional talent is expressed in the precocious preface (addressed to the "Gentlemen Students of Both Universities") Nashe wrote for Greene's *Menaphon* in which, as a young unknown, he casts up the accounts of English literature. In this document (composed, it would like to have thought, for a select group of readers), Nashe targets not only dull "mechanical mate[s]" (3.311), authors of "two-pennie Pamphlets" (3.316) "that feed on nought but the crums that fall from the Translators trencher" (3.312), but academic ink-hornists: "give me the man whose extemporall veine in any humour will excell our greatest Art-maisters deliberate thoughts" (3.312). What is advanced is a relative outsider's power, personal, noninstitutional, idiosyncratic, which neutralizes Establishment power. Yet it is a subtle game that Nashe plays: if he seeks to distinguish himself from those stigmatized as jumped-up, laborious pedants of the Harvey type (the son of a rope-maker, as he liked to remind his readers), he also aligns himself with "the indevours of Art" (3.315), energetically praising that "Nurse of all learning, Saint Johns in Cambridge" (3.317)—his college. The idiosyncrasy of Nashe's style, especially the proliferation of coinages, suggests a straining for distinction: on his exceptional linguistic innovation, see Jürgen Schäfer, *Documentation in the OED: Shakespeare and Nashe as Test Cases* (Oxford, 1980), 7, 60–63. On Nashe's stylistic individualism, see Paul Salzman, *English Prose Fiction: 1558–1700: A Critical History* (Oxford, 1985), 83–86, and Margolies, *Novel and Society*, 3, 86. For his scorn for "common" writers like Deloney, see Wright, *Middle Class Culture*, 93–94.

112. See the epilogue, lines 17–18, to *Arden of Faversham* in M. L. Wine's edition (London, 1973).

113. *The Elizabethan Pamphleteers: Popular Moralistic Pamphlets: 1580–1640* (Rutherford, N.J., 1983), 255.

114. Elizabethan dramaturgy and stage practice was probably rather heavily stylized, combined with realism of detail where possible: see Bradbrook, *Elizabethan Tragedy*, 16–28. On Shakespeare's "theatrical shorthand," see Alan C. Dessen, "Shakespeare and the Theatrical Conventions of His Time," in *Cambridge Companion to Shakespeare Studies*, ed. Stanley Wells (Cambridge, 1986), 90 and passim.

115. "Degradation, whether parodical or of some other type, is characteristic of

Renaissance literature" (Bakhtin, *Rabelais,* 21).

116. Weimann, *"Fabula* and *Historia,"* 191: in *The Unfortunate Traveller,* Nashe "sacrifice[s] Renaissance decorum [Sidney's "Universall Consideration"] for . . . historiography" (186).

117. "Fishermen" are addressed as the audience (3.223; see also 3.223–25), and it is proclaimed that their "kannes shall walke to the health of *Nashes* Lenten-stuffe" (3.225), in commemoration of the author's service.

118. Cf. the complaint about "deepe reaching wits . . . Moralizers . . . that wrest a never meant meaning out of every thing, applying all things to the present time" in *Summers Last Will and Testament* (3.235).

119. For Hibbard, Nashe's subject is always his "virtuosity as a writer": *Thomas Nashe,* 64.

120. Pamphlets had a low status, appealing mostly to "a kind of middle-class" ("tradesmen, merchants" and so on) whose "tastes and values" differed "significantly . . . from those catered for by writers like Sidney and Spenser": Clark, *Elizabethan Pamphleteers,* 22, 23, 176–77.

121. "Her [Nature's] world is brazen, the poets only deliver a golden": *Defence,* 78.

122. Weimann, *Shakespeare,* 14.

123. Cf. the way penury leads Greene's well-educated Francesco into the clutches of the players: "Thus every way destitute of meanes to live, . . . he calde to minde that he was a scholler, and that although in these daies Arte wanted honor, and learning lackt his due, yet good letters were not brought to so lowe an ebbe, but that there might some profite arise by them to procure his maintenance. In this humour he fell in amongst a companie of Players": see *Francescos Fortunes; Or, the Second Part of Greenes Never Too Late* (1590), in vol. 8 of *The Life and Complete Works in Prose and Verse of Robert Greene,* ed. Alexander B. Grosart (1881–86), 128.

124. On Pierce and Nashe, see Stanley Wells, ed., *Thomas Nashe* (London, 1964), 5; and Weimann, *"Fabula* and *Historia,"* 190.

125. *Endeavors of Art,* 29.

126. Hibbard, *Thomas Nashe,* so describes *The Terrors of the Night* (118).

127. The idea of popular carefreeness is linked to that of "the sufferings of the great," which Stephen Greenblatt calls "one of the familiar themes in the literature of the governing classes in the sixteenth century": *Shakespearean Negotiations,* 54. Gemulo, the shepherd in *The Maydes Metamorphosis* (pub. 1600; thought by Bond to be only doubtfully Lyly's) articulates this theme: "So did *Apollo* walk with shepheards crooke, / And many Kings their scepters have forsooke: / To lead the quiet life we shepheards know / Accounting it a refuge for their woe" (Bond's edition of Lyly, 3.351). Cf. the observation of Elizabeth (quoted in Rowse, *England of Elizabeth,* 267): "To be a king and wear a crown is more glorious to them that see it, than it is pleasure to them that bear it."

128. *Thomas Nashe,* 84.

129. For Morton W. Bloomfield, *The Seven Deadly Sins: An Introduction to the History of a Religious Concept, With Special Reference to Medieval English Literature* (Ann Arbor, Mich., 1952), the Sins are "threads in the medieval fabric" (243). I think the import of the allegory invoked in this part of *Pierce* is its medievalism (felt as a certain vagueness or insubstantiality), but it must be admitted that much medieval allegory, *Piers Plowman,* for instance, displays the vividness and specificity *Pierce* values as modern.

130. *"Fabula* and *Historia,"* passim. Cf. his conviction of the new empiricism of Renaissance literature: the Elizabethan and Jacobean period saw "the art of poetry . . . integrated . . . with a new sense of the world of empirical reality" (*Shakespeare,* 196).

131. *Defence,* 112.

132. See Margolies, *Novel and Society,* 85. The revolting descriptions of Greediness and Dame Nigardize are high (or low) points in this materialistic technique (1.166–68).

133. Terence Cave finds "prodigality and self-consciousness" characteristic of sixteenth-century writing, in which "proliferation becomes a theme . . . itself": see *The Cornucopian Text: Problems of Writing in the French Renaissance* (Oxford, 1979), ix.

134. Stephen Greenblatt, *Renaissance Self-Fashioning: From More to Shakespeare* (Chicago, 1981). For Weimann's remarks on Tarlton, see *Shakespeare,* xviii.

135. Will's mixed social character is emphasized by Hibbard, *Thomas Nashe:* he embodies "the popular tradition," but expresses the attitude of a sophisticated London wit (102).

136. Cf. Will's address to Nashe himself (probably holding the prompt book) on 3.290.

137. He strongly recalls the Will Summers of the later play *When You See Me, You Know Me,* whose "liberty of behaviour," not to mention impudence, in and about the court is striking: see introduction, n. 19.

138. Hibbard, *Thomas Nashe,* 19; on literary patronage generally ("obsolescent" by 1600), see Miller, *Professional Writer,* 94, 94–129, and Margolies, *Novel and Society,* 11.

139. See the second part of *The Return from Parnassus,* lines 69, 2222.

140. Curtis, "Alienated Intellectuals," 27–28, 39–41.

141. "Low Style," 49.

142. As an example of this approach, Kaula speaks of Wilton's "low style" opposing, debunking or exposing artificial styles (49–50), although he notes that Surrey is treated with "a bemused, even affectionate condescension" (45), and that Wilton's "scepticism" toward high styles combines with "sheer delight in reproducing" them (49).

143. The complexity of Autolycus's social character has already been mentioned as relevant to Nashe's personae: he "serv'd Prince Florizel," and once "wore three-pile" (4.3.13–14), but essentially he stands apart, unencumbered by social distinctions.

144. A place of execution: Wells, ed., *Thomas Nashe,* 373.

145. *Bartholomew Fair,* ed. Jamieson, 1.2.113–14.

146. Tragedy, A. P. Rossiter points out, "in Shakespeare's own usage, seems to mean 'an alarming calamity, usually bloody, and often determined by the plotted designs of someone'": see *Angel with Horns: Fifteen Lectures on Shakespeare,* ed. Graham Storey (London, 1961; repr. New York, 1974), 254. But the likelihood that Nashe exploits a social irony in applying the word "tragedy" to artisans seems greater when we recall that "catastrophe" is a theater word (*OED,* 1), Heywood using it thus technically in the *Apology* to refer to the fourth part (before the conclusion) of a comedy (49). Cf. Edmund in *Lear:* "Pat! he comes like the catastrophe of the old comedy" (1.2.134).

147. Weimann's suggestive article, *"Fabula* and *Historia,"* on the relation between poetic and historiographical discourses in *The Unfortunate Traveller,* has influenced my analysis in the following pages, though I am more interested in the text's social-rhetorical contrasts than he.

148. The Jonson/Shakespeare dichotomy (despite Jonson's good-natured "To the Memory of My Beloved . . .") involved just such social distinctions.

149. Surrey and Wilton are wrongly imprisoned in Venice, and encountering there the innocent Diamante, wife of a merchant, Surrey indulges his passion for romantic rhetoric by temporarily substituting her for Geraldine. Wilton comments: "he wold praise her beyond the moone and starres, and that so sweetly and ravishingly as I perswade my self he was more in love with his own curious forming fancie than her face; and truth it is, many become passionate lovers onely to winne praise to theyr wits" (2.262).

150. "Realism" is a tendentious word that rather clouds the issue: it often implies a superiority and opposition to "non-realistic" modes. Although the term usefully describes some aspects of Nashe's work, its polemical connotations need deemphasizing.

151. Weimann, "*Fabula* and *Historia,*" observes the absurdity of the tournament and its "emblematic language of knighthood" (190).

152. *The Dialogic Imagination,* 19.

153. Cf. M. W. MacCallum, *Shakespeare's Roman Plays and Their Background* (London, 1910; repr. New York, 1967), 1–2.

154. Cf. G. K. Hunter, "Shakespeare and the Traditions of Tragedy," in *The Cambridge Companion*: I am indebted to his analysis of history and modernity in *Lear, Macbeth,* and *Hamlet* (136–40).

155. Foxe provides an interesting contrast: although including plebeian martyrs, these nonelite lives are read as instances of the history of the true church rather than for their own sake—are assimilated, that is, to a master narrative.

156. The social complexity of this episode is perhaps deepened by a further incongruity, that between town content and aristocratic pretensions of form (though Heraclide is "a noble & chast matron" [2.287]).

157. Jones, "Inside the Outsider," notes how Nashe "frames [this and other] episodes with sign-posting comments that make their literariness, their status as generic performances, clear" (66).

158. See Harold Jenkins's discussion of the role of the First Player's speech in his *Arden* edition, 478–79.

159. On the "Gothic" tradition of fortune in English Renaissance tragedy, see Willard Farnham, *The Medieval Heritage of Elizabethan Tragedy* (Oxford, 1936). "The vulnerability of the man of high estate is the central theme of Elizabethan tragedy as of medieval": F. P. Wilson, *English Drama*, 128.

160. Cf. 2.241: "This tale [of the Anabaptists] must at one time or other give up the ghost, and as good now as stay longer."

Chapter 2. "No Glorious State": The Social Interplay of Bourgeois Tragedy

1. Wine, ed., *Arden of Faversham,* limits the play tentatively to 1588–91 (xlv). Charles Dale Cannon, ed., *A Warning for Fair Women* (The Hague, 1975) provides limits for that play of the mid-1580s and 1599 (48). Authorship of these plays is unknown, and Robert Yarington, the supposed author of the *Two Lamentable Tragedies,* remains little more than a name (and even that may be "fictitious"; see the article on Yarington in the *Dictionary of National Biography*). The text is printed in vol. 4 of A. H. Bullen's *A*

Collection of Old English Plays (London, 1885); Sidney L. Lee, "The Topical Side of Elizabethan Drama," *Transactions of New Shakspere Society* 11 (1887), notes that the London murders dramatized in the play occurred about 1599 (23). A. C. Cawley and Barry Gaines, ed., *A Yorkshire Tragedy* (Manchester, England, 1986), suggest that the play "was composed shortly after the event which it depicts," that is, late 1605 (2). Heywood's *A Woman Killed with Kindness* was first performed in 1603: see the edition by R. W. Van Fossen (Cambridge, Mass., 1961), xv. All quotations and references are to these editions and are included in the text: *Arden, A Yorkshire Tragedy,* and *A Woman* are referred to by scene and line number; *Two Lamentable Tragedies* by page number; *A Warning* by line only. One of the first attempted definitions of the genre was H. H. Adams's *English Domestic or Homiletic Tragedy: 1575–1642* (New York, 1943), which located the plays in the morality tradition. A. P. Rossiter, *English Drama from Early Times to the Elizabethans: Its Background, Origins, and Developments* (London, 1950), also sees their orientation toward "ordinary ethical and social problems" as an outgrowth of the moralities (161). Wright, *Middle Class Culture,* distinguishes them as realistic, nonsatirical studies of bourgeois domestic life (631–37).

2. "Confusion underlay all Renaissance genre-theory, even the simplest": Colie, *Resources of Kind,* 9.

3. Prologue, *Tamburlaine the Great,* Part One, in *Christopher Marlowe: Complete Plays and Poems,* ed. E. D. Pendry and J. C. Maxwell (London, 1976).

4. For a classification of kinds of Elizabethan tragedy (into *De casibus,* Italianate, and domestic), see Doran, *Endeavors of Art,* 115–47. G. K. Hunter stresses "the variousness of tragic experience" in Shakespeare in "Shakespeare and the Traditions of Tragedy" (*Cambridge Companion,* 125).

5. In *Kinds of Literature: An Introduction to the Theory of Genres and Modes* (Cambridge, Mass., 1982), Alastair Fowler criticizes essentialist or Platonic models of genre, proposing instead a historicized, diachronic generic theory (45–52 and passim), an approach validated by the actual diversity of Elizabethan tragedy.

6. See Wine's edition, lix, n. 1. Catherine Belsey shows this comparison to have been more or less contemporary with the play: see *The Subject of Tragedy: Identity and Difference in Renaissance Drama* (London, 1985), 141.

7. Sanders, the murdered husband in *A Warning,* is a London businessman who spends his days at "the Exchange" (324); Arden, a not insubstantial landowner; Merry, tavern keeper and notorious, or "Saint-like," as a waterman disgustedly puts it, Puritan (83); Master Frankford, a country gentleman, "possess'd of many fair revenues" (4.5). The Husband of *A Yorkshire Tragedy* comes from a famous old county family. *Bourgeois,* therefore, is used not in the strict sense in which it may be applied to Sanders or Merry, but to express the middling station of the heroes of these plays, occupying a rank different from both the lowest and the highest in society.

8. The "bulwarks" of the stage were "royal favour and popular demand": Bradbrook, *Rise of the Common Player,* 81. On the protection of the stage by Royalty and the Privy Council, see Chambers, *Elizabethan Stage,* 1.3, and F. P. Wilson, *Elizabethan and Jacobean* (Oxford, 1945), 91. On the close relation between the theaters and the court, see Gurr, *Shakespearean Stage,* 12, 28–31, and on the City fathers' hostility to the stage as a menace to law and order, see Margot Heinemann, *Puritanism and Theatre: Thomas Middleton and Opposition Drama under the Early Stuarts* (Cambridge, England, 1980),

31–36. Cohen offers a Marxist interpretation of this complex of social relations in *Drama of a Nation*, which views the London public theater as "an institutional battleground" for fundamental social contradictions decisively contested in the next century (161–62).

9. Spelling modernized from "Robert Greene's attack on Shakespeare," *Riverside Shakespeare*, 1835. The players' status gradually improved: Gerald Eades Bentley, *The Profession of Player in Shakespeare's Time: 1590–1642* (Princeton, 1984), 8–11; except for a few stars most were poor (5). The City did not regard acting as legitimate work, and the players' social position was uncertain and untraditional, but they enjoyed a rise in status following James's patronage of the King's Men: Bradbrook, *Rise of the Common Player*, 47, 40–41, 64. Notwithstanding, however, "the upward social mobility of Elizabethan actors," acting remained "a profession never wholly distinct from vagabondage": Peter Thomson, "Playhouses and Players in the Time of Shakespeare," *Cambridge Companion*, 78.

10. Cf. Cohen, *Drama of a Nation:* the theater "was a socially composite organization" (151).

11. Alfred Harbage argued that "Shakespeare's audience . . . was a cross-section of the London population of his day"; see *Shakespeare's Audience* (New York, 1941), 90. This has been the standard view: see, for instance, Ashley Thorndike, *Shakespeare's Theater* (1916; repr. New York, 1960), 406, and is still commonly encountered: cf., for example, Heinemann's conviction as to "the broad social basis" of Elizabethan drama in *Puritanism and Theatre*, 12. The opinion that Shakespeare's audience was "essentially popular" (Thorndike, *Shakespeare's Theater*, 430) has been strongly challenged by Cook, *Privileged Playgoers:* "the privileged represented the most consistent patrons of the drama, no matter where or when it was performed" (273). Cook's view, based upon an analysis of economic evidence, is supported by Michael Hattaway in *Elizabethan Popular Theatre: Plays in Performance* (London, 1982), 49. Martin Butler, *Theatre and Crisis: 1632–1642* (Cambridge, England, 1984) has argued against Cook: "the presence of the privileged" (who, unlike the poor, will have left record of their attendance in the theaters) "does not logically entail the absence of the unprivileged" (298). However, he does not address the implications of the economic data Cook presents. A new approach is in Gurr's *Playgoing in Shakespeare's London*, which, while taking into account Cook's objections to Harbage, considers her conclusion an "oversimplification" (4) in the opposite direction, and argues for a "division of social classes" among "different types of playhouse" (79, 75).

12. The full title (reproduced in Cannon's edition, 93) runs: *A Warning For Fair Women Containing, The most tragicall and lamentable murther of Master George Sanders of London Marchant, nigh Shooters hill. Consented unto By his owne wife, acted by M Browne, Mistris Drewry and Trusty Roger agents therin; with their severall ends.*

13. As in, for example, *All's Well*, 2.5.91, 3.3.11, or *Coriolanus*, 1.9.42–44, 3.2.113

14. I am much indebted here to Hunter's analysis of the play's self-consciousness in his forthcoming *English Drama*.

15. On this "anti-literary" rhetoric of fact in the plays, see the still useful article by Lee, "The Topical Side of Elizabethan Drama," 23–25.

16. "To the Readers" in *Sejanus*, ed. Jonas A. Barish (New Haven, Conn., 1965), 27

17. There is of course some esteem for the "infinite jest" and "most excellent fancy" of a witty court fool such as Yorick (5.1.185)—the type of figure, encountered in Nashe whose essence involves existing outside conventional social classifications.

18. See the chapter "The Sense of Overdoing It" in Clifford Leech's *Tragedy* (London, 1969).

19. Dieter Mehl, *The Elizabethan Dumb Show: The History of a Dramatic Convention* (Cambridge, Mass., 1966), observes that the dumb shows of the play, which "draw on the style of the moralities" (92), serve the function of "moral exegesis" (94): throughout "realistic tragedy and instructive morality alternate in a way not unlike the technique of 'fading in' in films" (94).

20. Such an order is conspicuous in the repentant gallows speeches at the end of the play, carrying the monitory Christian message about "the launces that have sluic'd forth sinne" (Tragedy in the epilogue [2718]); in such moments tragedy is vindicated as truth rather than distanced as artifice.

21. See M. C. Bradbrook, *The Growth and Structure of Elizabethan Comedy* (1955; new ed. London, 1973), 27–28.

22. *Shakespeare*, 202, 197.

23. See his edition, lxix.

24. Moretti, "'A Huge Eclipse,'" comments on the concrete sense of "tragedy" in these lines, such that it "is largely synonymous with misfortune or death" (17). Bradbrook, *Elizabethan Comedy* (27) observes that "tragedy was sometimes loosely applied, rather in the manner of the modern journalist, to any violent action ending with physical death"; and see my chapter on Nashe, n. 146.

25. *Queen Elizabeth* (New York, 1934), 30.

26. Raymond Chapman, "*Arden of Feversham:* Its Interest Today," *English* 11 (1956): 17.

27. *Subject of Tragedy*, 132.

28. See his edition, lxii.

29. See Belsey, *Subject of Tragedy*, 133–35; at times "the play presents Alice Arden's challenge to the institution of marriage as an act of heroism" (134).

30. The phrase is Henry James's, in "The Art of Fiction": see *Henry James: The Critical Muse: Selected Literary Criticism*, ed. Roger Gard (Harmondsworth, England, 1987), 195.

31. We have seen that *Arden, A Warning,* and *Two Lamentable Tragedies* have a highly ambiguous relation to tragic idealization.

32. *Defence*, 96, 115, 113.

33. The play insists upon the Husband's "honoured stock and fair descent" (9.4), stressing his "father's and forefathers' worthy honours, / Which were our country monuments . . . " (2.136–37): he is "of a virtuous house" (2.170), and an "ancient seat" (3.91), but "ancient honour" (5.4) has been ruined by one who is "the blot / Upon his predecessors' honoured name" (9.33–34).

34. Heywood, *Apology*, 17.

35. The savage ethos of this scene is illuminated by Lawrence Stone's comments on England's violent elite in *The Crisis of the Aristocracy*, 223–34.

36. Peter Ure discusses this parallel between main plot and subplot in "Marriage and the Domestic Drama in Heywood and Ford," in *Elizabethan and Jacobean Drama: Critical Essays by Peter Ure*, ed. J. C. Maxwell (U.S.A., 1974), 149–50.

37. Cf. Robert Ornstein, "Bourgeois Morality and Dramatic Convention in *A Woman Killed with Kindness,*" in *English Renaissance Essays in Honor of Madeleine Doran and*

Mark Eccles, ed. Standish Henning, Robert Kimbrough, and Richard Knowles (Carbondale, Ill., 1976), on this balance between "bathos" and "irony" (139).

38. *Apology,* 49.

Chapter 3. Shakespeare and the
Social Symbolism of Art

1. *An Essay of Dramatic Poesy,* in Dryden, *Essays,* 1.79.

2. "The myriad-minded man . . . Shakspeare": in vol. 1 of Samuel Taylor Coleridge, *Shakespearean Criticism,* 2d ed., ed. Thomas Middleton Raysor (London, 1960), 89.

3. *Shakespeare,* 246; see also 177.

4. Greer, *Shakespeare* (Oxford, 1986), 18, 85, 125. Shakespearean "negative capability" has been formulated diversely. Margot Heinemann in "How Brecht Read Shakespeare" (*Political Shakespeare: New Essays in Cultural Materialism,* ed. Jonathan Dollimore and Alan Sinfield [Ithaca, N.Y., 1985]), observes Brecht's modeling of his epic theater on "the many-sided, dialectical, argumentative style of Shakespeare" (211). W. R. Elton, "Shakespeare and the Thought of His Age," in *A New Companion to Shakespeare Studies,* ed. Kenneth Muir and S. Schoenbaum (Cambridge, England, 1971) sees Shakespeare's dialectical art as giving appropriate form to a contradictory, transitional age, articulating the "complexity and variety, inconsistency and fluidity" of Renaissance thought (180; see 197–98). Otto Ludwig's comment that "Shakespeare's entire art is based on contrast" is cited by Weimann, *Shakespeare,* 245; Clemen, "Characteristic Features of Shakespearian Drama," stresses contrast and the combination of "opposite and diverse material in order to form a new unity" as essential (202; 202–3). Rossiter, *Angel with Horns,* formulates the dialectical spirit of Shakespearean tragedy less as an argument than as a matter of "diabolical" irony and "Gothic" grotesque (292): in Shakespeare's "comic-ironic" universe "the tragic includes its seeming opposite"; the "view is the double-eyed, the ambivalent: it faces both ways" (270, 272, 292). Norman Rabkin in *Shakespeare and the Common Understanding* (New York, 1967) analyzes the "principle of complementarity" in the plays and finds that the "true constant" of Shakespeare's texts is their "dialectical dramaturgy" (27, 11, and passim); see also his *Shakespeare and the Problem of Meaning* (Chicago, 1981) on the irreducible "existential complexity" of the plays (32 and passim).

5. See Raymond Williams, *Marxism and Literature* (Oxford, 1977), 55–75, 128–36: "structure of feeling" is a concept intended to "go beyond formally held and systematic beliefs" to include "meanings and values as they are actively lived and felt" (132). See also Peter Erikson, "The Order of the Garter, the Cult of Elizabeth, and Class-Gender Tension in *The Merry Wives of Windsor,*" in *Shakespeare Reproduced: The Text in History and Ideology,* ed. Jean E. Howard and Marion F. O'Connor (New York, 1987), 117–18.

6. The social "inclusiveness" of Shakespearean theater in general, but above all of the *Henry IV* plays, is stressed by Barber in terms of the dramatic use of popular custom and ritual: see *Shakespeare's Festive Comedy,* 192 and passim.

7. Influential Marxist accounts of Shakespearean "comprehensiveness" are Weimann's *Shakespeare* and Cohen's *Drama of a Nation*. Both emphasize the period as an age of transition from feudalism to capitalism: see Weimann, 161–69 and passim; *Drama of a Nation*, 82–84 and passim. See also Szenczi, "Shakespeare's Realism." Bristol, *Carnival and Theater*, accepts that "the theme of transition" from feudalism to capitalism remains generally "a valid interpretive strategy for elucidating social change in the Elizabethan period" (47), but argues that it needs supplementing by an awareness of the conservatism and relative permanence of the forms of popular culture—"what Fernand Braudel has called '*longue durée*' or the 'structure of everyday life'" (48). Cohen defends "the quest for totality" (21) of Marxist modes of criticism in *Drama of a Nation*, 21–22.

8. In his edition: "every single character in Shakespeare is as much an Individual as those in Life itself": see vol. 2 of *Shakespeare: The Critical Heritage*, ed. Brian Vickers (London, 1974), 404.

9. *Shakespeare and Social Class* (Atlantic Highlands, N.J., 1988), 75–77.

10. Cf. Puttenham: "many a meane souldier and other obscure persons were spoken of and made famous in stories, as we find of Irus the begger, and Thersites the glorious noddie, whom Homer maketh mention of. But that happened (and so did many like memories of meane men) by reason of some greater personage or matter that it was long of"; from *Arte of English Poesie*, in *Elizabethan Critical Essays*, 2.45.

11. See Harbage, *Shakespeare and the Rival Traditions* (New York, 1952); Bradbrook, *Elizabethan Comedy* and *Rise of the Common Player*; and Barber, *Shakespeare's Festive Comedy*. "A pervasive mixing of popular and elite elements . . . characterized the immediate institutional context of the drama" (Cohen, *Drama of a Nation*, 19; also 405 and passim). The major contemporary statement of this position is Weimann's *Shakespeare*: Elizabethan drama was "neither farcical nor learned nor courtly," but a theater universal "in its social and aesthetic appeal" (173 and passim). Both writers, however, formulate this social-cultural mingling in terms of a larger contradiction between ruling and subordinate classes: "in the Renaissance theater . . . the popular tradition was free to develop relatively independent of, and yet in close touch with, the *conflicting* standards and attitudes of the dominant classes" (Weimann, *Shakespeare*, 169, my emphasis). For Cohen the essentially "artisanal" (181) social character of the Elizabethan playhouse suggests "the inherent subversiveness of the institution" (183): even in a play with an overtly aristocratic outlook, "the medium and the message were in contradiction, a contradiction that resulted above all from the popular contribution" (183). Weimann, "Shakespeare (De)Canonized," has similarly argued for tension between dramatic content and performative context on the Elizabethan stage: see Introduction, n. 32.

12. See *William Shakespeare*, 227–32. On John Shakespeare's public career, see 33–39.

13. For Greene's attack on Shakespeare: ibid., 151, and 143–59. For the title page to the *Farewell*, see vol. 9 of Greene, *Life and Complete Works*, 225.

14. Even by 1640, when their status had been much improved, playwrights were still not very highly regarded, according to Bentley, *Profession of Dramatist*, 43.

15. For a sociological reading of *Tamburlaine* and other plays in terms of the special position in society of the "University Wits," see G. K. Hunter, "The Beginnings of Elizabethan Drama: Revolution and Continuity," in *Renaissance Drama*, n.s. 17 (1986): 29–52.

16. C. L. Barber and Richard P. Wheeler, *The Whole Journey: Shakespeare's Power of Development* (Berkeley, 1986), 63.

17. Danby compares Sidney (as archetype of the aristocrat-poet) with "the tradesman's son from the country," Shakespeare, in *Poets on Fortune's Hill,* 73.

18. For a conception of the forms of literature as "institutionally objective," see Fowler, *Kinds of Literature,* 260.

19. Snyder, *Comic Matrix of Shakespeare's Tragedies,* shows that the upsetting of normal social arrangements can be comic or tragic in Elizabethan drama; thus the convention of social inversion in the romantic comedy of the 1580s and early 1590s, in which "women and servants" are commonly elevated above "their betters" (27), has a dark, ironic significance in *King Lear* (140–46).

20. I am grateful to Ayşe Agiş for drawing my attention to the different ways Titania and Oberon evaluate the Faerie Queene's infatuation.

21. "Shakespeare's plays are centrally, repeatedly concerned with the production and containment of subversion and disorder": Greenblatt, *Shakespearean Negotiations,* 40; see also Arthur F. Kinney, *Renaissance Historicism: Selections from "English Literary Renaissance,"* ed. Arthur F. Kinney and Dan S. Collins (Amherst, Mass., 1987), xi.

22. On the play's synthesis of courtly and popular materials and its use of social contrast generally, see David Young, *Something of Great Constancy: The Art of "A Midsummer Night's Dream"* (New Haven, Conn., 1966), 15, 30, 58–59; H. B. Charlton, *Shakespearian Comedy* (London, 1938; repr. 1959), 120; K. M. Briggs, *The Anatomy of Puck: An Examination of Fairy Beliefs among Shakespeare's Contemporaries and Successors* (London, 1959), 44; M. C. Bradbrook, "The Fashioning of a Courtier," in *Shakespeare Criticism: 1935–1960,* ed. Anne Ridler (London, 1963), 377–80; and R. W. Dent, "Imagination in *A Midsummer Night's Dream,"* *Shakespeare Quarterly* 15 (1964): 125.

23. The fairies in general "are a fantastic 'mingle-mangle' blending classical and Germanic mythology with native folklore" (Weimann, *Shakespeare,* 174), and "Shakespeare's Puck . . . at once a product of the popular imagination as well as a part of the more literary traditions of Cupid and Ovid's *Metamorphoses"* (196).

24. Compare with Puck's superiority to, yet association with, the common people, Diccon in *Gammer Gurtons Nedle,* whose mischief drives the play's complications: cleverer than his rustic victims, he nevertheless participates in much the same sphere of life as they.

25. Elliot Krieger, *A Marxist Study of Shakespeare's Comedies* (New York, 1979): "the play furthers the aristocracy's fantasy of its absolute social predominance" (61). Krieger proposes an ideological analysis of the "two-world" structure of much Shakespearean comedy: the "secondary" world (Arden, the wood outside Athens, Belmont) is a mystification of the class conflicts of the historical, "first" world of the plays; see his introduction, 1–8. This two-world theory of Shakespearean comedy (a movement from a "normal world," into a "green world," and back again to the "normal world") derives from Northrop Frye, *The Anatomy of Criticism: Four Essays* (Princeton, 1957), 182; see also 182–85.

26. Cf. Spingarn, *Literary Criticism in the Renaissance:* "the principle of decorum" necessarily entails the "much deeper question . . . of social distinctions": "The observance of decorum necessitated the maintenance of the social distinctions which formed the basis

of Renaissance life and of Renaissance literature" (87).

27. On the popularity of disguise in both genres, see Bradbrook, *Themes and Conventions*, 17.

28. Sly's reference to "a tumbling-trick" seems designed to signify a popular entertainment, as different as possible from the sophisticated "history" (or "story represented dramatically" [*OED*, sb. 6a]), of reasonably complex plotting, which the *Shrew* proper offers. But it is relevant to any discussion of the relations of "popular" to "aristocratic" culture in the period, and underscores the slipperiness of such distinctions, that tumbling or acrobatic performances were court fare as well: the Office of the Master of the Revels Account Book (1 November 1582 to 31 October 1583) records that "Sundrey feates of Tumbling and Activitie were shewed before her majestie on Newe yeares daie at night by the Lord Straunge his servauntes"; and the Book for 31 October 1584 to 31 October 1585 notes that "Dyvers feates of Actyvytie were shewed and presented before her majestie on newe yeares daye at night at Grenewich by Symons and his fellowes": see *Documents Relating to the Office of the Revels in the Time of Queen Elizabeth*, ed. Albert Feuillerat (Louvain, Belgium, 1908), 349, 365.

29. A similar status-consciousness is, of course, discernible in Hamlet's advice to the players: the speech Hamlet heard once "pleas'd not the million, 'twas caviary to the general" (2.2.436–37); there are the distinctions between "the judicious" and "the unskillful" (3.2.25–26), or "the groundlings, who for the most part are capable of nothing but inexplicable dumb shows and noise" (3.2.10–12). Aesthetic matters are thus discussed with a casual automatic reference to degree. Nonetheless, drama does not in *Hamlet* have the essentially conservative function it has in *A Midsummer Night's Dream* or, as I shall show, *The Taming of the Shrew*: in Claudius's court holding the "mirror up to nature" (3.2.22) is necessarily a disruptive act; the resources of theater are, as in Lear's scorching mock-trial of his daughters, the weapons not of the powerful, but of those striking back (from a position of vulnerability) at injustice.

30. G. K. Hunter discusses this irony in *William Shakespeare: The Late Comedies* (London, 1962), 14, 20.

31. The best-known study of a "Saturnalian" tradition of misrule or "topsy-turvydom" in English Renaissance theater is Barber's *Shakespeare's Festive Comedy*. An early consideration of Shakespeare's indebtedness to traditional pastimes and festivals (especially in the comedies but also in *Lear*) is Spens, *An Essay on Shakespeare's Relation to Tradition*, 35–52: thus Sir Toby in *Twelfth Night* recalls the Lord of Misrule of the court, an office, along with the play's title, suggesting the play's "link with a folk-festival," the Feast of Fools (43, 41–43). Weimann's political interpretation of the tradition, whereby "the inverted vision of the world" is "a means of criticizing society" (*Shakespeare*, 40) has been influential. Thus Bristol, *Carnival and Theater*, in an analysis of carnivalesque popular culture derived from Bakhtin, stresses the capacity of festivity to act as a mode of resistance to the dominant elite and its "power structure" (4). But topsy-turvydom has a learned history too: see E. R. Curtius, "The World Upside Down," in *European Literature in the Latin Middle Ages*, trans. Willard R. Trask (Princeton, 1953), 94–98.

32. On the "parallel between domestic patriarchy and absolute monarchy" in the thought of the period, see Belsey, *Subject of Tragedy*, 144, 137–48. If the concluding Christopher Sly scene in *The Taming of a Shrew* (possibly a memorial reconstruction of

Shakespeare's play) reflects an ending originally in some version of the text, the notion of Sly being subjected to order becomes less satisfactory—for, as a man, he also benefits from it, "know[ing] now how to tame a shrew": "I'll to my wife presently and tame her too an if she anger me"; see *The Taming of the Shrew*, ed. H. J. Oliver (Oxford, 1982), 235; on the textual problem of Sly, see 28–29, 40–43. But the play Sly watches still promotes order; and the Sly awakened by the Tapster, after the "dream" of being a lord (235), has certainly been put in his place.

33. Leonard Tennenhouse understands English Renaissance drama as an extension of elite power, or "a vehicle for disseminating court ideology," in *Power on Display: The Politics of Shakespeare's Genres* (New York, 1986), 39. Stephen Orgel's "Making Greatness Familiar," in *Power of Forms*, ed. Greenblatt, is a salutary reminder of just "how little we really understand," from a sometimes perplexing historical record, of "what must have been a very complicated and ambivalent relationship" between government and players in the period (46).

34. Cf. Tennenhouse, *Power on Display:* the induction "calls attention to the role of the dramatist and his power to produce and shatter the illusions in terms of which one understands identity" (46). One would have to qualify this by distinguishing among spectators: Sly is an especially naïve one, and the play explores such social differences; we may suppose that the lord would not be as vulnerable to the power Tennenhouse specifies.

35. Not only the art of the theater, either: note the ravishingly beautiful "pictures" (induction, 2.49) offered Sly, all Ovidian subjects (Adonis, Io, Daphne), and done with exquisite skill and workmanship (56, 60). This aesthetic language introduces a note of control and discipline into Sly's social metamorphosis that removes it from the more natural changes in the *Dream*.

36. Even Oberon's manipulation of Titania seems significantly different from the lord's playing with Sly, for here too, as with the other translations in the *Dream*, there is the strong suggestion, in an enchanted natural scene, of the disclosure of certain unobvious or paradoxical truths; but Sly-as-lord is a mere distorting trick.

37. Thus according to Young, *Something of Great Constancy*, the play undoes "conventional Elizabethan dichotomies" (115); see "Bottom's Dream," 109–67.

38. Bradbrook uses this term (*Themes and Conventions*, 110–11) to describe a conventional mode for orchestrating the speech of elite characters like Beatrice and Benedick, yet it is applicable to Grumio's quibbling.

39. Quoted from vol. 1 of *Narrative and Dramatic Sources of Shakespeare*, ed. Geoffrey Bullough (London, 1957), 112. On Shakespeare's use of Gascoigne, see Kenneth Muir, *The Sources of Shakespeare's Plays* (New Haven, Conn., 1978), 19–20, and Bullough, *Narrative and Dramatic Sources*, 1:66–68.

40. "Shakespeare's Primitive Art," in *Interpretations of Shakespeare: British Academy Lectures Selected by Kenneth Muir* (Oxford, 1985), 53, 60. See also Patricia Binnie's introduction to her edition (Manchester, England, 1980), 25–29.

41. George Peele, *The Old Wives Tale*, edited by Patricia Binnie, 43.

42. I spoke of a "popular" realism in Nashe's work challenging elite idealism. Such realism, as this passage shows, need not be "popular": the deflationary realism here comes from Madge's superiors (who, however, are still not to be identified with the elite). For Bakhtin, medieval and Renaissance folk culture expresses a "material bodily principle"

at odds with elite or official idealism: see *Rabelais*, 18 and passim.

43. "Engagement and Detachment in Shakespeare's Plays," in *Essays on Shakespeare and Elizabethan Drama in Honor of Hardin Craig*, ed. Richard Hosley (Columbia, Mo., 1962), 285. The Elizabethan audience of S. L. Bethell's *Shakespeare and the Popular Dramatic Tradition* (London, 1944) is similarly "alert and critically detached" (39): "Elizabethan playhouse psychology" is characterized by "the dual consciousness of play-world and real world" (41).

44. See Cook, "Shakespeare's Gentlemen," in *Deutsche Shakespeare—Gesellschaft West Jahrbuch* (1985): 9–28.

45. Thompson, *Shakespeare's Chaucer*, notes Chaucer's "solemn, intellectual" Elizabethan reputation (5), and its coexistence with the image of a "merry," bawdy writer (7): for Shakespeare, however, Chaucer is a "romantic and courtly" poet rather than "a comic naturalist" (82).

46. De Quincey thought the first and last acts "finished in a more elaborate style of excellence than any other almost of Shakespeare's most felicitous scenes"; quoted in Paul Bertram, *Shakespeare and "The Two Noble Kinsmen"* (New Brunswick, N.J., 1965), 263.

47. On the final plays as a revival of "popular art," and on *Pericles* as a return to "old-fashioned Romance," see Bradbrook, "Shakespeare's Primitive Art," 60–61.

48. Aristocratic high-mindedness also features in *Henry VIII*—as a way of exculpating the king: the play succeeds brilliantly in conveying the impression that almost everyone is on his or her best behavior, and that calamities, such as Katherine's fate, just "happen," blamelessly and of necessity.

49. There are a few exceptions to this noble manner (for example, the mild jesting of Emilia and her nurse at 2.2.118–52, or the similar exchange between Palamon and Arcite at 3.3.27–42), but they do not alter the general effect.

50. Cf. Philip Edwards, "On the Design of *The Two Noble Kinsmen*," *A Review of English Literature* 5 (1964), who sees a sexual contrast in the play, one posing "Emilia, with hardly any sexuality," against "the gaoler's daughter, all sexuality" (104).

51. *Some Versions of Pastoral* (London, 1935; repr. New York, 1974), 196, 199.

52. Reference to Ophelia raises the question of that character's social identity, with her madness, "fantastic garlands," "crownet weeds," "weedy trophies" (4.7.168, 172, 174) and quaint folk snatches. In her deepest disillusionment with her father's court, Shakespeare gives her a "popular" profile: in these scenes she is set apart from court society.

53. See Eugene Waith's edition (Oxford, 1989), 22.

54. For a discussion of the ways Renaissance literary texts display an awareness of the social function of art, it seems significant that this reconciliation of the Daughter to her "true" social level, or the reimposition of decorum, is effected by theatrical techniques: coached by a doctor, the Wooer makes a creditable Palamon, and the Daughter succumbs to his performance. Thus the Daughter's socially unacceptable desire is circumvented by a theatrical ruse. The parallel with Christopher Sly is evident: our attention is directed toward a conservative function of theater, that of buttressing social hierarchy and placing people in it.

55. For Levin, such material often forms a "third level" of the action of English Renaissance plays: see *Multiple Plot*, 55–58.

56. In Cordelia's words, the Daughter's madness is a "great breach in . . . [her]

nature" (*Lear*, 4.7.14), visionary and morally imaginative rather than ludicrous: so the compassionate vision of the shipwreck (3.4.5–11).

57. There are other ways in which tragedy is distanced as a social-cultural mode in this play: thus Hamlet is the hero of a revenge tragedy in which the "ethic of . . . revenge" is problematic: see Hunter, "Shakespeare and the Traditions of Tragedy," 139.

58. Both Lear and Gloucester "emphasize the need to share the lot of the poor" (Cohen, *Drama of a Nation*, 334). Cohen's brilliant reading of *King Lear* has influenced my own sense of the play as distancing the tragic. See also Dollimore, *Radical Tragedy*: "As unaccommodated man [Lear] feels what wretches feel" (189). Against this approach, however, it must be asked to what extent Lear can feel what wretches feel.

59. See G. Wilson Knight, "*King Lear* and the Comedy of the Grotesque," in *The Wheel of Fire: Interpretations of Shakespearian Tragedy with Three New Essays*, 4th ed. (London, 1949); and Rossiter's essays, "Shakespearian Tragedy" and "Comic Relief," in *Angel with Horns*.

60. *King Lear* "gives full weight to both" aristocracy and populace (Cohen, *Drama of a Nation*, 328); on the play's "crucial popular dimension" (333), see 332–45.

61. On Lear and Gloucester as "outcast," and for the possibly overhopeful judgment that Lear accedes to a "revolutionary understanding" of society, see Cohen, *Drama of a Nation*, 334, 334–37. It is paradoxical to speak of Lear as both an "outsider" and as having discovered a certain solidarity with the underprivileged: I shall suggest that this paradox is at the heart of Lear's experience on the heath.

62. Cohen discusses whether Edgar's firsthand experience of "the misery of the poor" (*Drama of a Nation*, 342) portends a break with injustice in the post-Lear world (342–45). Such speculation can seem idle (how many children had Lady Macbeth?), but it is fair to consider whether the play attaches any hopeful significance to Edgar's trials.

63. Brecht claimed that "Shakespeare gives the plebeians good arguments to answer back with" in the opening scene with Menenius: see his remarks on the play in vol. 9 of his *Collected Plays*, ed. Ralph Manheim and John Willet (New York, 1972), 380. For an analysis of Brecht's use of Shakespeare see Heinemann, "How Brecht Read Shakespeare." Cohen comments that Shakespeare "shows the legitimacy of lower-class grievances" in the play (*Drama of a Nation*, 303). For E. C. Pettet, however, "*Coriolanus* and the Midlands Insurrection of 1607," *Shakespeare Survey* 3 (1950), the play gives an "emphatically . . . unfavourable" portrait of a "fickle and unstable," and cowardly, "mob" (38). This is true in one sense (the plebeians are confused and easily manipulatable, though cowardly only by comparison with the superman Coriolanus), but Pettet does not take sufficiently into account the justice of the citizens' complaints.

64. Cf. F. N. Lees, "*Coriolanus*, Aristotle, and Bacon," *Review of English Studies*, n.s. 1 (1950): Coriolanus, whom the play presents through a mixture of animalistic and divine imagery (117), exemplifies the Aristotelian position that only beasts and gods do not need cities. Coriolanus is "unfitted for the life of a right social animal" (114).

65. For a succinct account of the military ideology of medieval and Renaissance elites explored in this play, see J. H. Hexter's introduction to *Utopia*, ed. Edward Surtz, S.J., and J. H. Hexter, in vol. 4 of *The Complete Works of St. Thomas More* (New Haven, Conn., 1965), xlviii–lv.

66. Coriolanus's "unsympathetic character . . . alienates audience and reader alike": B. A. Brockman, ed., *Shakespeare: Coriolanus: A Casebook* (London, 1977), 11.

67. "The instantaneous cessation of enormous energy . . . is like nothing else in Shakespeare" ("Character and the Imaginative Appeal of Tragedy in *Coriolanus*" [1912], in ibid., 67).
68. See his introduction to *Coriolanus* in *Riverside Shakespeare*, 1395.
69. "Character . . . " in Brockman, ed., *Casebook*, 55.
70. *Shakespeare and Social Class*, 157.
71. On Coriolanus's "inhumanity," see G. K. Hunter, "The Last Tragic Heroes" in *Later Shakespeare*, ed. Brown and Harris, 20. On Coriolanus as an "ultra," see Berry, *Shakespeare and Social Class*, 158. In "Livy, Machiavelli, and Shakespeare's *Coriolanus*," *Shakespeare Survey* 38 (1985), Anne Barton suggests Coriolanus's political attitudes reflect Jacobean absolutist ideology, but does not assume that the play therefore endorses James's, or Coriolanus's, antipopulism (128–29).
72. *Collected Plays*, 9.374.
73. Ibid., 385.
74. "The Failure of Orthodoxy in *Coriolanus*," in *Shakespeare Reproduced*, ed. Howard and O'Connor, 232.
75. For the view that the romances privilege plot over character, see Wells, "Shakespeare and Romance," 74.
76. See his Arden edition (London, 1976), 29.
77. "Livy, Machiavelli, and Shakespeare's *Coriolanus*," 119, 117. Coriolanus is a political "anachronism, out of line even with the other members of his class" (121).
78. Cf. Hunter's comments on "the political nature of the scrutiny to which these later heroes [Macbeth, Coriolanus, Antony] are subjected. . . . all feel the pressure to pursue a political course which runs against their natural individualities" ("The Last Tragic Heroes," 16–17).

Epilogue

1. Introduction to *The Historical Renaissance: New Essays on Tudor and Stuart Literature and Culture*, ed. Heather Dubrow and Richard Strier (Chicago, 1988), 10.
2. *Communist Manifesto*, quoted by Perez Zagorin in vol. 1 of *Rebels and Rulers: 1500–1660* (Cambridge, England, 1982), 12.
3. Zagorin, *Rebels and Rulers*, 1:16.
4. Introduction to *Rebellion, Popular Protest and the Social Order in Early Modern England*, ed. Paul Slack (Cambridge, England, 1984), 11. On the propensity of the London apprentices to attack marginalized "groups or activities" such as "brothels, servingmen, and stranger artisans," see Ian W. Archer, *The Pursuit of Stability: Social Relations in Elizabethan London* (Cambridge, 1991), 5. An anti-alien apprentice riot of 1517, Evil May Day, is often regarded as "the most serious riot of the sixteenth century in London": Susan Brigden, *London and the Reformation* (Oxford, 1989), 132. (Anti-stranger riots, though, argues Roger B. Manning, may not have been as common as protests "against the administration of justice": *Village Revolts: Social Protest and Popular Disturbances in England, 1509–1640* [Oxford, 1988], 194.) Two essays in the volume edited by Slack discuss the motivations of apprentice protesters, without recourse

to an explanation from social class, by exploring the predicament of youth in a gerontocratic and authoritarian society (for background, see Keith Thomas, "Age and Authority in Early Modern England," *Proceedings of the British Academy* 62 [1976], 205–49): Steven R. Smith's "The London Apprentices as Seventeenth-Century Adolescents," which vividly evokes the regimented lives apprentices led in their masters' houses, and Susan Brigden's "Youth and the English Reformation," which, among other apprentice hardships, notices the frustrations consequent upon the delay in marriage brought about by seven-year apprenticeships (see especially 83–91, 86). Geoffrey Holmes, also in Slack, does not discount "hooliganism" and "revelry" as factors in later disturbances in "The Sacheverell Riots: The Crowd and the Church in Early Eighteenth-Century London" (260). Steve Rappaport, *Worlds within Worlds: Structures of Life in Sixteenth-Century London* (Cambridge, England, 1989), considers the violent character of young male culture another probable cause of apprentice rioting (11).

5. See Derek Hirst, *Authority and Conflict: England 1603–1658* (London, 1986), 43.

6. See above, chap. 1, n. 74.

7. "Political Criticism of Shakespeare," in *Shakespeare Reproduced,* ed. Howard and O'Connor, 38. Cohen's criticism relates to Marxism's discomfort with postmodernism generally. See, for instance, Terry Eagleton's insistence that Marxism is either an "epistemological realism" or nothing at all: "Two Approaches in the Sociology of Literature," *Critical Inquiry* 14 (1988): 470–72.

8. Page references to this book are included in the text.

9. See Schoenbaum, *Shakespeare,* 232–37.

10. *Elizabeth I,* 145.

11. As John Guy notes, "despite careful preparation by the leaders, only four rebels assembled at the appointed time and place" (*Tudor England* [Oxford, 1988; repr. 1991], 405).

12. *Village Revolts,* 207. For another account, see Rappaport, *Worlds within Worlds,* 12.

13. Rappaport, *Worlds within Worlds,* 12.

14. Guy, *Tudor England,* 405.

15. "Most disturbances were brawls involving small numbers of youths and even they occurred infrequently" and "apparently involved little or no loss of life and minimal destruction of property" (Rappaport, *Worlds within Worlds,* 18).

16. Ibid., 14–15.

17. *Pursuit of Stability,* 9; numbers in brackets in the rest of the text refer to pages in this book. "Stability was the key-note in internal City politics": Frank Foster, *The Politics of Stability: A Portrait of the Rulers of Elizabethan London* (London, 1977), 4; see also Rappaport, *Worlds within Worlds,* 19.

18. Palliser, *Age of Elizabeth,* is also struck by "how few serious disorders" occurred in England (311). Disturbances there "after the . . . mid-sixteenth century . . . involved fewer people" and generally "were much less frequent and less violent than those in France," perhaps because of the lighter tax burden on the English "lower orders": Paul Slack, *Rebellion,* 12.

19. *Tudor England,* 30; see also Foster, *Politics of Stability,* 160.

20. Rappaport, *Worlds within Worlds,* 377, 378.

21. For Archer, the rulers' responsiveness "to pressures from below" (50) was a

fundamental cause of City stability; see also Rappaport, *Worlds within Worlds*, 19 and 380. That the elite was not regarded as unconcerned about popular hardship is stressed by John Walter and Keith Wrightson in "Dearth and the Social Order in Early Modern England," in Slack, *Rebellion*: "in the face of dearth . . . the initial reaction of the poor was not one of riot but of appeal to the local authorities to act" (127).

22. See Guy, *Tudor England*, 404.

23. Keith Wrightson, quoted by Archer, *Pursuit of Stability*, 99.

24. See Foster, *Politics of Stability*, 156. Derek Hirst also stresses the opportunities for political participation in the towns: citizens "had a wide range of minor offices in wards, parish and trade guild open to them" (*Authority and Conflict*, 47); see also Archer, *Pursuit of Stability*, 64, 74. Rappaport emphasizes the role that openings for "personal advancement" played in tempering popular envy and resentment of the rich: *Worlds within Worlds*, 387.

25. See Foster, *Politics of Stability*, 12; Archer, *Pursuit of Stability*, 50–51.

26. See Foster, *Politics of Stability*, 91; Hirst, *Authority and Conflict*, 50; Archer, *Pursuit of Stability*, 215–16.

27. Hirst, *Authority and Conflict*, 50.

28. Archer, *Pursuit of Stability*, 52–53, 56–57; see also 259. According to Zagorin, the patriarchal character of rural life inhibited the exploitative impulses of landlords: *Rebels and Rulers*, 1.84–85.

29. Zagorin, *Rebels and Rulers*, 1.70, 71, 85.

30. *Authority and Conflict*, 32; see also 50–51 for the "general acceptance" of hierarchy and patriarchy even among popular protesters.

31. Zagorin, *Rebels and Rulers*, 1.212; see also above, Introduction, n. 15.

32. See *The World We Have Gained: Histories of Population and Social Structure*, ed. Lloyd Bonfield, Richard M. Smith, and Keith Wrightson (Oxford, 1986).

33. Wrightson, "Social Order," 199.

34. Ibid., 198, 201.

Bibliography

Adams, H. H. *English Domestic or Homiletic Tragedy: 1575–1642.* New York, 1943.

Alexander, Peter. *Shakespeare's Life and Art.* London, 1939.

Archer, Ian W. *The Pursuit of Stability: Social Relations in Elizabethan London.* Cambridge Studies in Early Modern British History. Cambridge, England, 1991.

Aristotle. *Poetics.* Ed. D. M. Lucas. Oxford, 1968.

Atkins, J. W. H. *English Literary Criticism: The Renascence.* 2d ed. London, 1951.

Bakhtin, Mikhail. *The Dialogic Imagination: Four Essays.* Ed. Michael Holquist. Trans. Caryl Emerson and Michael Holquist. University of Texas Press Slavic Series 1. Austin, 1981.

———. *Rabelais and His World.* Trans. Hélène Iswolsky. Bloomington, Ind., 1984.

Barber, C. L. *Shakespeare's Festive Comedy: A Study of Dramatic Form and Its Relation to Social Custom.* Princeton, 1959.

Barber, C. L., and Richard P. Wheeler. *The Whole Journey: Shakespeare's Power of Development.* Berkeley, 1986.

Barton, Anne. "The King Disguised: Shakespeare's *Henry V* and the Comical-History." In *The Triple Bond: Plays, mainly Shakespearean, in Performance,* ed. Joseph G. Price. University Park, Pa., 1975.

———. "Livy, Machiavelli, and Shakespeare's *Coriolanus.*" *Shakespeare Survey* 38 (1985): 115–31.

Beaumont, Francis. *The Knight of the Burning Pestle.* Ed. Sheldon P. Zitner. The Revels Plays. Manchester, England, 1984.

Belsey, Catherine. *The Subject of Tragedy: Identity and Difference in Renaissance Drama.* London, 1985.

Bentley, Gerald Eades. *The Profession of Dramatist in Shakespeare's Time: 1590–1642.* Princeton, 1971.

———. *The Profession of Player in Shakespeare's Time: 1590–1642.* Princeton, 1984.

Berry, Ralph. *Shakespeare and Social Class.* Atlantic Highlands, N.J., 1988.

Bertram, Paul. *Shakespeare and "The Two Noble Kinsmen."* New Brunswick, N.J., 1965.

Bethell, S. L. *Shakespeare and the Popular Dramatic Tradition.* London, 1944.

Black, J. B. *The Reign of Elizabeth: 1558–1603.* 2d ed. The Oxford History of England. Oxford, 1959.

Blake, N. F. *Shakespeare's Language: An Introduction.* London, 1983.

Bloomfield, Morton. *The Seven Deadly Sins: An Introduction to the History of a Religious Concept, with Special Reference to Medieval English Literature.* Ann Arbor, Michigan, 1952.

Borinski, Ludwig. "Shakespeare's Comic Prose." *Shakespeare Survey* 8 (1955): 57–69.

Boswell, James. *Life of Johnson.* Rev. ed. by R. W. Chapman. Oxford, 1970. Reprint. World's Classics, 1980.

Bradbrook, M. C. "The Fashioning of a Courtier." In *Shakespeare Criticism: 1935–1960,* ed. Anne Ridler. London, 1963.

————. *The Growth and Structure of Elizabethan Comedy.* 1955. New ed. London, 1973.

————. *The Rise of the Common Player: A Study of Actor and Society in Shakespeare's England.* Cambridge, Mass., 1962.

————. "Shakespeare and the Use of Disguise in Elizabethan Drama." In *Aspects of Dramatic Form in the English and the Irish Renaissance.* Vol. 3 of *The Collected Papers of Muriel Bradbrook.* Brighton, England, 1983.

————. "Shakespeare's Primitive Art." In *Interpretations of Shakespeare: British Academy Lectures Selected by Kenneth Muir.* Oxford, 1985.

————. *Themes and Conventions of Elizabethan Tragedy.* 2d ed. Cambridge, England, 1980.

Bradley, A. C. "Character and the Imaginative Appeal of Tragedy in *Coriolanus.*" 1912. In *Shakespeare: Coriolanus: A Casebook,* ed. B. A. Brockman. London, 1977.

Braudel, Fernand. *The Wheels of Commerce.* Vol. 2 of *Civilization and Capitalism: 15th–18th Century.* Trans. Siân Reynolds. London, 1982.

Brecht, Bertolt. *Collected Plays.* Vol. 9. Ed. Ralph Manheim and John Willet. Associate editor Wolfgang Sauerlander. New York, 1973.

Brigden, Susan. *London and the Reformation.* Oxford, 1989.

————. "Youth and the English Reformation." In *Rebellion, Popular Protest and the Social Order in Early Modern England.* See Slack, Paul.

Briggs, K. M. *The Anatomy of Puck: An Examination of Fairy Beliefs among Shakespeare's Contemporaries and Successors.* London, 1959.

Bristol, Michael D. *Carnival and Theater: Plebeian Culture and the Structure of Authority in Renaissance England.* New York, 1985.

Brockman, B. A., ed. *Shakespeare: Coriolanus: A Casebook.* London, 1977.

Brook, G. L. *The Language of Shakespeare.* London, 1976.

Bullough, Geoffrey, ed. *The Famous Victories of Henry the Fifth.* In vol. 4 of *Narrative and Dramatic Sources of Shakespeare.* London, 1962.

Burke, Peter. *Popular Culture in Early Modern Europe.* London, 1978.

Bush, Douglas. *English Literature in the Earlier Seventeenth Century: 1600–1660.* 2d ed. The Oxford History of English Literature. Oxford, 1962.

Butcher, S. H. *Aristotle's Theory of Poetry and Fine Art.* 4th ed. 1911. Reprint. New York, 1954.

Butler, Martin. *Theatre and Crisis: 1632–1642*. Cambridge, England, 1984.

Byrne, Muriel St. Clare. "The Social Background." In *A Companion to Shakespeare Studies*, ed. Harley Granville-Barker and G. B. Harrison. New York, 1934.

Cannon, Charles Dale, ed. *A Warning for Fair Women*. The Hague, 1975.

Cave, Terence. *The Cornucopian Text: Problems of Writing in the French Renaissance*. Oxford, 1979.

Cawley, A. C., and Barry Gaines, eds. *A Yorkshire Tragedy*. The Revels Plays. Manchester, England, 1986.

Chambers, E. K. *The Elizabethan Stage*. 4 vols. Oxford, 1923.

Chapman, Raymond. "*Arden of Feversham:* Its Interest Today." *English* 11 (1956): 15–17.

Charlton, H. B. *Shakespearian Comedy*. 1938. Reprint. London, 1959.

Chaucer, Geoffrey. *Chaucer's Major Poetry*. Ed. Albert C. Baugh. Englewood Cliffs, N.J., 1963.

Clark, Sandra. *The Elizabethan Pamphleteers: Popular Moralistic Pamphlets 1580–1640*. Rutherford, N.J., 1983.

Clarkson, L. A. *The Pre-Industrial Economy in England: 1500–1750*. London, 1971.

Clemen, Wolfgang. "Characteristic Features of Shakespearian Drama." In *Shakespeare's Dramatic Art: Collected Essays*. London, 1972.

Coghill, Nevill. *Shakespeare's Professional Skills*. Cambridge, England, 1965.

Cohen, Walter. *Drama of a Nation: Public Theater in Renaissance England and Spain*. Ithaca, N.Y., 1985.

———. "*The Merchant of Venice* and the Possibilities of Historical Criticism." *ELH* 49 (1982): 765–89.

———. "Political Criticism of Shakespeare." In *Shakespeare Reproduced: The Text in History and Ideology*, ed. Jean E. Howard and Marion F. O'Connor. New York, 1987.

Coleman, D. C. *The Economy of England: 1450–1750*. Oxford, 1977.

Coleridge, Samuel Taylor. *Shakespearean Criticism*. 2d ed. 2 vols. Ed. Thomas Middleton Raysor. London, 1960.

Colie, Rosalie, L. *The Resources of Kind: Genre-Theory in the Renaissance*. Ed. Barbara K. Lewalski. Berkeley, 1973.

Cook, Ann Jennalie. *The Privileged Playgoers of Shakespeare's London: 1576–1642*. Princeton, 1981.

———. "Shakespeare's Gentlemen." *Deutsche Shakespeare—Gesellschaft West Jahrbuch* (1985): 9–28.

Cressy, David. "Describing the Social Order of Elizabethan and Stuart England." *Literature and History* 3 (1976): 29–45.

Crewe, Jonathan V. *Unredeemed Rhetoric: Thomas Nashe and the Scandal of Authorship*. Baltimore, 1982.

Cromwell, Otelia. *Thomas Heywood: A Study in the Elizabethan Drama of Everyday Life*. Yale Studies in English 88. New Haven, Conn., 1928.

Curtis, Mark H. "The Alienated Intellectuals of Early Stuart England." *Past and Present* 23 (1962): 25–44.

Curtius, E. R. *European Literature in the Latin Middle Ages.* Trans. Willard R. Trask. Princeton, 1953.

Cust, Richard, and Ann Hughes. "Introduction: After Revisionism." In *Conflict in Early Stuart England: Studies in Religion and Politics: 1603–1642,* ed. Richard Cust and Ann Hughes. London, 1989.

Danby, John F. *Poets on Fortune's Hill: Studies in Sidney, Shakespeare, Beaumont and Fletcher.* London, 1952.

Davis, Walter R. *Idea and Act in Elizabethan Fiction.* Princeton, 1969.

Dekker, Thomas. *The Roaring Girl, or Moll Cutpurse.* In vol. 3 of *The Dramatic Works of Thomas Dekker,* ed. Fredson Bowers. Cambridge, England, 1958.

———. *The Shoemaker's Holiday.* Ed. R. L. Smallwood and Stanley Wells. The Revels Plays. Ed. F. D. Hoeniger et al. Manchester, England, 1979.

Deloney, Thomas. *The Novels of Thomas Deloney.* Ed. Merritt E. Lawlis. Bloomington, Ind., 1961.

Dent, R. W. "Imagination in *A Midsummer Night's Dream.*" *Shakespeare Quarterly* 15 (1964): 115–29.

———. *Proverbial Language in English Drama Exclusive of Shakespeare, 1495–1616: An Index.* Berkeley, 1984.

Dessen, Alan C. "Shakespeare and the Theatrical Conventions of His Time." In *The Cambridge Companion to Shakespeare Studies,* ed. Stanley Wells. Cambridge, England, 1986.

Dollimore, Jonathan. *Radical Tragedy: Religion, Ideology and Power in the Drama of Shakespeare and His Contemporaries.* Brighton, England, 1984.

Doran, Madeleine. *Endeavors of Art: A Study of Form in Elizabethan Drama.* Madison, Wis., 1954.

Dryden, John. *Essays of John Dryden.* 2 vols. Ed. W. P. Ker. Oxford, 1900.

———. *The Poems of John Dryden.* 4 vols. Ed. James Kinsley. Oxford, 1958.

Dubrow, Heather, and Richard Strier. "Introduction: The Historical Renaissance." In *The Historical Renaissance: New Essays on Tudor and Stuart Literature and Culture.* Chicago, 1988.

Durkheim, Émile. *The Rules of Sociological Method.* Originally published 1895. 8th ed. Trans. Sarah A. Solovay and John H. Mueller. Ed. George E. G. Catlin. New York, 1966.

Eagleton, Terry. "Two Approaches in the Sociology of Literature." *Critical Inquiry* 14 (1988): 469–77.

Edwards, Philip. "On the Design of *The Two Noble Kinsmen.*" *Review of English Literature* 5 (1964): 89–105.

Eliot, T. S. *Elizabethan Essays.* London, 1934.

———. "*Ulysses,* Order, and Myth." In *Selected Prose of T. S. Eliot,* ed. Frank Kermode. New York, 1975.

Elton, W. R. "Shakespeare and the Thought of His Age." In *A New Companion to Shakespeare Studies,* ed. Kenneth Muir and S. Schoenbaum. Cambridge, England, 1971.

Empson, William. *Some Versions of Pastoral.* London, 1935. Reprint. New York, 1974.

Erikson, Peter. "The Order of the Garter, the Cult of Elizabeth, and Class-Gender Tension in *The Merry Wives of Windsor.*" In *Shakespeare Reproduced: The Text in History and Ideology,* ed. Jean E. Howard and Marion F. O'Connor. New York, 1987.

Evans, G. Blakemore. *Annals: 1552–1616.* In *The Riverside Shakespeare,* textual editor G. Blakemore Evans. Boston, 1974.

Farnham, Willard. *The Medieval Heritage of Elizabethan Tragedy.* Oxford, 1936.

Ferguson, Priscilla Parkhurst, Phillipe Desan, and Wendy Griswold. "Mirrors, Frames, and Demons: Reflections on the Sociology of Literature." *Critical Inquiry* 14 (1988): 421–31.

Feuillerat, Albert, ed. *Documents Relating to the Office of the Revels in the Time of Queen Elizabeth.* Louvain, Belgium, 1908.

Finkelpearl, Philip J. *John Marston of the Middle Temple: An Elizabethan Dramatist in His Social Setting.* Cambridge, Mass., 1969.

Fletcher, Anthony. *Tudor Rebellions.* Seminar Studies in History. 3d edition. London, 1983.

Foster, Frank Freeman. *The Politics of Stability: A Portrait of the Rulers in Elizabethan London.* Royal Historical Society Studies in History. London, 1977.

Fowler, Alastair. *Kinds of Literature: An Introduction to the Theory of Genres and Modes.* Cambridge, Mass., 1982.

Frye, Northrop. *The Anatomy of Criticism: Four Essays.* Princeton, 1957.

Gascoigne, George. *Supposes.* In vol. 1 of *Narrative and Dramatic Sources of Shakespeare,* ed. Geoffrey Bullough. London, 1957.

Gramsci, Antonio. *Selections from the Prison Notebooks of Antonio Gramsci.* Ed. and trans. Quintin Hoare and Geoffrey Nowell Smith. London, 1971.

Greenblatt, Stephen. "Murdering Peasants: Status, Genre, and the Representation of Rebellion." In *Representing the English Renaissance,* ed. Stephen Greenblatt. Berkeley, 1988.

———. *Renaissance Self-Fashioning: From More to Shakespeare.* Chicago, 1981.

———. *Shakespearean Negotiations: The Circulation of Social Energy in Renaissance England.* Berkeley, 1988.

Greene, Robert. *George a' Greene, The Pinner of Wakefield.* In vol. 2 of *The Plays and Poems of Robert Greene,* ed. J. Churton Collins. Oxford, 1905.

———. *The Life and Complete Works in Prose and Verse of Robert Greene.* 15 vols. Ed. Alexander B. Grosart. 1881–86.

Greer, Germaine. *Shakespeare.* Past Masters. Oxford, 1986.

Gurr, Andrew. *Playgoing in Shakespeare's London.* Cambridge, England, 1987.

———. *The Shakespearean Stage 1574–1642.* 2d ed. Cambridge, England, 1980.

Guy, John. *Tudor England.* Oxford, 1988. Reprint, 1991.

Haigh, Christopher. *Elizabeth I. Profiles in Power.* London, 1988.

Harbage, Alfred. *Shakespeare and the Rival Traditions.* New York, 1952.

———. *Shakespeare's Audience.* New York, 1941.

Hardison, O. B., ed. *English Literary Criticism: The Renaissance.* Englewood Cliffs, N.J., 1963.

Hattaway, Michael. *Elizabethan Popular Theatre: Plays in Performance.* Theatre Production Studies. London, 1982.

Heinemann, Margot. "How Brecht Read Shakespeare." In *Political Shakespeare: New Essays in Cultural Materialism,* ed. Jonathan Dollimore and Alan Sinfield. Ithaca, N.Y., 1985.

———. *Puritanism and Theatre: Thomas Middleton and Opposition Drama under the Early Stuarts.* Past and Present Publications. Cambridge, England, 1980.

Helgerson, Richard. *Self-Crowned Laureates: Spenser, Jonson, Milton and the Literary System.* Berkeley, 1983.

Hexter, J. H. Introduction to *Utopia,* by St. Thomas More. In vol. 4 of *The Complete Works of St. Thomas More,* ed. Edward Surtz, S.J., and J. H. Hexter. New Haven, Conn., 1965.

———. "The Myth of the Middle Class in Tudor England." In *Reappraisals in History.* London, 1961.

Heywood, Thomas. *An Apology for Actors.* Shakespeare Society edition. London, 1841.

———. *The Dramatic Works of Thomas Heywood.* 6 vols. London, 1874. Reprint. New York, 1964.

———. *The Four Prentices of London.* Ed. Mary Ann Weber Gasior. Renaissance Drama: A Collection of Critical Editions. New York, 1980.

———. *A Woman Killed with Kindness.* Ed. R. W. Van Fossen. The Revels Plays. Cambridge, Mass., 1961.

Hibbard, G. R. *Thomas Nashe: A Critical Introduction.* London, 1962.

Hilliard, Stephen S. *The Singularity of Thomas Nashe.* Lincoln, Nebraska, 1986.

Hirst, Derek. *Authority and Conflict: England 1603–1658.* The New History of England. London, 1986.

Holmes, Geoffrey. "The Sacheverell Riots: The Crowd and the Church in Early Eighteenth-Century London." In *Rebellion, Popular Protest and the Social Order in Early Modern England.* See Slack, Paul.

Hunter, G. K. "The Beginnings of Elizabethan Drama: Revolution and Continuity." *Renaissance Drama,* n.s. 17 (1986): 29–52.

———. *The English Drama: 1585–1642.* Oxford History of English Literature. Forthcoming.

———. "Flatcaps and Bluecoats: Visual Signals on the Elizabethan Stage." *Essays and Studies* 33 (1980): 16–47.

———. *John Lyly: The Humanist as Courtier.* London, 1962.

———. "The Last Tragic Heroes." In *Later Shakespeare.* Stratford-upon-Avon Studies 8. Ed. John Russell Brown and Bernard Harris. New York, 1967.

———. "Shakespeare and the Literary System." Unpublished paper.

———. "Shakespeare and the Traditions of Tragedy." In *The Cambridge Companion to Shakespeare Studies,* ed. Stanley Wells. Cambridge, England, 1986.

———. "Shakespeare's Tragic Sense As It Strikes Us Today." In *Shakespeare: Pattern of Excelling Nature,* ed. David Bevington and Jay L. Halio. Cranbury, N.J., 1978.

———. *William Shakespeare: The Late Comedies.* Bibliographical Series of Supplements to *British Book News* on Writers and Their Work. London, 1962.

Hunter, J. Paul. "'News and New Things': Contemporaneity and the Early English Novel." *Critical Inquiry* 14 (1988): 492–513.

James, Henry. "The Art of Fiction." Originally published 1884. In *Henry James: The Critical Muse: Selected Literary Criticism,* ed. Roger Gard. Harmondsworth, England, 1987.

Jameson, Fredric. Foreword to *The Postmodern Condition: A Report on Knowledge,* by Jean-Françoise Lyotard. Trans. Geoff Bennington and Brian Massumi. Manchester, England, 1984.

———. *The Political Unconscious: Narrative as a Socially Symbolic Act.* Ithaca, N.Y., 1981.

———. *The Prison-House of Language: A Critical Account of Structuralism and Russian Formalism.* Princeton, 1972.

Jones, Ann Rosalind. "Inside the Outsider: Nashe's *The Unfortunate Traveller* and Bakhtin's Polyphonic Novel." *ELH* 50 (1983): 61–81.

Jonson, Ben. *Bartholomew Fair.* In *Ben Jonson: Three Comedies,* ed. Michael Jamieson. Harmondsworth, England, 1966.

———. *Ben Jonson.* 11 vols. Ed. C. H. Herford and Percy Simpson. Oxford, 1925–52.

———. *Sejanus.* Ed. Jonas A. Barish. The Yale Ben Jonson. New Haven, Conn., 1965.

———. *Timber, or Discoveries . . .* In *Ben Jonson,* ed. Ian Donaldson. The Oxford Authors. Oxford, 1985.

Jupin, Arvin H., ed. *Mucedorus.* New York, 1987.

Kaiser, Walter. *Praisers of Folly: Erasmus, Rabelais, Shakespeare.* Cambridge, Mass., 1963.

Kaula, David. "The Low Style in Nashe's *The Unfortunate Traveller.*" *Studies in English Literature: 1500–1900* 6 (1966): 43–57.

Kearney, Hugh. *Scholars and Gentlemen: Universities and Society in Pre-Industrial Britain: 1500–1700.* London, 1970.

Kenyon, J. P. *Stuart England.* London, 1978.

Kermode, Frank. Introduction to *Coriolanus.* In *The Riverside Shakespeare,* textual editor G. Blakemore Evans. Boston, 1974.

Kinney, Arthur F., and Dan S. Collins, eds. *Renaissance Historicism: Selections from "English Literary Renaissance."* Amherst, Mass., 1987.

Knight, G. Wilson. "*King Lear* and the Comedy of the Grotesque." In *The Wheel of Fire: Interpretations of Shakespearian Tragedy, with Three New Essays.* 4th ed. London, 1949.

———. "Lyly as Shakespearian Precursor." Originally published 1939. In *Shakespearian Dimensions*. Brighton, England, 1984.

Knights, L. C. *Drama and Society in the Age of Jonson.* London, 1937.

Kolakowski, Leszek. *The Founders.* Vol. 1 of *Main Currents of Marxism: Its Origins, Growth, and Dissolution,* trans. P. S. Falla. Oxford, 1978.

Krieger, Elliot. *A Marxist Study of Shakespeare's Comedies.* New York, 1979.

Lanham, Richard. "Tom Nashe and Jack Wilton: Personality as Structure in *The Unfortunate Traveller.*" *Studies in Short Fiction* 4 (1967): 201–17.

Laslett, Peter. *The World We Have Lost Further Explored.* 3d ed. London, 1983.

Lee, Sidney L. "The Topical Side of Elizabethan Drama." *Transactions of New Shakspere Society* 11 (1887): 1–36.

Leech, Clifford. *Tragedy.* The Critical Idiom. London, 1969.

Lees, F. N. "*Coriolanus,* Aristotle, and Bacon." *Review of English Studies,* n.s. 1 (1950): 114–26.

Leishman, J. B., ed. *The Three Parnassus Plays: 1598–1601.* London, 1949.

Levin, Richard. *The Multiple Plot in English Renaissance Drama.* Chicago, 1971.

———. *New Readings vs. Old Plays: Recent Trends in the Reinterpretation of English Renaissance Drama.* Chicago, 1979.

Lewis, C. S. *English Literature in the Sixteenth Century, Excluding Drama.* The Oxford History of English Literature. Oxford, 1954.

Lyly, John. *The Complete Works of John Lyly.* Ed. R. Warwick Bond. 3 vols. Oxford, 1902.

MacCallum, M. W. *Shakespeare's Roman Plays and Their Background.* London, 1910. Reprint. New York, 1967.

Mack, Maynard. "Engagement and Detachment in Shakespeare's Plays." In *Essays on Shakespeare and Elizabethan Drama in Honor of Hardin Craig,* ed. Richard Hosley. Columbia, Mo., 1962.

McGinn, Donald J. *Thomas Nashe.* Twayne's English Authors Series. Boston, 1981.

McKerrow, Ronald B. "Marprelate Controversy." In *Encyclopædia Britannica.* 11th ed. 1910–11.

Mann, Thomas. *The Magic Mountain,* trans. H. T. Lowe-Porter. London, 1928. Reprint, 1948.

Manning, Roger B. *Village Revolts: Social Protest and Popular Disturbances in England: 1509–1640.* Oxford, 1988.

Margolies, David. *Novel and Society in Elizabethan England.* London, 1985.

Marlowe, Christopher. *Tamburlaine the Great.* Part One. In *Christopher Marlowe: Complete Plays and Poems,* ed. E. D. Pendry and J. C. Maxwell. London, 1976.

Marprelate, Martin. *The Marprelate Tracts: 1588, 1589.* Ed. William Pierce. London, 1911.

Mehl, Dieter. *The Elizabethan Dumb Show: The History of a Dramatic Convention.* Cambridge, Mass., 1966.

Meres, Francis. *Palladis Tamia* . . . In vol. 2 of *Elizabethan Critical Essays*, ed. G. Gregory Smith. Oxford, 1904.

Miller, Edwin Haviland. *The Professional Writer in Elizabethan England: A Study of Non-Dramatic Literature.* Cambridge, Mass., 1959.

Miller, Henry Knight. "The Paradoxical Encomium with Special Reference to its Vogue in England, 1600–1800." *Modern Philology* 53 (1956): 145–78.

More, St. Thomas. *The Confutation of Tyndale's Answer.* Ed. Louis A. Schuster, Richard C. Marius, James P. Lusardi, and Richard J. Schoeck. In vol. 8 of *The Complete Works of St. Thomas More.* New Haven, Conn., 1973.

———. *A Dialogue Concerning Heresies.* Ed. Thomas M. C. Lawler, Germain Marc'Hadour, and Richard C. Marius. In vol. 6 of *The Complete Works of St. Thomas More.* New Haven, Conn., 1981.

Moretti, Franco. "'A Huge Eclipse': Tragic Form and the Deconsecration of Sovereignty." In *The Power of Forms in the English Renaissance,* ed. Stephen Greenblatt. Norman, Okla., 1982.

Muir, Kenneth. *Shakespeare's Comic Sequence.* New York, 1979.

———. *The Sources of Shakespeare's Plays.* New Haven, Conn., 1978.

[Munday, Anthony, and Henry Chettle?] *The Downfall and The Death of Robert Earl of Huntingdon.* In vol. 8 of *A Select Collection of Old English Plays* . . . *by Robert Dodsley* . . . 4th ed. Revised and enlarged by W. Carew Hazlitt. London, 1874.

Nashe, Thomas. *The Works of Thomas Nashe.* 5 vols. Ed. Ronald B. McKerrow. 1904–10. Revised by F. P. Wilson. Oxford, 1966.

Neale, J. E. *Queen Elizabeth.* New York, 1934.

Norton, Thomas, and Thomas Sackville. *Gorboduc.* In *Chief Pre-Shakespearean Dramas,* ed. Joseph Quincy Adams. Boston, 1924.

Orgel, Stephen. "Making Greatness Familiar." In *The Power of Forms in the English Renaissance,* ed. Stephen Greenblatt. Norman, Okla., 1982.

Ornstein, Robert. "Bourgeois Morality and Dramatic Convention in *A Woman Killed with Kindness.*" In *English Renaissance Essays in Honor of Madeleine Doran and Mark Eccles,* ed. Standish Henning, Robert Kimbrough, and Richard Knowles. Carbondale, Ill., 1976.

Owen, John Isaac, ed. *The Rare Triumphs of Love and Fortune.* Renaissance Drama: A Collection of Critical Editions. New York, 1979.

Palliser, D. M. *The Age of Elizabeth: England under the Later Tudors: 1547–1603.* Social and Economic History of England. London, 1983.

Patterson, Annabel. *Shakespeare and the Popular Voice.* Cambridge, Mass., 1989.

Peele, George. *The Old Wives Tale.* Ed. Patricia Binnie. The Revels Plays. Manchester, England, 1980.

Perkin, Harold. *The Origins of Modern English Society: 1780–1880.* Studies in Social History. London, 1969. Reprint, 1976.

Pettet, E. C. "*Coriolanus* and the Midlands Insurrection of 1607." *Shakespeare Survey* 3 (1950): 34–43.

Pope, Alexander. Preface to *The Works of Shakspear*. 1723. In vol. 2 of *Shakespeare: The Critical Heritage: 1693–1733*, ed. Brian Vickers. London, 1974.

Puttenham, George. *The Arte of English Poesy*. In vol. 2 of *Elizabethan Critical Essays*, ed. G. Gregory Smith. Oxford, 1904.

Rabkin, Norman. *Shakespeare and the Common Understanding*. New York, 1967.

———. *Shakespeare and the Problem of Meaning*. Chicago, 1981.

Rabkin, Norman, and Russell A. Fraser, eds. *Mucedorus*. In vol. 1 of *Drama of the English Renaissance*. New York, 1976.

Rappaport, Steve. *Worlds within Worlds: Structures of Life in Sixteenth-Century London*. Cambridge Studies in Population, Economy, and Society in Past Time 7. Cambridge, England, 1989.

Rhodes, Neil. *The Elizabethan Grotesque*. London, 1980.

Rossiter, A. P. *Angel with Horns: Fifteen Lectures on Shakespeare*. Ed. Graham Storey. London, 1961. Reprint. New York, 1974.

———. *English Drama from Early Times to the Elizabethans: Its Background, Origins, and Developments*. London, 1950.

Rowley, Samuel. *When You See Me, You Know Me . . .* Ed. Karl Elze. Dessau, Germany, 1874.

Rowse, A. L. *The England of Elizabeth: The Structure of Society*. New York, 1951.

Sacks, David Harris. "Searching for 'Culture' in the English Renaissance." *Shakespeare Quarterly* 39 (1988): 465–89.

Salzman, Paul. *English Prose Fiction, 1558–1700: A Critical History*. Oxford, 1985.

Schäfer, Jürgen. *Documentation in the OED: Shakespeare and Nashe as Test Cases*. Oxford, 1980.

Schlauch, Margaret. "The Social Background of Shakespeare's Malapropisms." In *A Reader in the Language of Shakespearean Drama: Essays Collected by Vivian Salmon and Edwina Burness*. Amsterdam, 1987.

Schoenbaum, S. *William Shakespeare: A Compact Documentary Life*. Revised edition. New York, 1987.

Shakespeare, William. *Coriolanus*. Ed. Philip Brockbank. London, 1976.

———. *Hamlet*. Ed. Harold Jenkins. London, 1982.

———. *Much Adoe About Nothing*. Ed. H. H. Furness. Vol. 12 of *A New Variorum Edition of Shakespeare*. Philadelphia, 1899.

———. *The Riverside Shakespeare*. Textual editor G. Blakemore Evans. Boston, 1974.

———. *The Taming of the Shrew*. Ed. H. J. Oliver. The Oxford Shakespeare. Oxford, 1982.

———. *The Two Noble Kinsmen*. Ed. Eugene Waith. The Oxford Shakespeare. Oxford, 1989.

Sidney, Sir Philip. *The Countess of Pembroke's Arcadia (The Old Arcadia)*. Ed. Jean Robertson. Oxford, 1973.

———. *A Defence of Poetry*. In *Miscellaneous Prose of Sir Philip Sidney*, ed. Katherine

Duncan-Jones and Jan Van Dorsten. Oxford, 1973.

Slack, Paul. Introduction to *Rebellion, Popular Protest and the Social Order in Early Modern England.* Ed. Paul Slack. Past and Present Publications. Cambridge, England 1984.

——. *Poverty and Policy in Tudor and Stuart England.* London, 1988.

——. "Poverty and Social Regulation in Elizabethan England." In *The Reign of Elizabeth I,* ed. Christopher Haigh. Athens, Ga., 1985.

Smith, Steven R. "The London Apprentices as Seventeenth-Century Adolescents." In *Rebellion, Popular Protest and the Social Order in Early Modern England.* See Slack, Paul.

Snyder, Susan. *The Comic Matrix of Shakespeare's Tragedies: "Romeo and Juliet," "Hamlet," "Othello," and "King Lear."* Princeton, 1979.

Sorge, Thomas. "The Failure of Orthodoxy in *Coriolanus.*" In *Shakespeare Reproduced: The Text in History and Ideology,* ed. Jean E. Howard and Marion F. O'Connor. New York, 1987.

Spens, Janet. *An Essay on Shakespeare's Relation to Tradition.* Oxford, 1916.

Spingarn, J. E. *A History of Literary Criticism in the Renaissance.* 2d ed. 1908. Reprint. New York, 1954.

Stephen, Sir Leslie, and Sir Sidney Lee, eds. "Yarington, Robert." In *The Dictionary of National Biography.* 22 vols. Oxford, 1921–22. Reprint. 1949–50.

Stevenson, Laura Caroline. *Praise and Paradox: Merchants and Craftsmen in Elizabethan Popular Literature.* Cambridge, England, 1984.

Stone, Lawrence. *The Crisis of the Aristocracy: 1558–1641.* Oxford, 1965.

Stone, Lawrence, and Jeanne C. Fawtier Stone. *An Open Elite? England 1540–1880.* Oxford, 1984.

Suzuki, Mihoko. "'Signiorie over the Pages': The Crisis of Authority in Nashe's *The Unfortunate Traveller.*" *Studies in Philology* 81 (1984): 348–71.

Szenczi, Miklós. "The Nature of Shakespeare's Realism." *Shakespeare Jahrbuch* 102 (1966): 37–60.

Tawney, R. H. *Religion and the Rise of Capitalism.* 1926. Reprint. West Drayton, England, 1948.

Tennenhouse, Leonard. *Power on Display: The Politics of Shakespeare's Genres.* New York, 1986.

Thomas, Keith. "Age and Authority in Early Modern England." *Proceedings of the British Academy* 62 (1976): 205–49.

Thompson, Ann. *Shakespeare's Chaucer: A Study in Literary Origins.* New York, 1978.

Thomson, Peter. "Playhouses and Players in the Time of Shakespeare." In *The Cambridge Companion to Shakespeare Studies,* ed. Stanley Wells. Cambridge, England, 1986.

Thorndike, Ashley H. *Shakespeare's Theater.* 1916. Reprint. New York, 1960.

Tillyard, E. M. W. *The Elizabethan World Picture.* London, 1943.

——. *Shakespeare's History Plays.* 1944. Reprint. Harmondsworth, England, 1969.

Ure, Peter. "Marriage and the Domestic Drama in Heywood and Ford." In *Elizabethan and Jacobean Drama: Critical Essays by Peter Ure,* ed. J. C. Maxwell. English Texts and Studies. U.S.A., 1974.

Walter, John, and Keith Wrightson. "Dearth and the Social Order in Early Modern England." In *Rebellion, Popular Protest and the Social Order in Early Modern England.* See Slack, Paul.

Weimann, Robert. "*Fabula* and *Historia:* The Crisis of the 'Universall Consideration' in *The Unfortunate Traveller.*" In *Representing the English Renaissance,* ed. Stephen Greenblatt. Berkeley, 1988.

———. "History and the Issue of Authority in Representation: The Elizabethan Theater and the Reformation." *New Literary History* 17 (1986): 449–77.

———. *Shakespeare and the Popular Tradition in the Theater: Studies in the Social Dimension of Dramatic Form and Function.* Ed. Robert Schwartz. Baltimore, 1978. Reprint. 1987.

———. "Shakespeare (De)Canonized: Conflicting Uses of 'Authority' and 'Representation'." *New Literary History* 20 (1988): 65–83.

Wells, Stanley. "Shakespeare and Romance." In *Later Shakespeare.* Stratford-upon-Avon Studies 8. Ed. John Russell Brown and Bernard Harris. New York, 1967.

———, ed. *Thomas Nashe.* The Stratford-upon-Avon Library 1. London, 1964.

Williams, Raymond. *Marxism and Literature.* Oxford, 1977.

———. *Modern Tragedy.* Stanford, Calif., 1966.

Wilson, F. P. *Elizabethan and Jacobean.* Oxford, 1945.

———. *The English Drama: 1485–1585.* Ed. G. K. Hunter. The Oxford History of English Literature. Oxford, 1969.

———. "The English History Play." In *Shakespearian and Other Studies,* ed. Helen Gardner. Oxford, 1969.

———. "Shakespeare and the Diction of Common Life." In *Shakespearian and Other Studies.*

———, ed. *The Oxford Dictionary of Proverbs.* 3d ed. Oxford, 1970.

Wilson, John Dover. "The Marprelate Controversy." In *Renascence and Reformation.* Vol. 3 of *The Cambridge History of English Literature,* ed. Sir A. W. Ward and A. R. Waller. 1909. Reprint. Cambridge, England, 1949.

Wine, M. L., ed. *Arden of Faversham.* The Revels Plays. London, 1973.

Wright, Louis B. *Middle Class Culture in Elizabethan England.* Chapel Hill, N.C., 1935.

Wrightson, Keith. *English Society: 1580–1680.* New Brunswick, N.J., 1982.

———. "The Social Order of Early Modern England: Three Approaches." In *The World We Have Gained: Histories of Population and Social Structure. Essays Presented to Peter Laslett on his Seventieth Birthday.* Ed. Lloyd Bonfield, Richard M. Smith, and Keith Wrightson. Oxford, 1986.

Yarington, Robert?] *Two Lamentable Tragedies.* In vol. 4 of *A Collection of Old English Plays,* ed. A. H. Bullen. London, 1885.

Yates, Frances. "Elizabethan Chivalry: The Romance of the Accession Day Tilts." In *Astraea: The Imperial Theme in the Sixteenth Century.* 1975. Reprint. London, 1985.

Youings, Joyce. *Sixteenth Century England.* The Pelican Social History of Britain. London, 1984.

Young, David P. *Something of Great Constancy: The Art of "A Midsummer Night's Dream."* New Haven, Conn., 1966.

Zagorin, Perez. *Society, States, and Early Modern Revolution: Agrarian and Urban Rebellions.* Vol. 1 of *Rebels and Rulers: 1500–1660.* 2 vols. Cambridge, England, 1982.

Index